THE ART OF DISAPPEARING

Elisabeth Hanscombe is a psychologist and writer who lives and works in Melbourne and has published a number of short stories, personal essays and book chapters about memory, psychoanalysis, shame, trauma and memoir. She blogs at https://www.sixthinline.com where she explores the fine line between fact and fiction, and the ways in which frail memory plays havoc with past experience to allow new ideas to emerge.

The Art of Disappearing

ELISABETH HANSCOMBE

Glass House Books
Brisbane

Glass House Books
an imprint of IP (Interactive Publications Pty Ltd)
Treetop Studio · 9 Kuhler Court
Carindale, Queensland, Australia 4152
info@ipoz.biz
http://ipoz.biz/ipstore

First published by IP in 2017
© Elisabeth Hanscombe, 2017

Printed in Sabon Next, Bely Display and Sauna.

National Library of Australia
Cataloguing-in-Publication entry:

Creator:	Hanscombe, Elisabeth, author.
Title:	The art of disappearing / Elisabeth Hanscombe.
ISBN:	9781925231588 (paperback) 9781925231595 (eBook)
Subjects:	Hanscombe, Elisabeth--Childhood and youth. Adult child abuse victims--Australia--Biography. Abused children--Australia--Biography.

To my family, to my parents, to my sisters and brothers.

This book has been many years in the making and as a consequence there are so many people to thank, I cannot name them all. In no particular order there are those from my writing life, including my beloved mentor and writing teacher Janey Runci who has helped me from the start and continues to this day, alongside other members from my writing groups, Helen Macrae, Cath James and Favel Parrett. And from days gone by, Stephen Renfree, Kim and Ian Bear. I also thank my fellow Thorn Bird writers: Ruth Clare, Julie Twohig and Magdalena McGuire as well as all my Tuesday Writer and CAE friends and teachers from many years ago, too many to list by name. Special thanks go to my friend, Carrie Tiffany who has supported me with guidance, writerly advice and friendship throughout this book's gestation as well as to my old and very dear friend Lesley Borland who has been a constant companion since early adulthood and together we shared many writing adventures. I also owe enormous thanks to Gerald Murnane with whom I have shared a rich and regular correspondence since 2005. My special thanks go to Barbara Turner Vesselago who introduced me to the freedom of freefall writing in 2003 and I have not looked back since. I owe much of my capacity to persevere with my writing to my analyst, Eve Steel, and more so to both my family of origin, my sisters and brothers and my parents. Finally, I want to thank my four daughters, Tessa, Rosemary, Amelia and Eleanor for sharing their lives with me, and more recently the sons-in-law who have joined us, Tim Fluence, Stephen O'Neill and Jarrod Woodward. To the fourth man to join our family, Will Robertson, I owe thanks for his excellent editorial help in earlier stages of this book and particularly to Tim Fluence who has worked as graphic designer to create the beautiful book you hold in your hands. I especially thank Tim for introducing me to Kurtis Adamson whose haunting artwork features on the cover. I also thank my grandsons. They give me perspective and last, though by no means least, I owe my greatest thanks to my husband, Bill Hanscombe. He has been by my side throughout this long journey.

Earlier versions of sections from this work have been published in:

All that's forbidden, *Meanjin* · Spring 2017

Even if it kills me, *The Stockholm Review of Literature* · March 2016

Peeping Tom, *Bluestem Magazine* · September 2015

A trip to the beach, *Lane Cove Literary Award Anthology* · 2014

In my father's house, *Griffith Review 40* · Winter 2013

Letters to Nietzsche *Axon Journal*, Issue 2 · 2012

Do you remember, *Hidden Desires: Australian women writing*, eds Christina Houen and Gina Woodhouse, Ginninderra Press, 2006

A strip of negatives, *Tirra Lirra*, Vol. 13, No. 1&2 · 2003

Contents

Touch

THE DAYS of leaning over my father to say goodnight and to receive the scraping of his thumb on my forehead flit across my memory. My father scraped a sign of the cross on the foreheads of each of his children at bedtime. My forehead bears the mark. The long frown down its centre, worn away through the years, and a reminder to avoid touch. To stay invisible.

My father's yellow nicotine-stained fingers; the nails clipped short and clean, the smell of his brandy breath, the scrape of his accented words across my ears.

'*Goede nacht,*' he says in Dutch. 'Goodnight,' we say in English.

My thought then: we are safe. But later in the darkness when each has scattered off to bed, and my father starts to wander the hallway and check out the rooms, I freeze over and turn into the white wall of a refrigerator.

MY FATHER taught me fear, my mother escape. She escaped into books, any books, any words that could take her away from the ranting of her husband and the clamours of her many children. And in the thick of this, I learned to withdraw into myself. I could squint my eyes so that any light available — a chink of sunlight through the curtains, the glisten of baubles on a Christmas tree, the reflections of the moon through my bedroom window — could shift from their sharp and cruel clarity into a blurry brilliance that took the edge off everything. When I opened my eyes again, they could offer the thrill of something new and exciting to help me escape the sound, sight, smell of my father and the prospect of his touch. I learned to disappear.

The Flood

DURING THE 1940s in Haarlem, Holland where his first babies were born, my father had read about the bringing up of children. He read Freud and Jung and Spock. But most of all he took in the teachings of Truby King, a medical doctor and psychologist, who developed what was called the Plunket system, which involved 'controlled feeding'. By all means feed the baby well, Truby King taught, but after each feed put him down immediately, after the nappy change if necessary, and then do not pick him up again for at least four hours. Even if he cries, no matter how distressed. The baby needs to learn patience. He needs to learn to hold on. If you cannot bear it, close the door. No long hugs. In this way babies learn to disappear, even from themselves, from their inner torments. They learn to go into fast freeze. They learn that no amount of crying, no amount of calling out will get a response.

YEARS LATER my mother told us how she had shuddered outside the door, her heart aching with each sob from her baby's room. She dared not go in. She waited and she prayed, 'Let him fall asleep, dear God. Soon I can hold him again.'

IT WAS easier when my father was away at work or at war, and later when the other babies came along, including me. By then my father had lost the energy needed to be a disciplinarian. By then he was past caring and it was easier for me to stay invisible. He lost interest in babies, yet expected heroic achievements from his sons as they grew. From his daughters he expected something else. Something unspoken.

My father arrived in Australia six months before the rest of his family on 17 September 1950, on the *SS Almkerk*. He wasted no time meeting up with my mother's brother who had arrived sometime earlier and together arranged for bed and board on the Hickling's chicken farm in Diamond Creek in exchange for weekend work. After the war, my father had wanted to work as a chemist in Holland but once in Australia he took whatever jobs he could. He worked as a builder's labourer and saved his earnings to buy a block of land on which to build his first home.

Before my mother arrived in Melbourne, pregnant, with four children following behind, the Hicklings had offered my parents the use of a derelict two-roomed incubator (a chook shed) as home. It was a long, rectangular building with a concrete floor, bare wooden walls, one entrance, one window at each end, sealed with fence wire and a galvanised tin roof. It was filthy with the stench of dead chickens and piles of chicken poop across the concrete floor. Yet my father managed to clean it, with the help of my older brothers. This chook shed was my first home.

Inside, my father hung three curtains to form a kitchen/living area, a tiny master bedroom and a larger area at the other end for the children's room, all six of us. We lived here until my father finished work on a house he built nearby in Arthur Street. This house was a pale blue weatherboard, Mary's blue, one among a row of neat houses, each similar in design, though painted a different colour and squatting among the eucalypts and wattle near Elder Street. On the front porch, my father had included an alcove to house the statue of the Virgin Mary, our own personal grotto. She was always there to greet you. And visitors would know this house protected a Catholic family, one that took its faith seriously.

The front of the house looked out across a dusty road, full of potholes in summer and mud in winter, to unsown paddocks, filled with wild grasses that stretched to the horizon, interrupted only by a dark, ragged line of barbedwire fence or rippled by the wind. Sometimes a farmer might let loose his horse or set the cattle to graze. They scarcely made a dint in the sea of grass.

In Australia it was dry and hot. And although my mother told us the winters in Holland had been hard, she also loved them for the ice-skating she and her brothers enjoyed everyday on the frozen canals near to where they lived. How she missed her home and her parents.

There was a book in my father's library in the Greensborough house with a cover made up of a stretched black and white photo of swirling water. I could not read the story in Dutch but the pictures told me something terrible had happened. One day, when I was small, I asked my mother to tell me more.

She told me then about *de ramp*, the flood in Holland, which happened soon after my parents had arrived in Australia. In 1953, storms raced across Europe and broke down the dykes, those high walls that kept out seawater. In the book, you could see people lining up sand bags to build extra protection. But the sand bags were useless and large parts of Holland wound up under water.

My mother looked sad when she first told me this story. I shifted from her face and her distracted eyes to other pictures inside the book, of cows with bells around their necks stranded on high ground, of photos taken from above: roads under water, people in boats rowing past chimney-stacks and drowned horses in a field.

My father was different. He had no family he told us. No family to miss.

'Look into my eyes,' he said one day, as I sat upon his lap, begging him to tell me stories about his childhood.

'Where are they now? Your parents, your brothers, your sisters? Where have they gone?'

'I come from nowhere,' my father said. 'Look into my eyes, they're black and evil.'

How could that be? I slid off his lap and into my bedroom, sobbing. I shook my fists heavenward, convinced my *Oma* who must be dead by now would hear me. If only my father's family were not invisible, he might be different and I could come out of hiding. I was four years old and it felt wrong that my father should see himself as evil. Although his moods and formality frightened me, I had plans at that time to marry someone just like him, a tall Dutchman with fair hair and blue eyes who could speak several languages, build houses and drive a motor bike.

Babies lost in limbo

ONE DAY when I was five, I wandered away from my sister, Hannah, and my brothers, Gerard and Henry, to the edge of the Plenty River pool. Someone had piled rocks there to create three depths: a shallow wading area, a deeper section for beginners and in the far corner, a deep end.

I had watched as Hannah and the boys took their time to get wet. My brothers were like twins, even though they were a year apart, and skinny in their loose swimmers. They seemed so much older than me, so much more able, as they dipped in their toes and splashed water up to their knees. Why not just jump in? I wondered.

There were signs around this pool but I could not read them. I could not tie letters together, even as I could make out the letter D on the sign above my head. D was for dog. How was I to know that the water in the pool that looked the bluest was also deeper than a man's height, and if I jumped in it would be over my head?

Hannah heard the splash from the other end of the pool. I did not. I was swamped by it, under water now, eyes wide open, enough to see the reeds at the bottom, enough to see the light trickle in and out on the surface above. There were bubbles all round, floating to the top before they popped.

The best part of being underwater was the silence, muffled, as if by earplugs. For once the noisiness of my five-year-old life settled. I had not yet tried to breathe, and the thought of opening my mouth to take in water clashed with the seclusion I felt at that moment, until something pulled at my hair. Twice. A pain on my scalp, just as water was entering my lungs.

Hannah dragged me out and onto the edge of the creek. She could not swim, she told me later, but she had seen my hair floating on the surface, enough for her to reach out as far as she could and grab a handful. The air outside when it hit my skin was cold and I disliked the rough feel of the ground, as Hannah pummelled my body to make me breathe. I spluttered and belched out water until there was nothing left inside of me. The air inside hurt my throat.

They would tell me the story later with enthusiasm, and everyone would laugh. But I hid my part in this disappearing.

THAT NIGHT there were noises coming from my parents' bedroom and I opened my eyes to see what was happening. My mother was crying. If the noises had come from the kitchen I would have crawled down from the top of my bed and tiptoed there. But my father was in the bedroom, too, and I knew to stay away.

I fell asleep again until the dog next door began to bark and I figured enough time had passed for me to go to my mother. She was quiet now. When I reached their room, I pushed open the door enough to see her on the edge of the bed. She was gripping the sides of her dressing gown together and rocking.

'Momma,' I said through the crack in the door. I hoped my father, who stood with his back to me, would not notice.

At the sound of my voice, my mother stopped rocking and yanked at the bedspread to cover herself with the sheets. They were smeared red.

'*Ga maar terug naar bed, schat. Ik ben* okay. Okay?' I could see the strain on her face and wanted to believe her even though I knew she was not okay. But I did as she told me and dawdled back to bed. When I slid under the blankets, my little sister,

Juliana, asleep in a cot against the wall, opened her eyes, stared at the ceiling for an instant, fluttered her eyelids and then fell back to sleep. I pulled the covers up to my chin and squeezed my own eyes closed to keep out the images of bloody sheets and my father glaring down at my mother.

Later that morning, when Juliana woke crying in her cot, my mother did not come. My father came instead and took her off to their room. He did not notice me. Hannah came a few minutes later and told me to get up. She was already dressed for school. Her grey jumper with the gold and blue lined V-neck hung low over her checked dress.

'You better be good this morning. Momma's sick.'

Inside the kitchen, Gerard and Henry were sitting at the table along the bench. I slid in to join them. The bigger boys, Dirk and Ferdi, had already left for school. Their bowls were smeared with leftover porridge.

'I don't want any of this muck,' Henry said as Hannah put a bowl in front of him. Gerard said nothing. He was the quiet one. Even at breakfast time he sat with a book in his lap. Henry loved animals and to be outside, but Gerard preferred to be indoors. He was only a year and a bit older than me and could read chapter books when I could not even figure out the alphabet.

My father came into the kitchen and just walked past us. We all went quiet. He was carrying a towel rolled into a bundle. It was stained red. He walked across to the sink where he pushed aside the dishes, put down the towel and crossed himself, 'In the name of the Father, of the Son and of the Holy Ghost.' Then he picked up the towel again and walked out through the back door. The screen banged behind him.

'What's he doing?' Gerard stopped his spoon midway between the bowl and his next mouthful.

'He's baptising Momma's baby,' Hannah said. She was standing over the stove, a wooden spoon in her hand ready to ladle out the next scoop from the saucepan. Strands of porridge had spilt over its edge and turned black at the bottom where the pan met the flame. It gave off a burnt smell.

'Momma had a baby last night. It wasn't ready to be born yet. It wasn't big enough.' For an eight-year-old, Hannah knew a lot. 'Dad told me all about it. And now he's gone to the back yard to bury her.' She paused and looked around at each of us in turn as if she was testing our reaction. We must have looked interested, because she went on. 'The baby will go to Limbo because Dad was too late.'

I knew about Heaven and Hell but not this other place.

'What's Limbo?' I asked. Hannah had just spooned out my bowl of porridge and it sat steaming in front of me. The steam made my eyes water.

'Limbo is where babies go when they haven't had a chance to get baptised before they died. And because it's not their fault, God made Limbo. It's as good as Heaven. You get to eat whatever you like, whenever you like. You don't have to work or anything and you can play all day. The trouble is, in Limbo you don't get to see God.' She moved to the sink, turned on the tap and poured water into the empty porridge pan. 'In Heaven, God's around you all the time, but not in Limbo. You can have a good time but you're on your own.'

Through the kitchen window, we watched our father force a heavy spade into the ground, digging up clumps of dirt. They fell in a heap beside him and soon changed colour from dark brown to khaki yellow. My father brushed away flies with the back of his hand. The goat, Hettie, who was tied to a eucalypt at the far end of the yard, dragged on her rope to reach the edge of the hole, but our father waved her off with his spade. Hettie tottered away. Even the goat knew to keep her distance and to hide.

OUR FAMILY was bookended by dead babies. My mother lost her first daughter during the war and twenty years later her last daughter was stillborn. In between, my mother had this miscarriage, somewhere between my two younger sisters.

In my imagination I saw it all. Years later my mother told me about the sudden rush of pain; premature contractions; the doctor in the morning; the blood on the sheets. My mother passed the foetus into a potty and kept it safe in water in the sink for the doctor to examine. She described a tiny creature cocooned in a bubble of jelly.

It was a good thing, my mother told me later, although she was sad at the time. In the morning after her miscarriage, the doctor sent her for a curette and during the procedure they detected a small lump near her womb, which they removed. If she had not lost the baby, in time the lump might have killed her.

My mother had a way of turning bad into good. Like a jumbled up version of the mysteries of the rosary, the sorrowful mysteries that tell of Christ's journey to crucifixion and the joyful mysteries that detail his miraculous conception and his mother's eventual ascent into Heaven. My mother had a way of turning my father's behaviour into a blessing, a burden sent to try us, but one that would make us better people in the end. One we could overcome through miracles.

Leeched out

I SPENT the fifth year of my life in Healesville on the Myers Creek Road, where my father, mother, and my mother's brother and his wife had gone into business. They bought a series of huts as accommodation in the mountains for city visitors and a café-cum-milk bar. It lasted a year.

The property was called 'Sunspot', which puzzled me because the sunlight had such trouble reaching through the tall gums and ferns to touch the ground. Even at the height of summer it could feel cold. It was different at school. At my first school, St Brigid's Primary in the main street, I never felt the cold.

At lunch times, I sat on a narrow bench against a red brick wall. Trees surrounded us. There, the asphalt could be hot even on overcast days and pink balls of Lilly Pilly seeds spread across the playground. I watched the other children run about in groups, children who sat in pairs, in threes or fours. They kicked at the pink seeds. Unlike them, I was content to sit alone and nibble at my sandwich. It came in a brown paper bag, wrapped in greaseproof paper and spread with jam, and although the bread was crusty around the edges, I didn't care.

Even then I was preoccupied with my own inner workings. I might look at others — consider what it was like to live inside their heads, walk in their shoes — but keep myself hidden. On weekends I walked along the creek in single file with as many as six of my brothers and sisters. Below the thick tangle of ferns and the wall of gum trees overhead I looked onto the shiny pebbles of the creek. I was one of the luckiest people alive. I had a ready-made cohort of friends living at home with me. I need never feel lonely. Like my mother, I became adept at turning bad into good. This made disappearing easy. Not only could I hide from view, the tough spots of life could become invisible, too.

'We do as if nothing is wrong,' my mother said when my father cut the telephone cord and she could not make calls back to her family in Holland, or when my father refused to drive her to Mass on Sundays, or yelled at her for burning the potatoes.

MY MOTHER worked the iron over my father's trousers on the low coffee table with its green tiled inlay as her board. She'd covered the uneven surface with a layer of grey army blanket, which she'd first folded over several times and topped with a white sheet. Not quite white anymore. The sheet was marked in criss-cross patches from times when the hot iron had been left too long face down. My mother spat on her finger and tipped the surface of the iron. It let out a hiss.

These days, for his work in the city, my father travelled for over an hour every day from Healesville where he worked as an accountant for Mr Brignell. The business was only just beginning and my parents needed the money. My father alternated between wearing two suits, both identical, both black and shiny. My mother squeezed out an old tea towel, which she had dunked into a bucket of water, then she twisted out the excess and placed it flat along the folded trouser line. She pressed down hard. Steam hissed.

She worked in the lounge room, perched on the edge of her armchair and left so much space behind her and the back cushion that I could have folded up in there, snug against her wide back, but I did not. It would have irritated her. Ironing was one of those jobs my mother hated; but it had to be done and, therefore, was done without any fuss. If she could have read while she ironed she would have, but since that was impossible, she settled for watching the television.

It was still too early for the midday movie. We turned on the screen to the ABC clock pattern, a grid of black and grey lines, roughly spaced like a robot's face, and listened to the background music.

'I had a letter this morning from Holland,' my mother said. She had folded my father's trouser legs over the metal coat hanger and hung them from the mantelpiece beside a long line of his white shirts. Henry and Gerard were playing chess in a far corner and they paid her no attention. Baby Bec crawled from one end of the room to the other. I had to interrupt my knitting from time to time to drag her out whenever she got stuck under the dining table. I looked up at my mother from my cross-kneed position on the floor, my ball of wool unwinding in my lap. I knew already. I had brought the mail inside, only one letter in a blue-bordered envelope with an aeroplane in the corner.

'It's from my cousin, Miecke,' my mother said. 'She's had a prolapse on the dance floor.'

What was that? I didn't ask. My mother had a way of saying things that left me feeling I should have known and if I didn't, it was probably not the sort of thing I should know.

As my mother spoke, her fingers rested on the handle of the iron, and her eyes stared into space. In my mind I could see Miecke's insides fall out onto the dance floor like sparkling red jewels around her knees.

'The doctors stitched her back in place,' my mother said, but I knew that Miecke would always need to walk carefully from then; desperate to hold her insides in, her knees knocking together.

My mother leaned over to take up a white shirt from the overflowing wash basket. She jabbed an open flap of the shirt shoulder against the corner of the table to iron, first one side then the other. Pins and needles were running up to my knees. I dragged myself up and over to the couch, pulling the loose wool behind me. For knitting I used an empty cotton reel onto which I had nailed four tacks. I held another longer nail firmly between my thumb and forefinger to lift the wool over each nail in turn. The knitting came out of the hole at the end of the reel like a colourful snake. When I had knitted several yards I planned to coil it round and round itself to make a rug for my doll, a round rug to put on the floor. It was hard work not taking off two threads of wool at the same time but rather lifting the one over the other. Two threads at a time would leave a hole in the middle of the coil.

My mother stopped talking and I worried now about a hole in our conversation. I wanted her to keep on talking, to keep filling in the spaces of her old life and I tugged at the dark blue snake spilling from my cotton reel.

Becca squawked. 'Grab her?' My mother jabbed at the shirt back seam with the point of the iron. I pulled Becca out from under the chair. Her leg was twisted under the chair rail and she could not get it free. Her nappy was wet through and was cold and clammy to touch. Layers of fat rolled down her thighs, around her middle and under her chin. She smiled up at me when I lifted up the chair over her head and released her foot. Most of the time I thought of her as my baby, like one of my dolls. But today I was annoyed. I was busy with my knitting and I wanted my mother to go on talking. My question disappeared.

The afternoon wore on. The midday show came and went, followed by *Happy Days* and cartoons. My mother worked her way through the ironing basket. The mess of clothes was now folded neatly in piles of school shirts and shorts.

'When's dinner?' Gerard asked.

'It's too soon to eat. I'll put it on later.' My mother folded the army blanket over itself and pushed the coffee table back in front of the couch. She piled shirts and trousers over her arms and left the room, returning five minutes later with a smear of red lipstick stretched across her lips. She had taken off her dressing gown and replaced it with a green floral summer dress. Signs that my father would soon be home. She picked Becca up from the floor and felt her wet nappy with the flat of her hand.

There was a footfall in the hallway — the cue to disappear — and we scattered off to our rooms. No one ever said leave. But we knew we had to slip away and out of sight if we were to avoid the changing moods of my father.

IN HEALESVILLE one school day, we walked down the stony driveway beside the rhododendron bushes, splashed with red, to the other side of the road and the bus stop. Our mother thought we were standing there to wait for the McKenzie's school bus that took us the five kilometres to St Brigid's, but we hid instead among the tree ferns on the other side of the road until the bus had passed. No one told me why we were hiding but I sensed my older brothers and sister disliked school more than me. So it wasn't my fault. I was too little. I just followed the others.

Without the bus or a car, the only way to get to school was to walk. The bitumen road ran like a silver ribbon through the bush. Tall gum trees with scraggly bark that peeled on all sides when you looked up to the sky underneath the masses of tree fern, whose tiny green centres curled and sprung like babies about to be born. In between there were palm trees with umbrella tops that shaded out the sun. Looking up I saw only splinters of blue against the green brown of the bush.

The road curved so sharply in places you could not see ahead. So we walked alongside it, just out of view. A car might come along and run us over. Besides, we did not want to be seen or for anyone to offer us a lift. If we kept walking we would get to school by lunchtime. We would miss half a day of school. We scrambled and hopped over fallen logs and broken off branches, over anthills, past wombat holes, past the hollowed out houses of foxes.

I didn't see the leech on my leg until it was fat. It had sucked in so much blood it was nearly ready to fall off. In Healesville there were thousands of leeches. They lived in the creek on the other side of Myers Creek Road.

'Don't touch it,' Henry said. 'It'll leave its sucker inside and you'll get poisoned.' Gerard wanted to flick it off my leg, but I did not want to have a poisonous hole there.

In the distance where the road came back into view between the thick ferns of the bush, we saw the house of Mrs Schmidt. Smoke curled from her chimney. My brothers knew Mrs Schmidt from our church.

'We can ask her to help,' Gerard said.

I took care not to let the edge of my sock rub against the place where the leech rested as I hobbled to her door. I did not want to disturb the leech. I did not want to leave a hole in my leg.

Mrs Schmidt was surprised to see us. 'Why aren't you at school?'

'We missed the bus and had to walk.'

'Come inside,' she said.

I didn't dare to bring the leech inside. It was full of blood and could make a mess on her carpet if it fell. Still the leech had to fall off otherwise its sucker would stay in my leg and I would have a poisonous hole there and the poison would get into the rest of my body and I would die.

All of this, I told Mrs Schmidt at the door. She laughed and said not to worry, and then went off to fetch a box of matches. When she came back, she lit a match and let the flame burn down till only the red-hot tip remained, then she put the tip against the back of the leech. In an instant, it curled into a ball and was on the ground at my feet.

'There,' she said. 'He's gone and he's taken his sucker with him.'

17

Before I had the chance to step inside the house, Henry trod on the leech. There was a pool of red, a splodge of black and my blood soaked into the ground.

A week later there was another leech, this time in Gerard's eye. You couldn't see it, but it was there. We knew because there was a line of blood spilling down Gerard's cheek and he was crying.

'We'll have to get it out,' my father said.

My father could not put his cigarette into Gerard's eye the way Mrs Schmidt had put a match to my leg.

'We'll just have to wait it out,' my father said. 'When it's had its fill, it'll drop.' I imagined the slimy leech sucking at the inside of my brother's eyelid, which was swollen shut. The blood went pink with Gerard's tears. He cried and cried till the leech plopped onto his cheek, fat and juicy, like a black worm.

'He's had his fill,' my father said and flicked it with his finger. It fell onto the veranda and he stepped onto it. When my father moved his shoe there was not much leech left. Just another splodge of red and black.

'At least he died happy.'

ON SUNDAY my father ordered us to line up for a treat. He had brought down a crate of lemonade from the shop and each one of us, my brothers, sisters, and cousins there on a visit, could choose from the red, green, orange and brown *Tarax* bottles with silver lids, which my father prised off one after the other.

I was last in line. If I had been first I would have chosen the raspberry or sarsaparilla but there were only two bottles of red lemonade and they'd already gone. The lime lemonades had gone too; my brothers chose them. By the time it was my turn the only one left was plain lemonade.

I didn't complain. Even plain lemonade was fun. It bubbled down my throat and made me burp. I pointed to the last few bottles and told my father I was happy with that one, the clear one. He looked at me strangely as though he was about to say something more.

'Here you are then,' he said, and popped open the top with his silver opener. The bubbles fizzed over the edge, just a little, not too much that I had lost any, just enough to make my mouth go wet inside with the thought of the lemonade. I stood under the rhododendron tree in the shade with my cousins. They had already drunk half their bottles and were slowing down to make them last. I tilted my bottle back to my mouth and swallowed hard.

It tasted terrible. Not like lemonade at all, more like salty water with bubbles. I had expected something sweet and the shock made me want to cry. I looked over at my father. He was laughing.

'It's soda water, you donkey.'

Why did he find it so funny? Why did he want to trick me?

'Come on, you can have another one,' he said.

I followed him into the shop at the top of the stairs that led up from the driveway. The screen door squeaked open. The room was cool and dark. My mother had pulled down the blinds to keep the sun off the counter and the shop smelt like new shoes, like lollies, like lemonade and more besides. I liked the smell of this shop especially on hot days when it was still cool thanks to my mother. But I did not want to be there with my father ever.

'Take your pick,' he said, and opened the fridge door. Inside there were rows of lemonade bottles, lined up in order of colour. I could not trust him enough to choose the red lemonade. I chose the clear lemonade again, only this time I looked at the label.

In my classroom all around the walls were the letters of the alphabet. L was for lamb, it was also for lemonade and lemonade was a long word, not like soda, which was a small word and sounded like it began with the letter 's'.

'You really did want lemonade?' my father said and I nodded.
'Okay, it's yours.' He pulled open the lid with a pop.
'Don't worry. This time it really is lemonade.'

I took the bottle outside. I did not want to drink it with my father standing beside me. My cousins had finished theirs and were waiting to explore the hole in the ground, which my father had dug out for a swimming pool. It had no water in it yet and was lined with grass and dandelion flowers. It was good for sliding.

I tried my lemonade. My father was right. It was lemonade but no longer tasted sweet. I drank a few more mouthfuls and rested against the rhododendron tree, and then went off with my cousins. Later in the day, I saw the lemonade bottle there, still half full, with a fly floating on top.

Do it in the Dark

THE THIN man in a grey suit from the real estate office around the corner in Canterbury Road told my mother the house at number two was built in 1912 for a ship's captain. It was the first house in the street, he said, planted right in the middle of market gardens and orchards, and it was grand.

'A real gentleman's residence,' my mother said.

'Why?' I asked. 'It's too big for only one man.'

'Not just for one man,' my mother said. 'It's called a gentleman's residence because in the old days only rich people could afford such houses.'

Although my parents had sold their first house in Greensborough before we moved to Healesville, the man who bought it could not afford to pay back all the money he owed straight away. He paid up years later after my father called in lawyers to help, but in the meantime, the Healesville business had failed and we needed to move again. This time we had to rent.

I knew renting was bad, like not having enough underpants so you could wear a fresh pair every day, or plastic sandals on your feet at school instead of brown leather lace ups. One day, Helen Breznik, who was captain of the class relay team, told me I was poor. She said the word 'poor' like it was a bad smell. She said it after I had dropped the baton and made us lose the race, even though I had practised my running the night before in the laneway behind our house.

Later my mother said it wasn't true. 'If you have a roof over your head and food in your stomach, you're not poor.' So I went to school the next day and said this to Helen Breznik. She didn't believe me.

We lived in a grand house, but we didn't own it, which made me think my mother might not be telling the truth. With four big bedrooms and an outside laundry, Number 2 Wentworth Avenue was big enough for nine children with my mother expecting again, though not one of the men in my family could be called a gentleman, not even my father.

There was a scullery in the kitchen, near the briquette heap, where we washed dishes in a sink against the wall. My mother said the servants would have washed dishes there. Rich people would not have wanted to see dirty dishes so the servants hid them. There was room enough for only one of us at a time to wash dishes in the scullery. The bells in the hallway near the kitchen were once used to call for the servants. Beside the scullery was another tiny room called the pantry. My father thought it was perfect for a dark room.

In his spare time, my father took photographs, mostly of us. He spent hours each weekend arranging the lounge into a photographer's studio, which matched the pictures in the books he had collected: *How to take Great Pictures with Your Pentax* and *Do it in the Dark*.

One Sunday my father wanted us all to stay home after Mass to mark my parents' twentieth wedding anniversary with a photo session. He started with group sittings on the slatted bench in the backyard. Henry scowled into the camera as my father told him to smile. Gerard looked the other way.

An hour later, we took turns for our individual portraits. No time to stop for lunch. The lounge, its walls yellow from my father's cigarettes and with only one window, was bright against the shadows. Two lights stood on poles at opposite sides of the room like umbrellas. It became a hot house with the faint whiff of burning as insects drawn by the light were sizzled in the heat. From the floor to the ceiling my father had draped a white sheet from his bed against the double doors as a backdrop.

He was happy enough for us younger ones to stay in Sunday clothes but Hannah had to change her dress all the time, as did my mother. My father had made my mother's dresses himself, bright floral dresses that came in at the waist. I hated these dresses, the way they plunged at the neckline, the way my mother sometimes dug her fingers into her cleavage in search of crumbs at meal times.

Hours later, when the photo shoot was over, my father took his camera into the dark room, heavy with the smell of chemicals. We were not allowed to watch. He needed to work in the dark, he told us, with only the glow of a special orange light or else the film would be spoiled.

Once inside he would turn off the bare bulb that hung overhead and close the door. In the glow of that light he spread out his roll of film and lay it in a doll's sized bath of chemicals to make the negatives. Then he hung the thin strips, which he attached with clothes pegs to coat hangers, from the shelves.

After school the next day, Juliana and I crawled under the kitchen table, when no one else was around. We had opened out the grey army blanket along the floor and pretended we were on board a ship, enjoying a tea party with our dolls. The waves crashed against our boat when by accident I dropped my toy yellow cup. It skittered across the linoleum and landed against the wall of the dark room.

Usually, my father left the door open unless he was working there. I switched on the dark room light to rescue my cup, holding my breath against the stink. I needed to duck to avoid a strip of negatives, tiny squares of black and white that were silhouetted against the light. There was an image of my mother in each window, row upon row of my mother without clothes down one half of the negatives, and on the other side rows in which she wore only her black cobweb shawl pulled into her cleavage. I don't remember my mother taking her turn on the high-backed chair. My father must have photographed her naked in their bedroom.

I did not tell Juliana what I had seen. I did not tell a soul, but it made me want to hide even more. My mother's body without any clothes made me worry about my own body, that would one day be like hers, fat and full, and as raw as a baby.

Later that night before dinner, I jumped over puddles one after the other under a chalky grey sky. The street was lined with the rotting leaves from the plane trees that lined Canterbury Road. I hadn't bothered to tell anyone I was going out, not like the other kids from my school whose parents insisted they account for their every movement. It gave me a sense of being free even though it was different at night.

The park was covered with a shimmer of wet and although I had managed to avoid the puddles I could not avoid my school shoes sinking into the grass and soaking through the holes underneath. I tried to ignore the dampness underfoot. So many things I tried to ignore as I swung higher and higher on the swing, high enough to swing level with the trees and then back down to earth again. High enough not to notice the thoughts that ran through my mind about mothers and babies and the things grown-ups did in the dark.

After I came home my mother asked me to run back down to the milk bar. A lump of butter and a bottle of milk. My mother's words repeated in my head. The milk bar man was about to close when I pushed through his screen door to the loud ping of the overhead bell.

'Just in time,' Mr Harris said and set about to get the butter from a refrigerator behind the counter. Alongside the milk and butter, I had included a bag of caramels.

'Did your mother say you could have these?' the milk bar man asked.

'Yes,' I lied. He handed me the bag and I took hold of its frilled edge, now twisted into a handle. I put the milk under one arm and took up the butter in the other hand, in which I also carried my lollies.

The rain was not heavy. I could sit on the swing in the park nearby to eat the caramels—one, two, three—in a rush. I needed to get rid of the evidence, even as I knew the milk bar man had written it down on the account—three caramel cobbers. If my father were thorough when he worked his way through the list of things we bought each month, he would notice. But maybe he would not.

The swing seat was wet. It left a dark patch on my school dress. Sudden panic, I'd been away too long. I ran back up the hill. My fingers, sticky with caramel juice, slid along the wetness of the cold milk bottle. I gripped hard to stop it from slipping out of my hands.

Lights flashed on and off at the zebra crossing. I waited until every car that approached from either direction had slowed down or stopped. I stepped out. Then everything else stopped.

When I woke up I found myself on the floor of the butcher's shop, sawdust in my hair. My mother was standing over me, her eyes glazed with worry.

'You've been hit by a car,' she said. 'They've called an ambulance.'

'She may have concussion,' the emergency doctor said. 'We'll keep her overnight for observation.'

In the ward the other children sat up in bed like dolls under white sheets and grey blankets. They looked expectantly as a woman in pink uniform wheeled in breakfast trays. There was none for me.

'What are you doing here?' a nurse with a gold and red badge in the shape of a cross on her collar asked, when she reached the foot of my bed. She took up the clipboard that hung there and flipped over sheets of paper.

'I got skittled.'

'You look okay to me.' She put the clipboard back in place. 'I suppose you'll want breakfast. I'll see if I can get you something.'

My mother did not send me to school the next Tuesday after I came home from hospital. She bought me a jigsaw and a set of pencils instead. I knew that my mother knew about the caramels, about the sickness in my stomach from too much sugar, but she blamed it on the car.

MY MOTHER's purse was black, in crinkly leather, with a silver buckle that snapped tight when she pressed it together with her thumb and finger. It was a sturdy purse, but she left it lying around, and like her reading glasses, it was often missing.

Mostly my mother's purse was empty. We lived on credit. Not only did we have an account at the milk bar, we had one at the grocer's, at the chemist, the newsagent's and at the green grocer's. This type of credit left us children feeling as if our parents had plenty of money, but every month the bills came in and any sense there was enough to go around disappeared. Every month, my father, pen in hand, went down the list of items in each account and complained about whether we really needed these things. To his mind we did not. On other days, my father simply wrote out cheques for the lot. There were months, perhaps because there was not enough money left in his cheque account, when he ignored the bill altogether until the following month, when it had doubled. Debt piled up in our house like dirty washing.

There were a few days, after my mother had insisted my father give her money for things she could not buy on credit, when her purse bulged with left over coins. I only ever raided my mother's purse when it was full. Just a shilling or two, not much more. Back down to the milk bar, but this time with money in hand, I gorged on *Aeros*, expensive chocolate bars that left me sick after

I had eaten the lot. There was nowhere to eat in secret. Instead, I gobbled everything up as I wandered the streets, aware of my sins, but too sugar-hungry to care.

One morning my mother had no coins left in her purse to pay the milkman who delivered our milk. No milk for tea, no milk for cereal or for porridge. Money was coming the next day, pay-day, so perhaps it would not matter if we borrowed milk from the neighbours a little further up the road, my mother said. They wouldn't notice a missing bottle or two.

So my mother sent Gerard off to help himself to two bottles from one couple up the road who had no children and more milk than they needed. The next day he returned the missing bottles full.

After the milk-snatching episode I no longer limited my stealing to home. I figured I could walk into the milk bar and ask for something my mother had asked me to collect and while Mr Harris was out back getting it I could slip one or two chocolate bars into my pocket.

There were always trays of chocolate bars, *White Knights, Flakes, Crunchies*, on display at the counter. These were chocolates we could never afford, but the price didn't matter any more, now it came for free.

I went stealing alone, when my mother was away at work and the others were at home in front of the television. I took myself off for many more walks to the milk bar. No one ever asked questions, not even Juliana.

Stealing had the odd effect of taking me outside my body. Feet off the ground and I was floating. I was nervous whenever I walked to the milk bar preparing what I would say. I felt chilled even when the sun was hot and shining.

First I needed to ask for something obvious that Mr Harris kept at the back of his shop: a pound of flour or rice, a tin of peaches, a pack of biscuits. Mr Harris disappeared for a minute, enough time to fill my pockets. I tried not to be too greedy, or make it look as though the contents of the trays on the counter had changed.

A few Saturdays later, Mr Harris said, 'I know you've been stealing things behind my back. I should report it to the police.' He glared at me and wiped his hands on his apron as if he was trying to clean something off. 'I won't this time. I'll tell your mother instead. She'll have to deal with you.'

If I had once been flying high on the excitement of my success, my stomach full of fluttering butterflies, followed by the over fed sickness of gorging myself, I felt heavy then, chained to the ground with the weight of being caught.

The next day my mother stopped me in the hallway. All day long the question had been hovering there, hanging onto the threads of silence or her sighs. All day long I knew it must come eventually. And here it was. In the shadows of the late afternoon, the hallway felt like a tunnel with no light at either end.

'Mr Harris tells me you've been stealing lollies from his shop. Is this true?'

I nodded my head, my cheeks burning.

'When he told me I didn't believe him. I thought maybe Becca or Juliana but not you. Was it you?'

I nodded again. My eyes to the floor, I could not bear to look at my mother's face.

'I thought you were better than that.'

I shuffled on the spot and my plastic sandals squelched with the heat and perspiration of the day. My toes curled. They slid against the grime.

There was nothing to say. I waited for her punishment.

'I won't tell your father but it won't happen again. Will it?'

'It won't.'

It did not. I did not dare. Still there were other forms of stealing I could not so easily give away.

I had wandered home from school one day, several weeks later, through the Magpie Park and into the side street that runs adjacent to Mont Albert Road, and found a red ball, abandoned on the nature strip. Like a huge apple, I couldn't resist it. I bounced it home, all the way expecting a voice behind to shout: 'Stop thief.'

No one did. Inside my head I heard police sirens, and saw their flashing lights. But whenever I turned around there was no one there.

I reached home and escaped being seen, or had I? I hid the ball in the garden. I was still muddled by the laws of finders-keepers and the duty of any finder to return lost property. I wanted the ball to be mine but the accusing voice in my head told me I had stolen it.

Buried out back, behind the wilting hydrangeas, the hidden ball followed me. That night I dreamt of it spinning towards me when suddenly the moon replaced it. I was travelling with others in a spaceship, high above the earth, safe inside a metal bubble, chrome and shiny with bright red and gold lights that flashed. We floated along pulled by the moon's gravity towards its centre. My companion, an old man who nursed a baby on his knees, pointed out the bright pink-red lights on the moon's surface. I told the baby she should take a long, hard look at this sight of the moon now because she would never enjoy so close a view again.

The curve of the moon, its silver craters and shadowed mountains, beamed at us through the window and I sensed the greatest pleasure at my discovery, until we were out of control. We had lost our gravitational connection with the mother planet and were plummeting, like a heavy stone, back to earth.

Broken Teeth

IT WAS a thick, foggy day when my mother took us to the dentist. Six of us abreast at the green tram stop for our journey to the city. I rolled my tongue across the top of my teeth and forced the tip into the holes on either side of my mouth. The edges were rough and flaky. I had tried to keep the inside of my mouth a secret, but now they'd find out.

Hannah was not with us that day but she had been to the dentist many times earlier. She had shown me the inside of her mouth where the dentist had put a gold filling onto her front tooth. It shone whenever she smiled. My two front teeth were crooked. There was a gap between them but no holes in them yet, not that I could feel with my tongue.

My mother nursed Jacob on her lap. He was half asleep and sucking on his thumb. Jacob was plump, so much so we called him Friar Tuck after the round and jolly abbot in the story of Robin Hood. Jacob was lucky like Becca. The dentist only saw children once they were five. I would have liked to sit at this tram stop for a good while longer. I would have liked to stay there all day. I would have even liked to go back to school. The tram rattled to a stop and we climbed on board one after the other. Gerard helped my mother with the pram.

On the tram, my brothers read their schoolbooks; my mother took Jacob from his pram and nursed him on her lap. She closed her eyes and slumped forward. I wondered whether my brothers and sister were scared. It did not show. The tram passed my school. I could see the red bricks of the cloakroom. They were like teeth, lined up in a row, teeth without holes. The picket fences of the houses that lined the street were like teeth, too. The advertisements on signposts above the tall buildings were like teeth. So many things were like teeth. I tried to block them all out.

I opened the pages of my book, *The Happy Mariners.* I'd reached the part where Martin took himself off from the others. He was the youngest of four children who sailed in an ancient ship to a tropical island in search of pirate treasure. He had finally reached the town of clocks. There was a black and white etching in the middle of the book. It showed six-year-old Martin as he walked along a cobbled street with high old-fashioned buildings on either side and bright stars twinkling in the sky. The second oldest of the happy mariners was a girl named Elizabeth, not the same spelling as my name, though I was travelling in her shoes to this magical place as well.

I wished I could have been like the children in my book and not go to the dentist with my mother and my sisters and brothers. Instead I could have been on an adventure in search of treasure on an old sea ship. The tram rattled past factories and shops, past gardens and bridges. I closed my book shut just as my mother opened her eyes.

'We change trams here,' she said.

Again we waited but this time at another tram stop, and this time we were surrounded by people, women mostly, with shopping bags and men in suits. There were no big children now, only babies and toddlers. I wondered if the other people at the tram stop were wondering why children like us were not at school. No one asked my mother and she did not tell them why we were all there together making our way up the wide street that led to the dental hospital in the middle of a school day.

A wind built up as we got off the second tram. My mother held onto her skirt with one hand while she tried to push the pram in a straight line onto the footpath. The dental hospital was like a giant box filled with windows, each the same size in row upon row, like teeth.

I thought about the children in my book, how excited they were to be setting off on the ship. I did not feel like them. I felt the way I always felt when it was my turn to recite my seven times tables to the rest of my class. I did not know my seven times tables. After I got to five times seven I forgot the rest. Big gaps in my mind, like the gaps in my teeth.

The receptionist handed my mother a number on a square sheet of cardboard and told her to take a seat in the waiting room. We waited and waited. There were other families in this room who waited with us. I looked at these other children and tried to work out which ones were going to see the dentist like us. These children looked happy enough. I expected to look at their faces and see the same terror I felt inside my stomach but none of them looked pale or sad or worried or anything.

'Number nine,' the receptionist called and my mother stood. It was our turn but again we were led to another room, this time a room that was long and rectangular. On one wall there were chairs, and we sat in them six in a row. On the other side there were doors. These doors were white and on each one in the middle was a small board on which was written the name of the doctor from that room, Dr Jones, Dr Smith-Wilson, Dr Bennett. Too many names to absorb. I wondered which door would be our door, and which doctor would call our number or name. How would we all be able to fit into the same room? One door opened and a woman in the uniform of a nurse came out.

'We'll take you one at a time,' she said. 'Oldest first.'

Henry disappeared behind the door. We waited. I listened for the noise of the drill but all I could hear was the murmur of voices. Gerard disappeared next through another door. Then it was my turn, and finally Juliana's.

My mother could not be in all these rooms at once. She stayed instead outside in the long corridor with Jacob and Becca and I walked behind the door to Dr Bennett's room alone. The doctor was standing at the window his head bent over a silver tray. A nurse told me to climb onto the high chair. I held my breath. I was waiting for the time when the dentist would walk over to me and tell me it was time to look into my mouth. Hannah had told me I must open my mouth as wide as possible. It would not hurt she said, only a little.

It was not the pain I feared. It was the gasp of horror in the room when the doctor looked into my mouth and saw all the holes in the back of my teeth.

'Brush your teeth, night and day,' the television advertisements said. In these advertisements for toothpaste the children smiled all the time. They stood at the bathroom sink frothing up their mouths with white bubbly toothpaste and they laughed.

'Have you brushed your teeth?' my mother asked each night.

'Brush your teeth,' Hannah said.

I might go into the bathroom. I might splash the water. But I did not brush my teeth. It was too much bother. Too much cold water and the taste of toothpaste too sickly on my tongue. I lied and said I'd brushed my teeth, amazed my mother could not see through my lie.

This dentist at the dental hospital in his long white coast with his long pink fingers would soon know the lies I had been telling.

'Dental cavities in children,' the advertisements said, 'are significantly reduced by using Colgate tooth paste.' I did not use Colgate toothpaste. I had cavities, instead, great big holes in my teeth.

I opened my mouth. I opened it wide. Long fingers went in. The dentist did not gasp, but he grunted and muttered. Then he called out numbers to the nurse who wrote them down on a yellow sheet of paper. I waited for the injection. I waited for the drill. Nothing happened.

'Right,' the dentist said. 'I'll need to speak to your mother.'

My mother had not spoken to any of the other dentists about the others. I expected the dentist to speak to me, to tell me how bad I had been. Now he would tell my mother instead.

I slid off the chair and went back to the corridor where my mother was rocking Jacob to sleep in his pram. The nurse called her in.

'You wait here with your brother,' my mother said and I took her place on the seat. It was warm from her bottom. She passed the pram to me and went into the room. The nurse had left the door open a fraction but I could not hear the dentist's words.

'You'll need seven extractions,' my mother said, when she came out. 'Your baby teeth should have fallen out by now. They're rotten.' My two brothers and Juliana only needed nine fillings, three each, and just one extraction, which the dentist could do straight away.

I waited again with my mother in another room outside another line of doors. My brothers and Juliana each went through one of these doors to dentists whose new names appeared on their doors: Drs Rogers, Shengold and Rope. This time I heard the sounds of drilling.

'They'll do the extractions next month,' my mother said. 'They'll put you to sleep. You won't feel a thing.'

I opened my book again to read.

Spared.

Weeks later my mother and I sat on a long wooden bench in a room that reminded me of a church, but there was a pile of magazines in one corner and no crosses to be seen. We were in the Dental Hospital again but this time I was alone with my mother. I could feel the shape of her hip against mine even through the thick layers of her woollen skirt and coat. I was wearing Gerard's black duffel coat. One of the wooden buttons was loose so the coat gaped in the middle. I did not want to think too much about this word 'extraction' but my mother said I would not feel a thing. When I woke up it would all be over. I looked down at my feet to my First Holy Communion black patents. I had worn them for a long time, every Sunday, and they were beginning to wear out. There were holes in the middle of the soles on each shoe, but no one could see this, no one knew but me. Only when I knelt down for Holy Communion at the front of the church did I worry that other people might see. Then I tried hard to curl my toes under while I knelt to keep as much of the sole as possible concealed. My mother had told me I must not worry. I did not want to think about why I should worry, but the smell of chemicals and of toilet cleaner, the mothball smell of this place made my stomach hurt. I tried to breathe through my mouth and I ran my tongue over my teeth.

'Seven baby teeth have to go,' I heard the dentist tell my mother as his big hands prodded into my open mouth. He scraped against my teeth with a metal stick. 'Normally we wait till they fall out of their own accord,' he said. 'But these seven are too far-gone. She's not doing a good job of brushing her teeth, is she?' he asked my mother as though I was not there.

'I tell her to brush them every day,' my mother said.

Between the cracked bits my teeth felt furry most of the time but not that day. That day they had a shiny feel in the places where they were not broken. They had a shiny feel because I had brushed and brushed them. I knew the dentist would look again at my teeth and he must not know that I had not told the truth.

I told the truth in confession. Every week I told the priest about the lies I'd told—he never asked what lies—and about the sins of disobedience, even though I was not much disobedient. Not brushing my teeth when my mother had told me I should, could not be a sin of disobedience because I had included it among my sins of telling lies.

A sin only counted once.

I knew it was easy to wash my soul clean. One visit to confession and everything would be washed away and my soul, which was just under my stomach right down close to my bottom was clean and white again. But my teeth were not spotless.

The dentist told my mother to take me into the next area where the nurses would arrange for surgery. We waited some more until a nurse with a tight bun on top of her head called out my name and my mother and I walked into a cubicle where my mother helped me take off my clothes. Then she dressed me in a thin white dress, which had big holes for sleeves and no buttons. My mother tied the cords all the way up the back but the hospital gown gaped even worse than my coat and I was scared that people might see my bottom. As soon as I was out of the cubicle the nurse told me to lie down on a long bed with metal sides and she pushed my bed through slamming doors that snapped shut behind, down a long corridor of bright lights. I stretched out like a dead person. I felt numb the way I imagined a dead person might feel but my mind ticked over. My hands were cold. My stomach ached from the alcohol type smell. A man in a mask leaned over my arm and stuck in a needle. I watched the silver shine of the needle as it broke my skin, felt the sharpness that came with it, then I felt no more.

When I woke up my mouth was full of the metallic taste of blood. I was too scared to run my tongue along my teeth. My mouth had become a bloody hole. I could see myself in a mirror on one of the walls and I had shrunk. I did not look the same as I remembered. My face was white, and flat as a plate. My lips were bright red.

Some time later, my mother and I stood outside the dental hospital and waited for my father. He pulled the grey Holden into the curb and my mother bundled me into the back. Her hands were gentle as they brushed back my fringe from my forehead. My soul felt black that day as though all the times of not brushing my teeth had been lined up together for punishment.

'You can have ice cream when we get home,' my mother said. My father pulled the car into the traffic. I had never been in a car alone with my parents before. Where were my sisters and brothers? I hoped my mother had not told them. I hoped they would not know about my teeth, the holes and my bad ways. There was still a week before my next confession; before I could tell the priest and my sins could disappear again.

Things that Happen at Night

THE NUNS at my school covered themselves in top to toe — black in summer and white in winter — and I imagined underneath those folds of fabric were machines that operated the nuns' heads, legs and arms, and with no alimentary canal whatsoever.

I had never seen a nun eat until one day when my teacher asked me to take a message to the staff room. I knocked on the door as quietly as I could, to be heard and at the same time not sound too demanding.

Sister Beatrice answered the door. She looked down at my hands with their white folded note, which I was about to hand over to her, while I looked across the room to the head nun who was seated at my eye height. The nun held a fork in her hand and was about to pitch strands of spaghetti, the tinned variety, into her mouth. I handed over the note to Sister Beatrice in a state of shock at the sight of those pale red tendrils.

It made me question my notion of the nuns and their mechanical bodies but the idea had already cemented itself inside my brain and with it the belief that I too should treat my body in a mechanical way, as if its twitches and twinges were of no consequence.

'Your soul is more important than your body,' Sister Perpetua had said during religious instruction. 'Your soul is your connection to God. Like a tidy house you must keep it clean.'

It was the word 'clean' that led me then to locate my soul down low below my stomach and just above the place between my legs from which I peed and shat. I'd have preferred to put my soul closer to my head, to my brain and mind, but Sister Perpetua told us our souls existed deep inside and I couldn't shift it around at my whim.

I had learned about my soul in preparation for my First Holy Communion, when the priest put the round white host onto the tip of my stuck-out tongue and I drew it into my mouth and held it there careful to let saliva spread around so as to stop the host from sticking to the roof of my mouth.

If it stuck to my teeth or gums, I might need to slip in a finger to dislodge it. This was unthinkable, given we were not to touch the host with our human hands. Only the priest, as God's representative, could touch the host, which we learned was God's body turned into bread.

The host looked nothing like bread and tasted like the Farex flakes my mother mixed with water and served spoon by spoon to Becca. The host melted as you sucked on it and was mostly easy to swallow even without chewing.

Chewing was also forbidden.

'Hold the host on your tongue for a moment. Think of Jesus, then swallow, like you swallow an aspirin. One big gulp,' Sister Perpetua said. She told us we must bow our heads while the host travelled through to our stomachs and away to our souls, lodged down below and close to our bottoms.

A SERIES of paintings illustrating the mysteries of the rosary was lined up in order along the four walls of the church. At confession time, I sat closest to the sorrowful mysteries—the agony in the garden; the scourging at the pillar; the crowning with thorns; the carrying of the cross and the crucifixion. The titles rolled off my tongue. Once a month on Fridays each person in my class took turns to enter one of the two confessionals situated below the sorrowful mysteries to confess their sins to the priest.

Although I preferred the younger of the two priests from our church, Father Walsh for his Irish voice and his friendly manner, it suited me better to go to the older, Father Godwin, as he gave an impression of disinterest. He never questioned but simply let me rattle off my list of safe sins before he offered his absolution. Father Walsh was more likely to go into details, as if he had all the time in the world. He was more likely to unearth my real sins, the ones I tried hard to keep hidden, the ones that happened in my head.

I studied one image after the other of Christ in the garden at Gethsemane, drops of sweat on his face, his hands clutching his forehead, his sorrow at what was to come, and then in the next picture, Christ dragging his cross through the streets of Jerusalem as the crowds jeered him on. I scratched at a scab on my knee from the last time I had fallen over and worried I might make it bleed. I took a hanky from inside my pocket and dabbed at the scab to blot up any drips of blood.

In this second picture, Veronica bent over to wipe the sweat and blood from Christ's face underneath the crown of thorns that pressed into his forehead. I liked the blood from my own wound as long as I could keep it hidden. Trying to keep other thoughts hidden was harder. Those hot thoughts, the ones that made my underarms prickle, the ones connected with the games I played with Juliana on the weekends when the others were outside or away from home and the house was quiet.

We lay side by side on the bed and touched one another in the same way as we saw people touch one another in the movies; only we were careful to avoid our bottoms and had to pretend to have breasts. I had to pretend to have a penis as well because I was older and needed to take on the man's job.

Hot, exciting and wicked as these games were, we could not stop playing them every weekend while no one was around and then afterwards came the torment of knowing we had sinned.

The nuns never spelled out the nature of impure thoughts but told us often enough we must avoid them. Not only was I guilty then of impure thoughts, I was guilty of impure actions, of touching my sister's body and later my own, for the pleasures of such sinful arousal.

At night alone in my bed I crawled under the blankets and imagined myself as Maid Marion with her long hair and breasts as big as my mother's, the cleavage visible under her velvet gown. In my fantasy, the Sheriff of Nottingham came to take Maid Marion to his bedroom where he would do things to her that she did not want, and then Robin Hood raced in and fought the Sheriff till he ran away. Then Robin Hood and Maid Marion were left free to do things to one another that made me feel juicy inside, that made my legs tremble, that left me hot and excited enough to go to sleep until the morning when I woke in another welter of guilt.

To confess my impure thoughts and deeds to Father Godwin or even Father Walsh would have meant talking about parts of grown up bodies for which I did not even have names. But if I kept the impure thoughts secret inside and did not find a way of relieving myself of them, I would be in trouble with God.

God knew everything. He knew what I had been up to in the night. He watched me and was unhappy. I looked at his face in the pictures on the wall, the grimace, the sweat, the blood, and walked into the coffin shaped confessional ready to rattle off my safe sins.

SISTER PERPETUA told us about novenas the same year we made our first confessions. She told us in the nick of time. Just when

I thought my head would burst with the pressure of all those impure sins, she told me how I could wash my soul clean simply by going to Mass on the first Friday of every month for nine months.

Confessions were easier after that. Confessions became a way station to total cleansing once I had completed that first Novena and could start again with an unblemished soul.

'We have to stop doing this,' I said to Juliana one Saturday after she gave me the look. 'No,' I said, as proper as a nun. 'These things are sinful and we must never sin again.' Juliana was sad but I was not. Not anymore. I had found a way around the problem of my body. One Novena was enough to set me free, at least for a while.

ONE DAY when I was in third grade I sat in church sandwiched between my sisters and brothers on the wooden benches of Our Lady of Good Counsel and listened as the priest droned his way through ideas on how to be a better person. His sermon considered how to live a good life, how to honour God's teachings; but not how to stay awake or take his words seriously. So I tuned out and watched the people around me instead.

I had noticed my teacher Miss Anderson several rows in front of me on the other side of the church. I could see her side on, eyes to the front, as if she were concentrating hard on every word the priest said and needed to get a good look at him in order to take it all in.

Her face looked like an angel's, saintly and devout. Her skin was pale against her black hair, which she wore in one of those French buns my mother loved but could not manage in her own hair because hers was too curly.

As the priest rambled on I fell under a trance. I was in love with Miss Anderson, but I pulled myself up short with a set of rules on the nature of female beauty.

Based on what I had learned in church and at school, I decided that the Blessed Virgin Mary was the most beautiful woman who had ever lived. And, given she was an eternal saint, her beauty should dominate all others.

Next in line, I included my mother. My mother was more beautiful than any other woman I had ever seen beyond the Blessed Virgin, and although my mother's skin sagged around her neck and she complained about the wrinkles on her elbows, wrinkles that gave away a woman's age, she told us, I had also seen her younger photos where she looked like a movie star, with her own head of dark, curly hair, and although her skin was not the ivory of my school teacher's — my mother's complexion turned towards olive — she still radiated the beauty of the angels. So I gave my mother second place.

After her, in third place, came Miss Anderson. Because I was allowed thereafter to make my own choices, the next in line came from television, a movie star called Ava Gardner.

Every Sunday I looked around the church for other beauties to add to my list. Not only were they to exude a glow that belonged to the saints, they needed to be pure and unsullied in their demeanour. These words came to me from the nuns and the prayer books, which told me all I needed to know about truth and beauty.

The priest talked about parishioners who had complained about the church. He took these people to task. They were grumbling about their own church, he said. Their own church, one to which they belonged as though they were finding fault with someone else's church.

These people set a bad example for the rest of us. We were in this together and given that our religion was the one and only true religion, the pure religion, the One Faith, then it was important for all of us to honour that position and be loyal to our calling as God's children.

Purity overruled all other aspects of beauty. A pure mind was best of all and a pure mind was almost impossible to achieve, unless I stopped paying attention to what was on the outside and cared only about the whiteness of my soul.

The next day, on our way to school, the dew on the grass stood like tiny icicles as I jumped the footpath slabs in one leap.

'Avoid the cracks,' I told Juliana, 'and nothing bad can happen today.'

I did not tell her about the night times. Juliana shared a room with Rebecca and I had moved in with Hannah once Dirk had left home. That day, Mrs Lindsay, our next-door neighbour, was in her front garden pruning her rose bushes. She wore a high fronted apron and held the secateurs tightly as if she was frightened they might fall out of her hands.

Mrs Lindsay's kitchen window fronted onto the fence that separated her house from ours. Could she see into our bedroom? Did she know what happened at night? Unlikely. Mrs Lindsay could not see beyond her roses.

Clip, clip clip, clicked her secateurs and I watched the buds, withered and dead, fall at her feet. Mrs Lindsay wore slippers even in the garden and I could see the shape of her bunions as they peeped out from either side of her feet. My mother had bunions too. They ruined her shoes.

Would I get bunions? I wriggled my toes together and felt for the bones. Bodies and bones and things that happened in the night, things I could not understand.

THE FIRST time my father visited our room it was dark. I could see the moon through the corner of the window blinking at me like a giant eye. Clouds scudded across its face leaving the room one moment lost in shadow, the next immersed in light. Soon the shadows came together and took bodily form, my father's silhouette against the window. He was leaning over Hannah. Her bed ran parallel to mine with a narrow passage between, now occupied by him.

I heaved across to face the wall. I tried to make it look as though I was turning in my sleep. If he thought I was asleep, he might leave me alone.

I could hear the sound of blankets peeling back, the rustle of sheets, moans and murmurs. I could not bring myself to look, afraid of what might be happening.

Then as suddenly as he had come, I heard the soft thud of my father's bare feet across the room, the rattle of the door handle. He was gone. The moon had gone by now, too, lost behind the clouds. In the stillness I could hear Hannah sobbing and I wondered what might happen if my turn came around.

Angels, rubbish tips and toast

THEY TOLD me about angels when I was seven and I fell for them like a dog desperate for water. Just what I needed — a companion I could keep in my pocket, better even than my shadow.

I could call on my angel when I walked down the lane-way over the road from my house, a lane-way that looked onto the backs of other houses with great sealed or gaping garage doors, all the way down to the next street.

The lane was built in the days of the dunny man. No one needed a dunny man now to travel along the lane-ways to collect their pans from the outside toilets but the lanes stayed. This one was filled on either side with fennel gone to seed and dandelion flowers waist-high. It was a place where terrible things might happen in the form of strange men who wanted to do unspeakable things to my body.

Not that I ever met a strange man there, but every time I walked into it to take the short cut from our house to the park, I recognised the danger. Besides, the lane-way did a dogleg in the middle, which meant that, although it was not long, you couldn't see from one end to the other.

Unlike my angel, my conscience gave me trouble. It made me question everything I said and did. My conscience made me worry at night that I had become a sinner because I told lies to my mother about stealing money from her purse. My conscience reminded me, not only was I a liar, I was also a thief.

My conscience told me that thoughts about my body and other people's bodies were bad, that I should be like the nuns whose bodies, hidden under all those layers of black clothing, did not exist.

My conscience told me I should live my life like a nun, always thoughtful of other people, never interested in what I wanted, generous and kind to people and animals, never rude, never outspoken, in readiness for my trip to heaven when I should reach the grand old age of sixty, which would be a good age to die.

I WAS not thinking about my conscience or my guardian angel the day I went to the tip, the place where people threw out their rubbish under the bridge that scaled Canterbury Road. The area had once formed part of the rail track that travelled from Oakleigh and East Camberwell through to Doncaster, but the government shut it down to save money. The space where the tracks once ran, bright and shiny, had become a weedy overgrown path. We walked through it on our way to school in Deepdene, past high cliffs on either side, cliffs that held tall mansions on top. The people in the mansions never came down to where the tracks once ran; they threw their unwanted rubbish there instead. Wild rose bushes and irises sprouted from the piles of garden waste and geraniums self seeded among the weeds.

A man appeared from behind one of the piles of rubbish when Henry, Juliana and I were not expecting to see other people. We were looking for useful things to take home with us, a rusty scooter, the frame of an old Singer sewing machine, a doll with its arm missing, another without eyes. Some of them were good enough and not too heavy to take home with us.

I was trying to drag out a piece of red plastic from a pile of newspapers when I noticed the man several metres away. He stood in the shade of a tree but the sun caught on a glint of silver from his waist. He was beckoning me with a shiny coin, and used his other hand to wave his penis up and down as if he were inviting me over to talk about it.

I did not think about my guardian angel's advice at this moment, nor did I consider my conscience. I figured this man was offering me something in the form of money. A single silver coin in those days could buy a mountain of lollies and so when Henry disappeared out of sight in search of treasure, I looked at Juliana who shook her head and held back. She was more timid than me. I walked over to the man, propelled by some unspoken desire, even as I knew men like this might be dangerous. The coin in his hand was a promise too great to ignore.

'Hold this and watch the cream come out,' the man said. He held up the coin again. 'Then you can have this.' I followed his instructions. I held his hard thing in my hand and shook it until a line of cream spurted out and landed in a yellow paint tin nearby. The man handed me the coin, wiped himself, zipped up his fly and walked away.

The next day my conscience kicked in. By then I had spent the money on lollies, which I shared with Juliana and Henry. Henry had been suspicious about where the money came from but Juliana said nothing and so the three of us filled ourselves with sweetness and bliss. Once the lollies were gone I felt ill, so ill I could not go to school the next day, a Monday, and found myself alone at breakfast with my mother.

We sat together in front of the single bar radiator, toasting bread on the end of forks. If you left it too long, the toast turned black and even when you rotated it properly over the red bar of the radiator to an evenly spaced brown, it still had a burnt taste.

'I met a man at the tip yesterday,' I told my mother. Crumbs from her toast fell onto the newspaper in her lap. 'He asked me to hold his thing and watch the cream come out.'

My mother looked at me, her eyes blank, and then folded the newspaper neatly in half. She put it on the table and reached out her fork for another slice of toast. She skewered the toast with the prongs of her fork near to the crust and looked me in the eye.

'Take this to confession and tell the priest.'

My conscience swung into action. What had I done? A sin? Of what? And what would the priest say?

My guardian angel was no help to me when I pulled the latch back on the sliding door between the priest and me. I rattled off my rote learned mantra, the 'Bless me father for I have sinned ...' followed by my list of safe sins, the inconspicuous ones, the stealing, the lying and being disobedient, and then I told the priest how I'd held a man's thing and watched the cream come out.

The priest shuffled in his seat the same way my mother had done a few days earlier, but he had more questions. I wriggled on the hard wooden plank that went as a seat in the tiny confessional.

'What thing, my child?'

'That thing down there.' I pointed even though I knew the priest could not see in the dark.

'Three Hail Marys,' he said, and then rattled off the Latin words for absolution.

The gloss went off my guardian angel after that. If she could not keep me safe then how could she ever protect me from my conscience?

An Empty Pram

MY MOTHER was sitting on the edge of her chair, darning. The sewing basket by her side overflowed with socks that had holes in their toes or heels and she worked through each one with tight stitches. Whenever the thread ran out she took her time to change it. She raised the hole at the end of the needle up to the window light, then licked the end of the yarn to a fine point and squinted as she forced it through the needle's eye.

'I need glasses', she said.

My mother resisted the wearing of glasses because she thought they made her look old. We were sitting together but she might as well have been alone. I had the photograph album open on my lap. Its pages were worn. We all loved to go through the album from time to time to look at photos from the past, wedding photos, baby photos and photos from relatives I'd never met before back in Holland.

My mother kept muttering to herself about the thread and the needle and the glasses she couldn't find. For a moment my grip on the album slipped and a loose photo of a sleeping baby surrounded by flowers, one I hadn't seen before, fell onto the floor.

'Who's this?' I asked.

My mother stared at it and her eyes flickered. 'Your sister', she said and reached over to take it. 'She was our first daughter but

she died when she was only four months old during the war.'
My mother let the photo slide out of her hand to land face up
on her lap. 'She might have lived longer but it was during the
Hongerwinter when the Germans stopped food supplies into
Holland and many people starved. Many babies died.'

My mother broke off the cotton thread, pulled the needle
away and pushed its point into her pincushion ball of wool, and
then stared ahead.

'It's Nature's way,' she said, then dropped a finished pair of
socks into the sewing basket. 'During wars, women don't have
strength enough to make babies and feed them. They need all
their energy to stay alive. Still, I managed to carry two babies
during that war, fourteen months apart and only one of them
died.'

My mother seemed lost in her thoughts. She had a story to
tell and I knew better than to interrupt. I wanted to know about
my dead baby sister. Then my father walked into the room.
His body blocked out any sunlight through the window as he
towered over us.

He needed my mother's help in the dark room, he said. The
darning could wait. So she left off the story then, and came back
to it later only when I begged her to tell me more.

Each time she told me the story — for there were many times
when I pleaded with my mother to go over it again — she wasn't
so much sad as resigned. She never cried. She'd accepted the loss,
but it made me wonder how she could be so heartless. How
could anyone get over losing a baby?

'We were all so hungry when our second baby was born,' my
mother said one day while she peeled the onions and leeks for
dinner. 'We had no milk or butter. We lived on potatoes and
cabbage, sometimes even tulip bulbs. We chopped them up, and
then fried them like onions, but they didn't taste any good.' She
gestured towards the onion in her hand, and wiped tears from
her eyes.

'You needed a lot of salt,' she said. 'I wasn't strong enough to feed the baby myself, so I gave her warmed skim milk, made from powder. It wasn't good for her, but it was all we had. The little bit of cow's milk we sometimes managed to barter from farms nearby would have been too strong.' My mother put the onions into a pan hot with fat.

'We bartered everything for food then. Money meant nothing except on the black market, and they charged such high prices we wouldn't have had enough to pay even for a bunch of endive.' Once my mother started on the story she found it hard to stop. She stirred the pan up and down and then she added the leeks.

'Once a farmer wanted me to trade my wedding ring for a pound of sausages, some carrots and a bit of butter. I wouldn't hear of it. Hungry we were, but not that desperate. Can you imagine it: this farmer, who lived on the polders far away from the city, actually thought that I'd sell my soul for food? I could never be bought so cheaply.' My mother turned down the flame on the leeks and onions. They were soft and golden now and gave off a delicious smell.

'So our baby stayed thin and wrinkled like a newborn mouse. She slept a lot but cried very little. She was a good baby. So hungry all the time but never complaining, not even during the long cold nights.' My mother stirred the pan.

'One day when she was four months old, my cousin, Jo van Tongeren came to visit, riding on her bicycle without tyres, as we all did then. Rubber was needed for the war, for the trucks and tanks. No cars were left in our town. You couldn't afford the petrol. Every day you could hear the bikes clatter over the cobblestones. Such a noise and it was so painful to ride. I never got used to the battering my body took from the bicycle seat, my teeth chattering in my head because of the way the hard metal wheel rim hit against the bumpy cobbles. *Kinder hoofjes* (toddler's heads) we called them, smooth and round. Those cobblestones must have covered the ground of Haarlem for hundreds of years.'

My mother moved back to the bench and began to chop clean potatoes ready for boiling. 'Hours after riding my bike I still ached all over.' She rubbed her back with her free hand as if she was remembering the pain. 'As I was saying, Jo visited. She came to tell us about a good family she'd met, the Kuys family, who lived near to her parents' home in Heilo. The Kuyses were farmers and had more food than they needed. They wanted to help people like us who were starving in the city. So your father and I decided, if the only way we could save our baby's life would be to make that trip there and take the help offered, we would do it. Besides, I was worried for your brother, Dirk, as well. He was only eighteen months old and, although he was healthy, he was hungry all the time. Just like the rest of us, but in such a small child it was awful. His little ribs stuck out from under his singlet and his face looked hollow, like a skull.'

My mother took the chopped potatoes and put them into a pan she had earlier filled with cold water. Then she turned off the leek and onions, shifted the fry pan to one side and put the potato pot on to boil in its place. 'Heilo is 35 kilometres from Haarlem and there was no public transport. So I walked for more than three days with the baby in her pram. My Papa, your *Opa*, and my sister, Treesje, came for company. We stayed overnight in Beverwijk with a friend of my father's, the principal of the teacher's college there, and then in Castricum with another cousin. Finally, we reached Heilo and were welcomed by that kind family.

'You can't imagine what it was like to walk into that cosy kitchen at the back of the farmhouse and feel the glow coming off the fire after all that walking in the snow and the wind. There was a wood stove in the corner with a kettle always on the boil for tea. And they had plenty of milk — the Kuys family had their own cows — and special cakes Mrs Kuys baked herself.

The family even had a little sugar they had bought with their coupons, which they shared with us to honour our visit. Later, in the evening, we ate *stammpot* for dinner, mashed potatoes, carrots and onions with slices of *rookworst*. It was the first taste of meat we'd had in months, and was like the finest bacon my mother could have ever served us before the war. I only wished the rest of my family were there, too.'

The potatoes were boiling hard in the pan and my mother lowered the flame. 'At the same time that we left for Heilo, your father fitted Dirk's cot on wheels onto the back of his bicycle and together they travelled to the other side of that town where another cousin's family looked after Dirk while your father returned to Haarlem. The baby and I stayed with Jo.

'It was very cold. Even if I'd dressed warmly I could not have travelled every day across town to see Dirk. I had to be content knowing he was safe and well fed. It was all I could do to stay with the baby who seemed to be doing a little better since she was now old enough to feed properly on full cream milk. Of course, at first we diluted it. Her little stomach could never have tolerated solid milk when she was still such a tiny baby.'

My mother ran her hands under the cold tap and scraped under her fingernails of one hand with the nails of the other. The potatoes were still spluttering in the pan and I worried they might burn. My mother forgot things on the stove often enough, but I didn't want to remind her in case she lost track of the story. I flicked the stove off myself and she smiled her approval.

'One morning after we'd been in Heilo for several weeks and I was beginning to feel more hopeful, the baby didn't wake me with her usual cry at six o'clock. I didn't wake either until it was past daylight. As soon as I saw her, I knew something was wrong. Her eyes were open but staring out. Her skin was pale. By the time the doctor made his next visit later that morning, she'd lapsed into a coma. We could only wait, he said. If she came out of this sleep I needed to give her a spoonful or two of boiled water and call for him immediately.

'I stayed by her side all morning and prayed. 'At two o'clock in the afternoon she woke suddenly and looked straight at me as if she knew me. For an instant, I felt hopeful. Then she lifted her little head, murmured and fell back onto the pillow. I knew she was dead, but I wouldn't believe it. I scooped her up in my arms and ran to my cousin, Gre, next door. Gre took one look and said, "Ach, the little darling is in Heaven now."'

My mother stopped speaking. She took a fork and pierced one of the potatoes. Then she drained them and set them back in the pot alongside the leek and onion. She spoke more slowly now, but her voice didn't waiver.

'Gre took her from me. My little baby. Her face was like an angel's, her skin soft and pale. I knew her soul had left her body and she was in Heaven with the other angels. And Gre, who is usually such a happy person, always laughing, always joking, had nothing more to say. I watched as she washed my baby and then dressed her in the white embroidered dress of her baptism.

'Gre asked if I wanted to hold the baby a little longer before the doctor came back, and before the priest, but I could only keep her in my arms for a short time. I had to put her down because she was getting cold. I could not cry. There are no words for how I felt.' My mother looked as though she might cry then. Instead, she sighed and leaned down to drag out plates for dinner.

'Someone sent a messenger to Haarlem to collect your father who arrived the next day early in the morning on his bike. He'd ridden all night, risking his life through the curfew. My parents came a day later for the funeral. I wanted to take your sister home with me, but the German authorities wouldn't authorise her transport and so we buried her in Heilo.' My mother moved around the table to spread out the plates.

'On the day of the funeral some school children came to sing the Mass of the Angels and they scattered white flowers around the baby's head in the coffin. Afterwards we all walked together through the town, your father and I, followed by my mother and father who were then followed by my cousins. The undertaker carried the small, white box under his arm in front. And everyone who passed in the street stopped to bow their heads or tilt their caps.'

Again, my mother sighed, but she did not cry. 'I can't remember the burial. I had dysentery by then and everything was running out of me so I couldn't return to Haarlem straight away. I had to stay on with my cousins until I had the strength to walk home. And when I finally made that trip, I walked with an empty pram and an empty space in my heart.'

My mother's eyes looked sad when she mashed together the potatoes, leeks and onion, then mixed them with milk and butter. She took out the beater and began to pummel them together. With every plunge it was as if she was driving away the memory.

IN YEARS to come, the photo of my dead baby sister, also named Hannah, took its place on the third page of our family album, the one after my oldest brother's birth, and two pages after the wedding shots.

One day, I peeled out her photo from the corners of this album. There were two almost identical pictures of the first Hannah, side by side. I hoped no one would notice the space left behind.

'She's dead,' I said and held the photo out to a group of girls in the playground. My fingers had smeared the photo's surface. The other children peered at the image. They wanted to stare at this picture of a dead baby. Not one of them had seen a dead body before, and not one of them had been able to imagine the stillness. I didn't show my teacher. I thought there was something wrong in this way of getting attention from my classmates. I hid the photo from my sisters and brothers, too.

I have it still — my dead sister with wispy fine black hair. In the photo there are dark shadows underneath her closed eyes. She looks asleep.

If this dead sister had lived, I imagine that none of what happened to my older sister would have happened. It would have been different for me too; I would not have my mother's name, the name given to the second daughter and my living sister Hannah would not have had her maternal grandmother's name, the privilege of the first born girl. Everything would have been topsy-turvy, and I might not have needed to hide.

In my father's house

MY PARENTS' bedroom stood at the front of the house, opposite a statue of Jesus hanging from his crucifix on top of the piano in the front hall. Jesus' feet were cracked where the nail had been driven in and although someone had tried to glue them back into place, the plaster had split up to his knees. So Jesus hung freely from his arms and swung from side to side in the breeze whenever someone opened the front door.

Further down the hallway, there was no sign on my parents' bedroom to say, 'keep out', but somehow I knew it was not a place to visit, at least not for long. Yet I was still drawn to this room.

My mother made up the bed each day by dragging a thick maroon cover over the top to hide the rumpled sheets and blankets. She had dyed the bedspread the colour of dried blood, to hide the stains on what was once a white bedspread, which she had brought with her from Holland. The spread was too heavy for regular washing and gave off a musty smell.

On the wall opposite the bed my parents had put my mother's Queen Anne dressing table. Three oval mirrors were held by hinges such that you could pull the two outer wings together and sandwich your body in between to see the front and back of yourself reaching to infinity.

On the wall of my parents' bedroom that faced the front window was a print of a bronze cast of Atlas hoisting the world globe on his shoulders. The bronze cast gave his skin a dark complexion as if he were from some place like Africa, some place I had learned about at school where we prayed for the missions and fed coins to Sambo in his straw hat and red jacket, as he sat on top of our teacher's table. The nuns encouraged us to slide a coin onto Sambo's tongue and when you pressed a lever at the back, the penny disappeared.

I came into my parents' bedroom in search of coins, not for the missions but to spend on lollies. When my father was away at work I rifled through his suit coats in the tall wardrobe next to the picture of Atlas. Money was not the only thing that attracted me. My father's military uniform stood in the cupboard along with his dress sword, in its silver sheath with gold tassels. When you pulled it in and out it made a squeaking sound as if a balloon had been let free, and the blade itself surprised me. It was as blunt as my brothers' toy plastic swords.

By the time I was ten, my mother worked in a children's home in Burwood looking after other peoples' children. She worked to a roster that included Saturdays. She worked at a time when most mothers did not work. She had no choice, she said. We needed the money.

In those days, Hannah took responsibility for running the household. She washed clothes, load after load, a week's washing for eleven people, piled high on the laundry floor. She cleaned the house, vacuumed, scrubbed, and gave instructions to us little ones about how to pitch in. The boys took off to play, but she expected my younger sisters and me to stay.

By mid-afternoon on hot summer days, Juliana and I also made our escape to the local swimming pool, but not before we walked past the open hallway door and saw Hannah perched on our father's lap. He was whispering in her ear.

I looked away.

The banister that led down the five or six steps onto the concrete path that took you to the change rooms of the swimming pool was made of steel. Round and cold to touch. It bent to accommodate the slope of the ground as it moved down the hill beside the pool onto the entrance to the change rooms, which fitted underneath, cave-like. In the corners of the shower recess there were green slime marks from the constant dripping, which I imagined was the swimming pool leaking into the earth. The change rooms stank of chlorine. Chlorine was the smell of summer.

The water at the swimming pool was the bluest of blues. I thought the colour must have come from the stuff that was added to the water and gave it the chlorine stink, a stink that stayed on my skin long after I had returned home from the pool.

Summer was also the freedom of swimming, an escape from my father. He did not swim. He had diabetes and needed to take care of his feet. He would not go to the beach for the same reason. There could have been strange things in the sand, broken bits of glass, the sharp edge of an abandoned tin can that could have cut his feet and if his feet got cut, he bled and if he bled something happened to his circulation and he could have wound up with gangrene and they might have to chop off his feet.

How I wished they would do that so he would not be able to walk. In a wheelchair he could not roam the house at night.

During one of my trips to the swimming pool, on my way out from the change rooms, I used the rod of the banister as a monkey bar and hung upside down. I did this repeatedly until my hand slipped and I was on the ground with a crash. I felt it in my shoulder, the pain of a broken bone or some other internal damage but I did not tell the pool people. Not until I reached home did I complain to my mother.

This was a mistake. My mother told my father. My father went to examine me. We did not use doctors in our house. Our father saw himself as the medical expert. The worst of it was when he bandaged my chest round and round like a mummy.

After my father bandaged me up, ready for postage, I took off, glad to be spared any more handling when he called to the others that he was ready for a game of bridge.

My brother Ferdi scowled but said nothing as he lifted the coffee table into place between my parents in readiness for the game. Sometimes Ferdi played with my mother in opposition to Hannah and my father, and sometimes they swapped sides.

Bridge was a tricky game. I knew this not from playing — I was too young to join in — but from the way my father barked orders at my mother whenever he let her be his partner, and from the sighs and grunts he let out whenever his partner — usually Hannah — made a wrong move, or had not been able to hold in mind all the cards that had been played by other people.

They played bridge on the same table as my mother did the ironing and the same table that held the plates of biscuits when visitors came by, aunts and uncles and cousins, the same table at which my father studied for his accountancy exams.

My father once rested a microscope he brought home from work on this same table. He fitted it sideways in front of his chair, then sat behind it and we were allowed to come up one at a time to look at the slides he had bought from a laboratory somewhere: a squashed and petrified ant, a strand of hair, a grain of sand. These things became pieces of life from outer space when I looked through the hole of the microscope, pleased that, at times like this, when my father had found something of interest and wanted to show us the wonders of the world, we could all come out of hiding.

When the others played bridge it was safe again for me to hover around the edges of the lounge room out of sight. I felt bad for the ones my father had trapped into these games, even as my chest hurt from the bandages and I was too stiff to move much. At least I was free to come and go. They had no choice but to sit near him, to hang on his every word, to concentrate and not make a mistake, while I read my book in the corner of the room. But over the hours the tension rose and my father kept on drinking till there was nothing left in the brandy bottle beside his chair.

My mother stood to make another cup of tea, her third for the evening. 'Anyone else want a cup?' she asked. But no one else had a chance to reply.

'You stupid woman,' my father said. 'You can't stop the game again.' My mother sat back down. She picked up her cards and studied them in silence.

'You don't care about the cards, do you?' my father went on. 'You care only for your children and your cups of tea. You selfish lazy woman.' My father pushed the table away from him and cards scattered everywhere. The dregs of my mother's tea dribbled onto the carpet where the cup had fallen and my sister and brother stood to gather up the cards. My mother bent to pick up the cup. No one spoke. My father leaned back in his chair and closed his eyes. The game was over for another night.

BY THE time my cracked collarbone had healed, Ferdi left home, and Gerard and Henry took his place at bridge. Luckily my turn never came. Once I was old enough to play, my father had lost interest in the game in much the same way he had lost interest in the proper care of babies, leaving me free to disappear. I took after my mother then and found an escape in books.

In the front room of the Camberwell house there was a wall-to-ceiling-bookcase, filled with books, all shapes and sizes. Most of the spines were in Dutch, but there were a few whose titles stood out because I could read them. Günter Grass, *The Tin Drum. A University Anthology of Poetry*, A series of *Reader's Digests* on Japan, Italy, America and a fat book on Art by Gombrich. When no one was looking, I pulled the art book out from the shelf, pushed the other volumes together to fill the gap, and hid the book under my jumper. I carried it to my room and dragged the blanket up over my shoulders, tee-pee style. I sat cross-legged and put the book in front of me. It had a shiny cover that showed a stone statue of a naked man without a head or arms. His penis was like a bunch of grapes with the leaves still attached.

In time I came to know all the pictures inside. Somewhere near the middle, there was an old man in a red shirt. He held a small girl on his lap. He was reading to her. The picture was painted from close up, so you could see his every pore, like tiny blackheads. On the end of his nose there was a large warty lump, uneven, like two mountains pushed side by side. The girl on his lap had toffee-coloured curls that fell around her shoulders. Her eyes were brown like chocolate and she looked happy.

I would not have been so happy sitting on the old man's knee. I could imagine the smell of his breath. It was stale like left over wine. His skin was clammy like a warm dishcloth and his hair had the old man smell of my Dutch grandfather. I turned the page and there was *The Rape of Lucrece*. There were horses in this picture, strong white horses with hooves held high, and on their backs a fully clothed man held onto a naked woman. Actually he was dragging the woman off another horse ridden by another man and the two horses stood side-by-side, rearing and bucking, as if they were unsettled by this exchange — one woman, two horses and two men. The two men looked as though they were fighting over the woman and her long brown hair fell down over her shoulders. Her skin was milk white. Her breasts were huge and firm. I told myself I should not look at this picture. Nor did I want anyone to see me looking. It would only add to the black patches on my soul.

Eggs

ON SUNDAYS my mother passed around the eggs — we only ever ate eggs on Sundays — one for each child, one for her and two for my father. She cooked my father's first in the fry pan alongside a butter-soaked slice of bread. Then my brothers each took it in turn to cook theirs. Ferdi still came for breakfast sometimes, dressed in his red velvet jacket. He got Hannah to fry his egg for him. Hannah preferred to boil hers, hard-boiled, the yolk yellow as the sun. Finally, my mother scrambled baby Jacob's egg into a buttery spread at the bottom of a saucepan. I was in the middle, and old enough then to cook my own egg.

I took it to the corner of the kitchen away from the others and cracked it on the side of a teacup. I eased apart the shell with my thumb and finger, so that the inner skin held like a hinge when I pulled the shell back. I then tipped the yolk from one half of the eggshell to the other, letting the white slide into my cup. All the while I kept a close eye on the yolk, not only for blood blisters that might suggest a fertilized egg gone wrong — one I would not eat — but also for ruptures. The yolk glistened and slipped from one side of the shell to the other.

When all the white had slid away into the cup, I offered the yolk to one of my brothers to cook alongside his own, as if his egg had had twins. Then I took a fork and two spoons full of sugar and began to whisk. I tilted the cup to one side to get maximum egg white without spilling any. I did this for an hour or two. I did this till the kitchen was empty of breakfast eaters and well past the time when we needed to leave for church and it was too late to eat. We needed to fast for three hours before Mass and communion; otherwise we would be in sin.

Two hours later, when I came home from Mass and went to collect my egg white from the fridge, it still sat in the cup like a fluffy white cloud, but the cloud no longer stuck to the sides of the cup. It had come away and slid around the inside afloat on a trickle of liquid that had leaked its way out, like a rain puddle. It no longer tasted of meringue, but had a raw egg flavour that curdled my stomach.

Around this time, I saw that the hem of my school dress had unravelled. I needed to hold it up in the front with one safety pin, and in the back with another. I feared Mrs Wilson would notice at my piano lesson on the Wednesday. She would say to me:

'You should ask your mother to sew it up for you. A big girl like you, in a dress like that.' Then she would ask me how much I had practised.

'At least three times this week', I would lie; otherwise she would need to speak to my mother.

The next Wednesday, I collected my music from the piano stand. It was still open at the page where I had left it a week ago. The door to the lounge room was open. Through the crack I could see my father. He stared into the space in front of him and the smoke from his cigarette curled around his head. It was early for him to be home from work and he had not yet started to drink. Nor was he likely to drink on a Wednesday.

He sat as still as a statue, as still as the statue of the Blessed Virgin on the mantelpiece behind him. The white plaster was visible just at the point that her hand had snapped off the last time Juliana dusted it. We did not tell and no one noticed. Juliana hid the hand in the briquette bin and used her *Texta* colour to mark the white black, but the colour had faded and from my position at the door it stared back at me like an eye. My father looked up and saw me.

'Come here', he said. I watched his Adam's apple go up and down on his neck, under his collar and tie. My mother's new pink dressing gown was folded on his lap. He brushed over it with his spare hand as if he was straightening out the creases.

'You have a new baby sister', he said, 'but she died this morning.' My father flicked ash off my mother's new dressing gown. We had bought it only last week, my mother and I, in the lingerie shop where they took her away inside a cubicle to fit her for a new bra, so that she would be able to feed the baby more easily, she told me.

'What baby?' I had wanted to ask. Another baby. I hoped it would be a girl.

My father collected his keys and moved to the door. He did not break his stride to hesitate or say goodbye. His footfall in the hall way softened on the outside bricks. I slid my music books under my arm and followed him. Mrs Wilson did not complain about my hem when I told her about my mother's dead baby. She only sighed.

Two weeks later, I stood beside my mother in the front garden of our house.

The geraniums had wilted under the summer heat, and my mother picked at them. She plucked off the dead ones and threw them away.

Mrs Bruyn from up the street stopped at our fence.

'I was sorry to hear about your baby', she said, and my mother's eyes filled with tears. 'But you still have your other children. They must be a comfort to you.'

My mother nodded, her eyes misty with tears, and Mrs Bruyn walked away. I watched her floral dress billow in the breeze. I heard the clip clop of her heels on the concrete path. Like my parents, Mrs Bruyn came from Holland, the land of babies, my mother told me, the land of large families, even if there was not enough room.

Mrs Bruyn had room for babies but she had not made any. It was not her fault, my mother told me, something to do with her eggs. Eggs, I thought then, like chicken eggs that sit under the warmth of a fat hen, then one day crack open and out pops a baby.

WHEN MY mother was in her late seventies I asked her yet again about her lost baby, not just the first who died during the war, or the miscarriage in between but about this last still born child, Anna Maria. My mother thought it had happened around the Easter time but I was unsatisfied as to her accuracy and curious, I contacted the Registry of Births Deaths and Marriages. And there it was, my sister was born dead on 19 November 1962. On that same day I was just ten days clear of my tenth birthday.

The synchronicity of numbers appealed to me then, but the sense of what it had been like to lose another sister in my tenth year is another one of those I have deleted from the bank of my sensations, another of those disappearing emotions, with all but the outline of events and details to remind me.

I have many such memories, events that at the time filled me with a sensation of numbness. Too many to count. Only later in adulthood during my long years of therapy and analysis could I begin to make sense of this impulse to disappear and to avoid touch, alongside an increasing longing to be seen and heard.

And so it was, numbers frightened me. My parents were always adding babies or sometimes losing them. For the first ten years of my life, my mother was either pregnant or carrying a newborn, but I have no memory of these pregnancies, not until my mother lost her last baby and two days later Mrs Fitzgerald lined us up in front of the blackboard in order of second names.

We were working on our times tables. I had hung back to get in a few minutes practice before it came to my turn.

The scratch of her chalk on the blackboard as Mrs Fitzgerald wrote down the next sum panicked me. I did not know about the French Revolution then but thinking on it now it was as if we were heading to the guillotine, and our execution. Mrs Fitzgerald smiled with all the charm of the women who knitted as the knife fell. Unlike the beautiful Miss Anderson, from the year before, Mrs Fitzgerald, who came from Scotland and whose harsh voice matched her harsh manner, was strict and unyielding, especially when it came to numbers. Either you knew them or you didn't and if you didn't know them there was no hope for you.

Almost summer, and I felt my dress press to my back as I tried to focus on my body as a way to steady my nerves. The two times, the three times, the four times and five were easy. They made sense. They had a rhythm and if she gave me one of them I would be fine, but if she took a higher order number out of her lucky dip of sums then I was bound to fail.

The boy ahead of me, Joey Santamaria, was one of the smart kids in the class. It didn't help to have him one ahead. Our second names both started with S, which put us together all the time. I could see by the slope of his shoulders that he felt none of the terror that had locked my brain into a panic.

Joey was the nephew of an important man named Bob Santamaria, a politician. My father did Bob Santamaria's books. I should have been good at numbers. My father was an account-ant but none of his daughters were good at numbers, he said, because girls weren't good with them. But being a girl was not a good enough excuse for Mrs Fitzgerald.

Joey Santamaria stepped forward after Maria Rizzo went back to her desk with a smile on her face. I saw the shapes on the board, the number seven to be multiplied by seven. Joey cleared his throat and got it right. He strode back to his seat, a grin on his face wide enough to take in the whole room.

I watched Mrs Fitzgerald dust off the last sum. She scratched her marks on the board. I watched as she turned to face the class and then looked at me.

'Your turn.'

The numbers swam before me like fish in water. They wriggled and spun. If they had been anywhere below five I would have recognised them but I could not this time, even though there were twos and ones in the mix.

Mrs Fitzgerald coughed. 'It's a tough one,' she said. 'But you should be able to manage it. Twelve times twelve.' I stuttered out the wrong answer and hobbled back to my desk hoping the floor might swallow me up and desperate to avoid the smug look in Joey Santamaria's eyes.

MY MOTHER told me, in years to come, if someone tells you often enough, as my father told her, you are stupid and have no brains, you begin to believe them. As a child I tried to develop patterns in my head to understand the way of things. I believed the cleverest children in my family were the oldest with intelligence decreasing as you went down the line, and beauty the inverse. The two littlest, Rebecca and Jacob, may not have been so smart — but they were beautiful.

In such a way equations evened things out, but as the sixth in line, one below the exact middle, I was left with not much to go on.

Killing time

WE SAT in the green Farina on the side of Elgar Road. My mother had parked the car a few blocks down from the children's home where she worked. She said we could come with her to work that Saturday because we didn't want to stay at home with our father, but we would need to spend the day in her car.

'Not all the time in the car,' she said. 'You can go for walks, too.'

The children's home was a fifteen-minute drive from where we lived. It was over the road from another home for teenagers, called Orana and next-door was the Princess Elizabeth Home for Blind and Deaf Children. In between these places were ordinary houses where ordinary people lived. My mother parked her car outside one of these ordinary houses right on the edge of the Princess Elizabeth.

There were no shops nearby which was just as well because we didn't have any money. We had already made four rounds of sandwiches for our lunch. One round each. I would have made more but we ran out of bread. I made one of the sandwiches with Vegemite for Juliana and the others with plum jam. Thick slices of white bread covered in butter or jam, the jam my father brought home from the Monbulk factory where he worked as an accountant. My father got this jam for free. He did the books there and the woman in the office knew he had a big family so she kept the spoiled ones for him, the dented tins, some squashed in at the top, and many without their labels. Mostly they were of plum, but if you were unlucky you'd find a melon and ginger tin among the plums.

When this happened to me, I told no one, but took the tin, forced back the lid I had just prised open with the can opener, and carried it into the back yard around the side of the house where we kept the rubbish bins. I took a brown paper bag with me so I could hide the tin from anyone else who came out after me to throw away garbage. It was a waste to throw out good food but if I left the tin of melon and ginger jam on the bench, even if I did not eat any myself, we would not be able to open another tin of jam until the melon and ginger was empty. We all hated melon and ginger, except my mother, and so it took an age before we got to the bottom of the tin. This way was better.

On this Saturday, my mother did not need a sandwich. She would have a hot lunch with the children at Allambie. My mother was lucky to have this job, she told us after she got it. She told the man who interviewed her that she had no childcare training but she had nine children of her own. That was training enough. 'Besides, if you don't give me a job, there'll soon be another nine children coming to your centre.'

My mother needed the money, she told us often, to pay the school fees. 'Education,' my mother said, 'is the best thing you can give your children.'

'Be good,' my mother was looking at me. 'And stay together. I finish work at four.'

We should have bought more books to read but that was no good for Jacob who was only three. Becca was six and read slowly. Only Juliana and I could read books. It was better that we play *I Spy* or sing songs.

'Let's have half our sandwiches,' I said, an hour or so into our wait, 'for something to do.'

Eating was good. It made us feel full but only for a while. I had to stop Jacob from getting into the second half of his sandwich to save it for later. The sky was grey with swirls of thick clouds slipping through the silvery ones. Even though it was early spring and still cold outside it got hot in the car.

'Let's go for a walk,' I said and remembered not to lock the car. Our mother had taken the key. There was a park at the end of Elgar Road at the corner where it turned into Riversdale Road, full of wattles and gumtrees, called Wattle Park. In the middle of the park there was an old tram hollowed out of everything but its wooden seats and the posts that people used to hold themselves up. It had no wheels. We walked all the way uphill to the tram. It was easy to trip along the dirt path full of potholes and tree roots, especially with Jacob's short legs, so we dawdled. Halfway up the hill I gave him a piggyback.

'I want a piggyback, too,' Becca said. I swapped with Juliana. She took Jacob on her back. He was lighter, and I carried Bec. We puffed our way up to the tram and stepped inside. The kiosk on the tip-top of the hill had a "Closed" sign in front. It wasn't yet lunchtime. A car pulled up and a woman dragging bags full of potatoes stopped to unlock the door of the kiosk. She flipped over the closed sign. We sat for ages inside the tram until more people arrived, other children who wanted to climb aboard, other children whose parents made their way into the kiosk for tea and scones with jam and cream. I had never eaten a scone before but I could imagine the taste, especially the cream and the jam.

'Let's go back to the car to finish our lunch,' I said.

The trip back was easy. We made it in half the time. We even sang together, songs that helped us forget we were walking, because we had to concentrate on the words. Songs that made the two little ones laugh. Soon we were back inside my mother's car, where we ate the last of our sandwiches and for a few more minutes were happy and full.

The afternoon dragged. 'Time for a nap,' I said to Jacob. 'Put your head on my lap.' We swapped places. Juliana moved to the front to read one of her war books and I moved to the back in the middle with Bec's head on one knee and Jacob's on the other. They fell asleep quickly. I felt drowsy too. A sliver of sunlight broke through the clouds. The car was warmer than ever. Juliana and I nodded off. Sleeping killed time.

I woke up with a cramp in both legs and watched as a bus pulled into the Blind and Deaf Home and a line of children scrambled out. They looked ordinary enough but I could tell some were deaf because they used finger signs to talk to one another, while the blind ones held white canes or were led by hand.

When my mother first got her job at the Allambie Reception Centre, I asked her what "reception" meant.

'It's where children go when the courts need time to decide where they'll live after their parents have separated or died. It's not an orphanage, though. Children in orphanages have no parents. Children at Allambie are trying to find parents, their old ones or new ones.' It was different with us, she said. We had Catholic parents who'd taken a vow and made a promise to stay together forever. Catholics did not separate. Catholics did not break their vows.

At Allambie my mother wore a grey dress for her uniform. It had buttons all the way up the front. It was as grey as the clouds in the sky that day. She liked it grey. Dirt wouldn't show. She liked her work, she told me. During her shifts she was responsible for over sixty children. My mother always liked children, babies best of all.

Jacob grunted in his sleep and Bec rolled over. The cramp in my legs got worse and my bum ached from too much sitting. I wanted to walk more but it was better for the others to stay asleep. Soon our mother would come and take us home. Soon this day would be over.

I fell asleep again and woke to the sound of the car door opening. My mother smiled, as if she'd only just left.

The following Saturday, I sat at the front gate of our house long enough for the thin sun to warm my skin. I sat still; hopeful no one might notice me. Hannah had issued house-cleaning instructions to me and to the others and I did not want to join them. I could have been clearing out lost objects from under my bed, or wiping over the dusty mantelpiece. Instead, I sat in the sun.

Why must I work? Why must I bother with the busy stuff when there was all this peace to be had at a gatepost in the early spring sunshine? The others must have been busy enough not to notice my absence, or they, too, might have taken to hiding. Only Hannah would be hard at it, cleaning and sweeping, mopping and dusting. Only she cared about these things. We stayed home all that morning while our mother was at work again, we younger ones avoiding the housework, until some time after lunch when Juliana and I snuck off to the station to await her return.

The slatted seat, still sticky from rain, stuck to our skin but there were no other seats left under cover and it was easier for Juliana and me to sit between train arrivals than to stand. In those days when she did not drive her car, our mother took the train from Alamein. It stopped at all stations to Camberwell and only there joined the Lilydale line to the city. Every Saturday when she was rostered to work, she took the train to Alamein and from there she walked to Elgar Road and the children's home. Most Saturdays at the end of the day, from four o'clock onwards, Juliana and I waited for our mother's train to make the return trip to the city, stopping at all the stations, including ours, in East Camberwell, from which she would eventually emerge.

Train after train came and went and each time I heard the thrumming on the line that signified a train approaching, I peered ahead filled with expectation. Then we watched after the train had stopped, while doors opened and passengers alighted, hopeful that our mother might soon step onto the station and then we would be safe.

As the last person left the station, we paused to take in that first rush of disappointment and began to hope again she'd be on the next train. The man in uniform blew his whistle and the train snaked its way on towards the city.

We sometimes waited for hours like this, until that particular Saturday when our mother came home from work early. We could not believe our luck, but her face, usually filled with smiles when she caught sight of us, was flat. My sister and I, one on either side, walked with her through the tunnel from the station that led up to the electricity output station, across past the scout hall and down through the park that eventually joined Canterbury Road and the final stretch home.

We did not tell her about our day at home avoiding the housework and our father. We had learned to keep our minds focussed on the happy things, the good things, the joy of walking side by side with our mother at last, the smell of pink blossom from the trees outside the scout hall, the first sprinkling of spring rain. We held our hands over our heads and sped up our steps to keep from getting wet before we reached the shelter of the shops.

I did not want to go home to my father, but there was no other choice. By now his mood, as typical on Saturdays, had dropped into one of darkness. The bottle at his side from which he took slurps was his one comfort.

Once home, we did not say hello but went straight for the kitchen where our mother took off her coat, hung it over a chair and pulled up the sleeves of her cardigan. She filled the sink with water and dropped in a pile of potatoes and then held each one in turn to scrub off the dirt with her fingertips, until her nails were black and each potato bare skin. She drained them and left the potatoes in the sink before taking them to the chopping board for peeling.

Our father staggered into the kitchen from time to time and each time he grew louder and angrier. Juliana and I crouched under the kitchen table holding onto our dolls as if they were safety harnesses until our father left the room, only to wait again for his return. We said nothing. We were trained in the art of pretence. We were good at behaving as though we were not there.

The potatoes were boiling in their water till there was almost no water left to boil, as our mother peeled a bunch of carrots and a couple of onions, which she had stripped and sliced, her eyes streaming. Once she'd mixed the potatoes and carrots altogether till they were soft, she added the fried onion and a splash of milk. She mashed the lot with globs of butter. We ate this *hutspot* together with sliced tongue for us kids, and steak for our father. My mother cooked his steak last in a river of butter that sizzled on the stove-top, while she boiled our meat, and then peeled off the layer of taste buds from the cow's tongue before slicing.

'I'm hungry,' our father said at the door. 'I wait all day for something to eat and you come in as though there's nothing to do.'

'I've got dinner ready,' our mother said and turned to serve onto plates.

'I don't want any of that shit,' he said. 'I've waited too long.'

Waiting was like that. You waited and you waited and the more you thought about the waiting, the worse it became. The more our father thought about the waiting, the angrier he became, too, and the more likely, when the thing he had waited for finally arrived, he didn't want it any more.

Falling

DURING THE school holidays, Juliana and I went one day to visit a friend whose father was a builder. Our friend's family lived in a red-bricked Edwardian mansion in Salisbury Street, which her father had renovated, with many secret rooms. On the top floor in one corner where the ceiling sloped down to the skirting board there was a half door that led into the roof cavity. It was held fast with a slide lock. Our friend, Suzanne, drew it aside and stepped in. She needed to hunch down to fit. Juliana followed and I was last in line.

'Lock the door behind you,' Suzanne called to me as I climbed inside. 'We shouldn't be doing this.' The space inside the roof cavity was so low we had to crawl on all fours to move along beyond the door. I could see chinks of light through the roof tiles overhead. It gave the place an eerie feel as if we were underground, and not high up, as I knew we must be. The air smelled of glue and dust mixed together.

We inched along like snails between the splintery roof beams and left behind a cleared path of pink insulation. In moments my knees began to itch, even as I tried to push the insulation aside. It fluffed into my nose and stuck to my lips. I tried to lick it off and wiped it with the back of my hand, but it hurt to touch, like splinters of glass.

'I'm not sure about this,' I called to Suzanne.

'It's okay,' she said. 'It's fun. Let's get to the middle.' Ahead I could see the slope of roof tiles where they met a distant wall and wondered whether this might be the middle. This crawling along the gritty floor seemed endless. I could see the outline of Suzanne's body ahead, her pink underpants smooth around her tight bottom. Juliana's underpants were fraying at the edge. There was a line of elastic that drooped down her leg. I had the urge to rip it clear, but could not reach. The palms of my hands were scratched and sore. At times my fingers dug through the *Insulwool* into something soft, as if in places the floor had given way.

Suzanne let out a shriek when one of my legs shot out from underneath me and dangled into space. Ahead Juliana had dropped out of sight. I looked through the hole where her body had fallen. She was lying on the floor below covered in plaster and pink insulation. She looked as though she could be dead, until I heard her gasp for breath.

Suzanne turned full circle to face me. 'We've got to get out of here.' She steered her way beside the hole my sister had made as one of her arms pushed through and made yet another crater in the ceiling surface. It was like looking through a colander down to the room below. Suzanne wrenched back her arm and forced her way past me. I crawled behind her, trying to make myself float. I wanted to think my body into non-existence, as if it held no weight at all.

The wooden beams that fixed the ceiling in place were like alleys we now crawled through. I held onto them to take my weight, but my legs pushed against the insulation and the floor crumbled with each drag of my body.

We reached the entrance and I followed Suzanne out through the latch door. We stood on the landing face to face with our horror. Suzanne was covered in plaster and *Insulwool*. I looked down at my arms and hands, which were also covered. Like pink ghosts, we fled down the stairs.

I could hear Suzanne's mother in the kitchen. My mind raced. How could we hide this? How could we fix it? I wanted to run out the front door. Leave it all behind. We raced from room to room looking for Juliana. We had no idea which ceiling she had fallen through. We wrenched open doors and slammed them shut. We found my sister on the floor of the rumpus room. Suzanne's father had made this room especially for Suzanne and her siblings, a playroom filled with toys and equipment.

'He just put a new ceiling in here,' Suzanne said as we looked up to the line of holes that spread in one direction across the length of the room. Bits of loose plaster and pink insulation trickled through like the padding from a torn stuffed animal.

Juliana looked like a broken doll as she hobbled to her feet and leaned against me.

'We'll have to tell my father,' Suzanne said.

Then the full weight of what we had done hit me. To tell her father was to tell my father.

'I'll go look for him.' Suzanne left us standing in the middle of the room and we waited for what seemed an eternity before they returned. Suzanne's father loomed in the doorway. He looked at us, he looked upwards to the ceiling, and he looked down at the floor.

'You two, go home,' he said, then turned to Suzanne. 'I'll deal with you later.'

After we arrived home we told our mother about the holes in the ceiling and her face puckered up with that worried look she had whenever something bad was about to happen, but she promised not to tell our father, unless Suzanne's father asked for money to pay the costs. I needed to find some way to escape the fear that at any moment he might knock on the door. For days afterwards I could feel the *Insulwool* prickle my skin even after my Saturday bath, and I was desperate to shake off the memory. I needed to find some way out of remembering and so each morning for the rest of the holidays I took off on my bike to travel as far away as I could.

The next week and still no phone call from Suzanne's father, I decided I would ride to Sydney, an entire state away. I told no one. No one needed know. And I took off full of confidence that I would be there by late afternoon and back by nightfall. I was on a mission. In the morning, I cut myself a sandwich, spread it with butter and Vegemite, wrapped it in greaseproof paper and dropped it into the basket at the head of my bike. The bike basket showed my bike was different from my brother's bikes. Only girls had bike baskets and mine had a plastic flower in front. Boys carried their belongings in their pockets.

Uphill was the worst. Burke Road past the turn to Doncaster, a good run down to the Yarra River, and then I stopped. I ate my sandwich and found a drink tap next to play equipment in a park, carved out of flat land near the river. I was thirstier than I'd thought, and my legs had taken on that jelly-like quality that comes out of too much exercise. The sun was mid sky and I had learned enough from nature study classes to know that it would only get hotter, but, in the shade of the gum trees and with a slight breeze skipping over the river, I cooled down.

I walked my bike to the edge of the paddocks that surrounded the river and left it there, climbed down the bank, took off my sandals and socks and then plunged my feet into the water. Mud oozed between my toes and twigs scratched against my legs. There was a light current, not enough to push me off balance but enough to make me want to stay close to the edge, close enough to be able to reach out to the thick tufts of grass that sprouted there.

My feet in the ooze and all I could imagine were dangerous creatures underneath, creatures that might drag me down if I stayed too long but it took a huge effort to drag myself back onto the shore. A cow in a nearby paddock looked up from chewing on grass. Even the cow had an ominous look in her eye as if she were unhappy that I should be there.

That's when I saw the man at the top of the hill, the man who stood looking down at my bike, sizing up the basket, as if he were looking for a rider and her belongings, as if he were looking for me. And what could a man alone on a hill near a river want with the rider of a small girl's bike, one he would know belonged to a girl because it held a basket? The man's silhouette on top of the hill, a black shape against a blue sky left me with a feeling I had broken rules. There were no signs around that said 'Do not trespass'. The river was free, or so my brothers had told me, but this man reminded me of the word 'no'.

I needed to hide. I took off on my bike as fast as I could pedal back along Burke Road through the junction back to Camberwell. When I reached home my brothers were in the back garden. They did not want to go inside, they said. Our parents were fighting and our father had hit our mother. We waited till dark until our mother called out to us that we should come inside for dinner. Our father was asleep by then and when Gerard asked her what had happened and why our father had hit her she said it was best to 'Do as if nothing has happened'.

In this way, I forgot about Suzanne's father, too. It was as if the hole in the ceiling had never happened and once the *Insul-wool* itch wore off, I had nothing more to remind me, but the faintest memory of falling.

Miracles and Saints

DURING THE term, at lunchtimes when no one else was around, I sat in the church of Our Lady of Good Counsel next door to my school. I could hear the others outside in the playground. The classroom was off limits during lunch but anyone could go into the church at any time. Catholic doors were always open.

I went into the church to pray. At the door, I dipped my fingers into the holy water font and splashed it on my forehead. It began to dry on my jumper when I tapped my chest and was gone by the time my fingers reached my shoulders. I glided up the aisle and genuflected on one knee. The movement was satisfying, like slow dancing. Then I sat in the corner of a pew in the middle of the church, on the left hand side nearest the centre aisle, and studied the altar. I had a suspicion that God was calling me, God the Son, not the Father. God the Son, the one who was spread-eagled on a wooden cross with a tortured smile on His face. I waited for Him.

The church was built of sandstone-coloured bricks. Its ceiling was made of dark wooden beams that crossed over one another like a ribcage. The light from the stained glass window behind the altar threw beams of colour onto the white altar cloth. There were two candles, one at either end. You could hardly see their black unlit wicks above the candle wax.

Behind the altar there was a free standing wall set several inches in front of the back of the church. It held the gold tabernacle, with the shape of a fish etched onto its door and a round keyhole. No one ever went behind the tabernacle wall. The priest and altar boys came into the altar space from doors on either side of the church. The space behind the altar wall was narrow. It cast a long shadow on one side. From there I imagined Jesus would arrive at any moment.

Was anyone else as lucky as me? If I had a vocation, then I had been chosen by God to do his special work on earth. I did not need to be out in the playground with the others. I had special work to do and was waiting to be called.

Even as I had read my share of the lives of the saints and was inspired by my patron, Queen Elisabeth of Hungary, I could never be so certain of my calling as the saints. Elisabeth of Hungary had loved the poor. I hated them. The little black Sambo on the teacher's desk with his bright bow tie and red metal tongue stuck out begging for a penny became a constant reminder of the miseries of being poor. Unlike the other children in my class, I never had a spare penny to offer to him or to the starving poor. If I had, I would most likely have kept it for myself.

My mother said our patron saint had married a tyrant. My mother and I had the same name. She told me the story of our namesake. In her version, Saint Elisabeth went one day to visit the poor with a basketful of food. She had taken bread, freshly baked from the palace kitchens, and fruit—green apples, yellow pears—plucked from the palace orchards and vegetables from the gardens. A riot of colours and smells neatly tucked inside Elisabeth's basket and covered with a latticed cloth, normally used by the cook for cleaning and mopping up spills.

The poor family, a widow with four children in rags, were huddled together around an open fire in the centre of the thatched cottage when Saint Elisabeth made her entrance. Before she had a chance to make her offering, horse's hooves could be heard in the background and a moment later Saint Elisabeth's husband swooped in through the door and ripped off the cover from the basket. He had forbidden his wife to give anything to the poor and was about to berate her when he stopped in his tracks.

Roses, red and yellow, spilled out across the dusty floor, their perfume overtaking the sooty fumes of the fire. Saint Elisabeth was spared her husband's rage. He was the one humiliated through the intervention of God's miracle. I took it as a message about the way I should live my life, a selfless and invisible life, in the service of others.

Inside the church I prayed for the sins on the souls of the sinners in purgatory in one corner of my mind; from the other corner of my mind, I stared at the empty seats along the pews looking for things. God the Son did not arrive, so I used this part of my mind to set my legs walking up and down the aisle of the church and explored the empty seats for objects left behind from Sunday Mass.

I avoided a direct line with the Altar. God was watching. At best I needed to genuflect each time I moved into the centre of the church in line with the altar. At worst, God would strike me down for my disrespect in roaming around the church. There was the usual collection of black covered missals, the ones with gold embossed pages and a shining cross on the front cover announcing the word Missal. These I ignored. The ones that caught my attention were the colourful prayer books left behind by children. These were the missals of rich children, gifts for their First Holy Communions, their Confirmation, books given to them to inspire them to keep up the work of prayer and penance, books inspired to encourage children to read.

I opened one with a pearly cover. It reminded me of the inside of a mother of pearl shell, without the rainbow colours. It was the colour of milk. Inside the front cover, which had been thickened, the manufacturers had cut out a square alcove inside which they had laid a gold figure of the body of Christ on the cross. I fingered its outline. A small figurine but not so small that I could not see the suffering in God's uplifted eyes as he gazed towards some imaginary sun, as he gazed towards Heaven. There was no name attached to the inside sheet of this missal. It was a case, therefore, of finders keepers.

As I prayed for the sins of the souls in purgatory another side of me fingered the gold metal clasp that held the pages together. I slipped it into my pocket. The missal felt heavy at my side. All the way home through the streets of Camberwell I struggled with the thought that my find was okay on the one hand, but on the other, it was theft.

I held my hands over my hair as I walked through the magpie park, fearful a magpie might swoop down and peck at my head, even though I knew I would be safe. It was winter. Magpies only swooped in spring. I once saw the top of a girl's head bloodied between patches of blond hair from the pecking of a magpie's beak.

This magpie had been sure that this girl, not much taller than a rose bush, was about to threaten her babies, about to steal the eggs from her nest. I buried the missal in the backyard behind the garage where no one would find it. I buried it like a dog buries a bone. I wrapped it in a plastic bag and slid it into a cardboard box that once held my mother's new shoes. I dug a hole as deeply as I could in the small stretch of land between the garage and the back fence and set it into the hole as though it was a coffin. Then I let it slip from my mind to disappear with all my other sins until I could clear them away again in confession.

AT OTHER times, I did not steal but took on loans. One day I borrowed a doll from a girl at school with more Barbies than she could manage and although she insisted it was only a loan, it was okay for me to take Barbie home for the night.

I could not let my brothers and sisters see this doll, which I tucked into the bottom of my school bag. All the way home I felt

I was carrying dynamite. Barbie's breasts meant she was no ordinary doll, round and cuddly, baby like or small girl in appearance. Barbie's breasts jutted out even more than her elbows and they were smooth rounded without nipples, but suggestive enough to leave me excited as when I played with my sister's actual body.

I took Barbie down the laneway behind our house where a neighbour had hollowed out an entrance way to their garage door, a space secluded from view and safe from passers by. That afternoon, I spent the hours alone before dinner disrobing and re-dressing Barbie into the two outfits that came with her, an evening gown in gold material that bunched in at the waist and floated half way down between Barbie's calves and ankles. Barbie could not walk far in such a dress and I worked hard at pushing her feet in small steps to give the illusion of movement. The other outfit, her casual day dress, was easier to manoeuvre and so in my games Barbie alternated as a secretary by day and a glamorous movie star at night.

Barbie's nakedness propelled me into shivers of pleasure and guilt. I needed to dress her back fast so that I would not feel too exposed, as if someone had taken my clothes off.

A loan for one night only. The next day I took Barbie back to school and my rendezvous with the glamorous world of beautiful women was over. Somehow games with Barbie felt less sinful than games with my sister though I was careful to hide her from others, as if they would see through my actions and into my desires.

Peeping Tom

SOME SUNDAYS, my father gave me ten shillings, enough to buy three packets of Craven A (filter tipped). The left over money could go to buy lollies for us all. My choice included a packet of Fags, those long white cigarette shaped musk tasting lollies with a sparkling red sugar dot at one end just like a lit cigarette. I held one between two fingers like my father and showed off my smoking skills to Juliana and Becca who begged for a turn.

One such Sunday while my father slept off the alcohol of the days before, I collected the cold butts from his ashtray, butts that still held enough tobacco to catch fire. When I had enough of these butts in my pockets I took off for the outside toilet, slid the lock on the inside door, sat on the closed toilet seat and arranged my butts on the ground in front of me.

I took the healthiest first and lit it from matches I'd snuck out of the kitchen drawer near the stove. The butts flamed red as I dragged onto them in turn, deep breaths, taking care to keep my throat sealed off at the top so that no smoke got inside. I did not want the smoke to reach my pink lungs. My lungs were pink my father had told me because I did not smoke. But if I was like him and smoked three packets of cigarettes a day, each day, my lungs would soon turn black like his.

I took the butt once lit and as fast as I could one after the other I applied the lit end to a fresh strip of toilet paper. I used the live butts like a pencil to form the shape of my initials, the hard lines of an E followed by the curly strokes of an S. It gave me satisfaction to see my initials laid out on the strip of toilet paper, the black edges of each letter a better way of blackening the paper than of blackening my lungs or my father's by then black heart.

That night from under my blankets I watched Hannah as she slipped out of her tunic and blouse into a nightie. She had started to wear a bra and the fine point of her breasts rose up from her chest like hills. I touched my own nipples, flat against my ribcage.

I knew one day I would grow breasts like Hannah and my mother. But I couldn't wait. In the daytime when no one was looking I had taken an old towel, one my mother kept for dishcloths, from the laundry cupboard. I tore it into one long rectangular strip. Then I took a piece of coloured ribbon from Hannah's sewing basket and tied it around the centre of the material to make a gathering where I could imagine my cleavage to be after I had tied the material around my chest like a bra.

While everyone slept I wore my bra under my nightie. I liked to feel it in place and imagined myself to be grown up like Hannah and my mother. In the morning I scrunched it up into a ball and stuffed the bra into an empty cigarette pack, which I hid between my bed and the wall.

WHEN I came home from school the next day, I found my mother in her usual chair beside the fire. Hannah sat beside her. They looked up when I walked in and Hannah smiled. They looked at one another and without knowing why, I sensed I was in trouble. Then I saw the cigarette box and the strip of towelling laid out on the table.

'What's this?' my mother said. She held my make believe bra up to the light. 'You know you're too little for one of these.' Then she threw it back onto the table. 'Never mind. You'll be big enough one day.'

Hannah smiled again; as if she knew something I did not. My hands were clammy and my singlet felt wet under my armpits. My cheeks were on fire.

'Now throw this out where it belongs. In the rubbish.' My mother picked up the cigarette box and stuffed the bra back inside.

'What are you doing?' Gerard asked, minutes later when he caught me at the rubbish bin with the cigarette pack. 'Have you been smoking?'

'No,' I said. My face was still red from my mother's discovery.

'You've been smoking,' Gerard said. 'Don't worry. I won't tell.'

THE NEXT day, Sunday, we three girls crossed the magpie park in harmony on our way to Mass.

'You take the second part, Lissie. I'll take the lead and you, Juliana, come in only when we get to the chorus. You're tone deaf.'

We ignored the looks from passers-by. We sang religious songs so no one could object. But we stopped our singing by the time we reached Whitehorse Road near the church, only because there were too many passers-by and, although she did not say so, Hannah would have been embarrassed if any of her friends came along.

Hannah was fourteen. She had childbearing hips. She was getting ready for adulthood, and to do so she needed to behave in ways that went beyond playing with dolls and on swings in the park like Juliana and me. She needed to become a woman.

We went round to the back of the church where Hannah knocked on the sacristy door. The curate, Father Walsh, came out. He took Hannah by the hand and walked her around to the side of the church where they had a secret conversation that only Hannah and the priest could hear. Father Walsh was helping my older sister with her problems. She did not talk to him for long on Sundays when Mass was about to start, but every weekday morning and most often on Saturdays, too, she got up early, as early as five o'clock in the morning when it was still dark and the birds had not yet started to sing and she walked on her own to church. She went to early morning Mass, she told me. She went to talk to Father Walsh afterwards. She went before school. She went to escape our father who visited her in the night, at the other end of the night when it was dark and the rest of the house was asleep. Except for me.

That night after I had undressed into pyjamas and crawled under the blankets, I waited for Hannah to join me. The lights were still on, or perhaps I'd turned them off. I looked across to the window on one wall and there in the darkness I saw the white orb of a face, a man's face, I was sure. I froze and although I stared at this face, the eyes scanned the room and then disappeared.

I leapt from my bed into the lounge room where my mother sat with my older brothers watching television. My father was asleep in his bedroom.

'There's a man looking through my window,' I said and Henry and Gerard fled out the back door of our house down the side laneway and up Alexandra Avenue in search of him.

'A Peeping Tom,' Gerard said. They couldn't find him but they swore later they could see him in the distance. At the time I had no doubt that I had seen him, too.

A WEEK later my mother and I took the yellow bus to Camberwell. It smelled of shoe polish and leather. I sat beside my mother near the front. That day there were just the two of us, my mother and me, and we were travelling to Camberwell to shop.

I had wanted to complain to my mother about her plans to buy Juliana pantyhose, but I said nothing. I was older than Juliana and I was still in socks. Why should she wear stockings before me? My mother hummed as if she was nervous. The bus turned the corners too fast and I slid across the seat right up against her. My mother's body felt hard and soft at the same time.

An ambulance siren split the air. My mother hummed on as though she had not heard it. I watched the bus driver's neck. It had uneven black stubbly bits that ran down and hid under his collar. He had fat stubby fingers that worked the gears whenever we slowed down to stop. My mother looked ahead, still humming. Her nose jutted out, hooked. She was proud of it. Aquiline, she said, like an eagle, and a sign of aristocracy. My mother may have been proud but she sat hunched over in her green mohair coat with her handbag on her lap. She did not wear pantyhose. She wore stockings held up with a girdle.

My mother fiddled in her handbag for her compact. It opened with a puff of powder; sweet and tacky like Lux Soap. She dabbed the powder on her nose. My mother did not like her nose to shine. She squinted into the compact's tiny round mirror and smeared on a line of lipstick. Glossy red.

The top of the bus brushed against the branches of street trees as we turned corners. At Stanhope Street it stopped for an old man who fumbled in his pocket for change and nearly fell over when the bus started again.

'Pull the cord,' my mother said. 'We mustn't miss our stop.' I stretched to my full height, taller than my mother, and pulled on the cord, which was slack like a skipping rope. A loud buzz and the driver slowed down. We walked towards the shops along an alleyway that led to the railway station.

My father will kill us all. The thought popped into my mind and I wanted to push it away but it would not go. *He will kill us all, one by one. He will start with my mother, move onto Hannah and then it will be my turn. He will work through the girls and then start on the boys.* I did not know how he would do it, but he would.

A train rattled through the cutting nearby, and my mother and I turned into the shop to buy my sister's pantyhose.

That night my father was at the bedroom door. He had been asleep. All day long and at night too, he had slept fitfully and when he woke he roamed. Our bedroom was at the centre of the house, a corridor away from the lounge. It had high ceilings and a dark fireplace, open like a lion's mouth. We did not light fires in it. Someone had sealed off the chimney. I was wearing pyjamas but I was not in bed. I was sitting on top of the bed and Juliana and Rebecca were beside me.

My mother sat at the end of my bed. Hannah was pushed up against the wall in the space between my little sisters along with Henry and Gerard. My mother perched on the edge of the bed with Jacob on her lap. All of us waiting.

We had turned off the light in the bedroom but I could see the outline of my mother silhouetted against the window. The sky outside had a yellow glow. The moon was big and my mother said we must pray.

'Hail Mary full of grace ...'

We said the rosary like a chant, but did not announce the decades first like I'd been taught at school: the Joyful Mysteries, the Sorrowful and Glorious. We just rattled out the prayers. The Hail Marys, the Our Fathers, one after the other. My skin was cold. I sat very still. We all sat still, mumbling our prayers.

The door flew open and my father was standing there.

'What a good woman you are. You'll go to Heaven. You and your ugly children. You'll all go to heaven.' He lurched forward and my mother pulled back. Jacob toppled off her lap and my father grabbed a handful of her hair.

'Leave off,' she said.

My father staggered, lost his balance and fell. I sat like a mouse on my corner of the bed and held my breath.

My father pulled himself up by the bed leg and tottered from the room.

'Henry,' my mother said. 'Go for the police. Tell them to come here.'

The police, I thought. Oh, please bring the police. Henry hesitated. He listened. We all listened. It was silent in the rest

92

of the house. Henry slid off the bed. He pushed up the window and clambered over the ledge. The night swallowed him up and we began again to pray. There were six of us now on the bed still waiting.

I wanted to sleep. My eyes were heavy. I wanted to pull the blanket up around my shoulders. But we were sitting on top of it. We did not dare move. My father was at the door again. He had taken off his clothes. His body was thin. It looked wrong. It looked cold. It looked like I should not look. I did not want to look. He had taken off all his clothes and in the darkness, my eyes fixed on the hairy place between his legs, the hairy, scary place where his shrivelled-up penis looked like a newborn mouse.

My father reached towards my mother and again I braced ready to push him away from her, but instead he pushed her aside and flopped into the middle of the bed. We squeezed up tight to make room. I squeezed up tight to disappear. I could not bear to touch him.

'What a lovely family you have — what lovely children,' my father's words broke up. 'And I am so bad.'

'Go back to your bed,' my mother said. But my father did not move. He rested his back against the wall. Now we were all waiting, as if we were holding a truce, knowing at any moment, my father might have changed his mind. After a few minutes, he slid off the bed, glared at my mother and left again.

The doorbell rang, a brittle chime in the middle of the night. My mother pulled her dressing gown tight around her waist and went to answer. Voices boomed through the house. The blood started to flow in my arms and legs. The cold began to thaw. So stiff, so frozen, it hurt to unwind. The police were talking to my father. They would put him straight. My mother's voice chimed in.

'I'm going to my bed now,' Gerard said. The other girls followed.

I slid under the blankets and listened. The police were about to leave. I heard the clatter of the front door as it opened. They were talking now to my mother on her own.

'I'm sorry, there's nothing more we can do,' one policeman said.

'It's a domestic,' said the other. 'He should settle down now. Call his doctor in the morning.'

Bloody drunk

ONE FRIDAY after school, Mother Mary John handed me a brown parcel.

'Take this home,' she said. 'Put it in your bag. Don't show anyone and give it to your mother.' I did as I was told.

My mother ripped it open and there inside along with two navy school jumpers with the white stripe against the V were two party frocks, one blue and one pink. The blue was smaller. It fitted Juliana. The pink was mine.

The next day I felt like a princess as I put on my new dress and Juliana watched. She was jealous I could tell because I was off to a party.

My father was already in his Saturday morning rage. I could hear him from the lounge room booming at my mother who was running late for work.

'I've left you a cup of tea,' she said.

'Is that all?' His voice droned on but I didn't listen. I was off to a party.

LIBBY KEATING'S house was a double story cream brick veneer on Burke Road, way past the school on the way to my uncle and auntie's house in Ivanhoe. It had been a long walk from home and I was tired and hungry. Someone had tied pink balloons in bunches at the gate and from the window frames inside. The table was full of food, chocolate crackles, patty cakes with lolly faces, lamingtons and chips. There were white plastic throwaway cups of coloured lemonade, green and red and yellow.

We stood around the table, a line of girls in party dresses, and reached out to help ourselves from the plates in the centre. I had never seen so much food. Libby's mother brought out sausage rolls and meat pies from the oven. The girls squeezed dollops of red tomato sauce onto their plates. The plates were made of cardboard. You could throw them away afterwards.

Most girls put one or two pieces offered on their plates and took a few bites. They left the rest for later. We were allowed to do this. To eat as much or as little as we liked. To go away and to come back.

I did not want to leave the food table. I wanted to stay there forever. I ate and ate and stopped only when everyone was called for games of musical chairs, pass the parcel and pin the tail to the donkey.

I did not like these games. I wanted to eat. In the end I was the only one who came back to the table one last time before Libby's mother started to clear away the plates, still full of half eaten food. I took the last Freddo Frog as she began to wipe down the tablecloth, which was also made of plastic. I ran my fingers across the surface. A plastic tablecloth made to look as though it was lace, with embroidery around the edge. The embroidery was not real either but made of raised bits in coloured plastic.

Libby's mother brought out a giant rose-coloured cake with cream and jam in the middle. On top in bold letters someone had written the words 'Happy Birthday Libby' and the cake was covered in blue candles. We sang happy birthday when the candles were lit and Libby beamed before she blew but she could not get up much breath and sprayed across the top of her cake. Her mother groaned but did not scold her and we all laughed. No one scolded Libby. Not her friends, not Mother Mary John, no one.

Libby had invited the whole class to her party, which is why I was there. If she had needed to choose, she would not have asked me. Once in the cloakroom at school, she pushed into me and made my head bang against the bricks in the window's alcove. I grazed my forehead but Libby did not care. I wanted to dob her in then but it would have been useless. Libby was a good girl and I was not. Not that I was a bad girl. I was a nothing girl. I sat in the classroom and said nothing much unless Mother Mary John asked me a question, which she hardly ever did, only when it was my turn to read out loud, during shared reading. I never stumbled over words like some of the others in my class. I could even pronounce some of the hard words. I did not need to ask Mother Mary John how to pronounce words. I could just roll on and on and on until she called out the next person's name and I had to stop.

At Libby Keating's birthday party I did not care about any of this. I only cared about the food, which I was beginning to regret. Libby's mother had put pieces of cake onto throwaway plates and urged us all to take a piece. My stomach ached. I sat down beside Anne Brown, while Libby opened her presents, one after the other. I hoped she would not mind the paint set I had wrapped for her. I saw in her bedroom she already had paint in tubes lined up in a box on her desk. Libby had a desk, and a bed with a pink chenille bedcover, the sort that dressing gowns were made of, and she had a bedroom all to herself.

After presents, Libby's father offered to take home the girls whose parents had not arranged to collect them. He dropped me off first because I lived the farthest away.

'We're having the house painted,' I lied as the car pulled into the curb. The paint was peeling off the gutters and the weeds were high in the middle of the front yard with only a few geraniums and arum lilies in flower. I walked around the back, relieved that Libby's father did not offer to take me in. I walked past the briquette heap beside the outside laundry, near the woodshed. Every morning one of the big boys or my mother lit the hot water service so we could wash dishes and have our weekly baths. The briquette shoot was squeezed between the woodshed and the laundry and filled with briquettes, black and sooty and shining like marble. Whenever I reached in to gather up briquettes my hands were chalked black.

When I opened the kitchen to come inside I was surprised to find everyone, all my sisters and brothers, including Ferdi, seated around the kitchen table. I knew there was trouble. I knew it before I had walked out to go to Libby's party because my father had been angry and I thought that he was maybe jealous, too, like Juliana, because I was going to a birthday party and I would get lots to eat. And I could dress up. I was happy at someone else's house. That was enough to make him cross.

The door leading from the hallway opened and my father staggered in. He swore at my mother and glared at the rest of us as if we were bad. Then he went out again and my mother said to us,

'Your father can't help it. He's sick.'

Ferdi went red in the face then, as red as his velvet jacket, the one that looked like the ones pop stars wore. 'He's not sick,' he said. 'He's bloody drunk.'

And then I knew. My father was drunk. Not sick, not crazy mad, just drunk.

THERE HAVE been many books written about the consequences of growing up in an alcoholic household. My mother's mantra became: 'Sons of alcoholics become alcoholics and daughters of alcoholics marry them.' We were doomed from the start. There was no way of escaping alcohol's grip.

At twelve I took the Sacred Heart Pioneer Total Abstinence Pledge to refrain from all intoxicating liquor until I was twenty-five years old. I took this pledge when I was confirmed in the second of the three pledges Catholics make, namely Baptism (when Godparents make promises on behalf of the baby), First Holy Communion and Confirmation. I was determined to set myself an example, but by nineteen and my first boyfriend I, too, had tasted of alcohol's forbidden fruit and I had enjoyed it.

I broke my pledge for the pleasure of alcohol. But my father's drinking always seemed to be driven more by desperation than by pleasure. He did not drink for taste or companionship, the loose, easy way that drinking can draw us out and dis-inhibit us. He drank for escape and to hide from his pain, much as I had learned to hide, but in doing so, we could not escape his rage and its trickle down effect on the rest of us.

Photo shoot

UNDER THE orange glow of my father's dark room, our images came to life on paper, first in sample size, tiny images that my father used as a type of tester. I can see us now in the bath, floating a couple of inches underwater where my father had laid us out. He washed our images there, washed off the chemicals and then spread us in strips over the edge of the bathtub to dry.

We were not to touch these images, but we could look and I took pleasure in studying each of my sisters and brothers down the line. I reserved my longest gaze for my own image. I did not see any more photos of my mother naked, which suited me, and I now shared some of my mother's pleasure in this idea of a beautiful family as revealed in my father's photographs. Twelve years old and already my face had taken on the look of someone who looked older. I did not know why this was. But this idea of moving up in the world, no longer one of the little ones, both frightened and pleased me.

When they were dry, my father collected his photos in another tray and took them back into his dark room. He studied us even more closely and held each of us in turn to the light that shone from the open dark room door. These tiny snap shots on sheets of paper revealed to my father the success or failure of his photographs and on the basis of these he decided which ones to enlarge and which ones to forget. Once he'd made his decision, he cast off the left over sheets into a basket at the back of a shelf where they collected dust.

I liked to scavenge from my father's cast offs and in time cut out individual shots of my various brothers and sisters, lining us up on the front page of my homemade album. Oldest to youngest. I preferred to use only facial shots because in these images the bodies were so small the person I knew as my sister or brother was scarcely visible. Not that this mattered much. I was the only one who looked inside my album.

I allowed each of my siblings a double page spread and treated myself to the same. I also tried to give us all descriptors, much as Ferdi had done in the album he built for our parents when they celebrated their twentieth wedding anniversary. Dirk was 'the philanthropist', Ferdi had written in white pen on dark grey paper, with a comment alongside: 'I hates everybody'. I could not understand this combination of meanings, so I could not use it myself. Dirk looked a lot like our father, and bore his name. He was also tall and wiry with a heavily lined broad forehead, which I also shared.

My own title from Ferdi was much better. He called me the 'Poetess', which sounded preferable to the title he chose for Juliana, 'Princess'. That I could do without. I reckoned my brother chose Princess because he thought Juliana was vain, like our mother, maybe because she was the one baby born who looked most like our mother: same dark curly hair, same round pixie face, same hooked nose. The rest of us were either a combination of both parents or, like me, more like our father: his long face, fair hair and bulbous nose.

Juliana spent a long time in front of the mirror, even longer than Hannah who needed mirror time because she wore makeup like our mother and had to adjust her hair and her clothes, especially during photo shoots when our father insisted she look her best.

On the last page of my album I included a photo of my family altogether, one that even showed my father. He had taken this photo in the days when he could time the camera to snap only when he could join the rest of us seated in line, this time in the back yard, the nature shots, as my father liked to call them.

There were other nature shots too, the ones my father took when we went on family outings to the Grampians, to the zoo, to Emerald Lake, shots where it was clear the camera was not always on you, which was easier than later when my father bought a video camera and followed us around.

He told us to be ourselves even as we knew his eye was on us and that we were to behave as though everything in the world was wonderful and we were a bright and happy family and no one could see what was underneath. It was enough the camera captured you, worse by far to be captured in his arms. The smell of cigarettes on his breath or the brandy smell at night after he had been drinking when, despite our wish to sneak off to bed unnoticed, our mother made us go into the lounge room one after the other and lean over him to wish him good night.

When my breasts began to develop my father still brushed his dry thumb against my forehead in the sign of the cross to say good night. Now, it was worse, this leaning over him. Now my father could peer down my cleavage.

ON THE night of Hannah's school dance, my father rested the white board against the bookshelf to take photos of Hannah in her evening dress.

'Sit there,' he told her. 'Sit straight. Now turn right.'

Hannah climbed onto the chair, our grandfather's high backed wooden chair with its tapestry seat. I sat at the other end of the room, pretending to read my book, *Emily Climbs*. I had reached the second volume of the three books and Emily was about to fall in love with Ted Kent, the first in a series of romances. I felt a thrill at the thought that something exciting was about to happen.

'I have to hurry,' Hannah said. 'I'm going to be late.'

'Hold on. I have to get this right.' My father put down his camera and took another lens from the table. He had a pile of lenses, all different shapes and sizes. He fitted the longest lens to the front of his camera and then clicked the whole thing into place on the tripod he'd erected in front of him. He stood behind his camera at one end of the room while Hannah perched on the edge of her chair at the other end. I could see the strain in her eyes, the fidget of her hands.

'Turn to face the door,' my father said. 'Now squeeze back into the chair and tilt your head.'

I could see the silhouette of Hannah's face, the way her nose turned, hooked like the prow of a ship. Although my mother reckoned such a nose was a sign of aristocracy and Roman, my sister looked anything but aristocratic. She looked like she was stuck there on that chair, itching to move on, but fixed in cement.

'Can't we finish now? Julian will be at the door any minute now.'

'He can wait,' my father said. He put down his camera, walked over to my sister and pulled her up towards him. He folded his arms around her, all the way around to adjust the zip that held the dress together. I couldn't quite see what he was doing; whether he was letting it loose or zipping it to the top but the look on Hannah's face was one of horror. My mother who sat behind her newspaper reading looked up once or twice, but she said nothing.

Hannah stood as stiff as the white cardboard backdrop, under my father's administrations, until he pushed her back into the chair, and pulled at the top of her dress to fix her cleavage. She had pinned a flower made of tissue paper like material just there at the centre of her dress. I thought she must have put it there to hide the mole in the middle of her breasts, an ugly

brown thing that looked like a miniature mountain and sometimes wobbled when she laughed, or otherwise moved up and
down with her breathing.

'You don't need this,' my father said as he unpinned the
flower. 'Much better without it.' All this attention to detail and
Hannah's eyes brimmed with tears that refused to spill over. She
clenched her hands together as if to hold back the dam when
our father took his place once more behind the camera.

What he saw was nothing like what I saw. I saw my frumpy
big sister in a mushroom brown dress that my auntie had loaned
her, a dress that came in tight at the waist to accentuate her
middle. It ballooned out into a full flowing skirt and exploded
on top into her bosoms, those things my father went to so much
trouble to capture.

The doorbell rang and Hannah leapt up.

'Stop. I almost had it,' my father said.

Hannah ignored him and shot off through the door. My
father looked surprised as if he was a kid and someone had just
taken away his favourite toy. Then he looked around the room.
My mother was still hidden behind her newspaper and so I
buried my face back inside my book. I pretended I had taken no
notice of all that went on before.

'You,' he said. 'Get yourself up here on this chair. 'I don't want
to waste the light.'

I looked down at my faded blue shorts, my baggy t-shirt.
Why take a photo of me? But I did as I was told. The chair was
still warm from my sister. I pushed my bum into it and felt its
wide arms enclose me. As long as my father stayed back there
behind his camera I was safe, but he looked into the lens and
up again, frustrated.

'This is no good.'

I froze as he moved towards me. His hot arms were around
my waist as he twisted me into place. He pulled at my t-shirt
first this way then that. He stank of cigarettes and of sweat. I felt

like a parcel wrapped in a hurry, a parcel that would not fit the sheet of paper my father had cut out for me, but I could not hide from his camera.

Pissing into bottles

WHEN REVEREND Mother Winifred at the convent up the hill from the primary school died, the nuns told us to pray to her. Pray to her and she might perform miracles. The Reverend Mother had lived a life of piety and good works. They laid her out in the chapel in a coffin near the altar but the younger students could not get up close enough to see her. Only the Reverend Mother's nose rose above the rim of white satin that peeped over the edge.

I decided if I prayed hard to Reverend Mother Winifred my father might be cured. She would lift up her hands in Heaven and ask God the Father to intercede on her behalf and stop my own father from drinking.

Two weeks after her death, after I had prayed hard to the Reverend Mother and nothing had happened, I decided to take more action. For my First Holy Communion an aunt had given me a set of rosary beads. Each bead was made of clear glass and in the centre sat a tiny statue of Our Lady in blue. The crucifix at the end was large relative to the rest of the beads. On the back there was a bubble of Lourdes water encased as a relic and set into the plastic.

I took my rosary beads out to the backyard and from the garage I borrowed one of my father's screwdrivers, which I used to prise off the clear plastic disc that held in the bubble.

My mother made tea at least ten times most days, so I waited between her visits to the kettle. On Sundays, our day of rest, when my father did not drink alcohol, he drank tea. The tray was always set. It was easy to pick out my father's cup, the unsugared one for the diabetic who dropped tiny white pills into his tea. The saccharin pills sat in their silver case beside his saucer. I took my tiny bubble out as my mother left the kitchen once more with a plateful of *Speculaas*. The bubble crushed readily between my thumbnail and finger. A tiny tear dropped into my father's cup.

My mother returned and then took it to him. I followed her into the lounge room and watched as my father sipped his tea, determined to be sure he had the right cup. There was no point in wasting a miracle on someone who did not need one. My father's nicotine-stained fingers lifted the cup by its handle and he sipped. He did not seem to notice anything different in his Lourdes-water-laced tea but I sensed already a glow in the room as if Saint Bernadette, the patron saint of miracles, was already at work. Bernadette, a fully-fledged saint, with the addition of some potent source like the Lourdes water, must surely be more effective than prayers to the Reverend Mother.

I kept notes on the changes in my father, notably his ability not to drink any alcohol from one week to the next for at least three weeks. I was almost ready to claim success when my father came home from work one Friday evening. We had grown complacent over those last three weeks. We had begun to feel safe and to imagine that it was okay to stay in the lounge room watching television even after our father came home. But there it was. Tucked inside his evening newspaper in a brown paper bag.

My father grunted a greeting. My mother rushed in and fussed over him for a minute or two before making her way back to the kitchen and her cooking. My father said nothing about the television. On this night he tolerated it. He did not insist we switch channels from *Doctor Who* and let us watch it right up to the end. By the time of the six o'clock news, when I had left the room, my father had pulled the bottle of brandy from its secret place beside his chair and poured a few slugs down his throat.

My miracle had failed. My prayers to Reverend Mother Winifred and Saint Bernadette had been a waste of time. I could not use my father as a case study to present to the nuns as one cured through the intercession of their Reverend Mother. I could not assist in the nuns' wish to get her to sainthood. Winifred was not a saint and my father was still a drinker.

FROM THE front windows of our house, at six o'clock on the next Saturday night, Wentworth Avenue was empty. It was winter. I knelt on the flat seat of the box bay window to watch and wait for my father. Somehow, even though I was only twelve, I imagined by standing guard I could stop his return. I could wish him dead; send sparks of death through the air by telepathy.

I wished hard that his car might have crashed and disintegrated and he would be squashed inside, but still his grey station wagon pulled into the curb. I watched him stride along the front path loaded down with two brown paper bags. My mother's humming reached down the corridor.

The front room, a bedroom now for the two little ones, stood next to the front door. It was a high-ceilinged room with an oak fireplace surrounding an unused hearth in one sliced-off corner. One of the four windows of the bay acted also as an extra door. I fiddled with its dark brass handle, smooth, oval and worn. When my father stepped through the front door, which fitted into an alcove on the side of the house, I went through the hallway to the kitchen and out into the back yard. I kept out of his sight.

IN THOSE days, my father pissed into bottles. We found them in the morning hidden in corners behind his chair. The bottle's orifice was small and he was so drunk, how did he direct his penis straight enough to piss inside the narrow circle of glass? There were never any tell-tale puddles on the floor.

In the morning my mother lifted each bottle with the tip of her thumb and forefinger and then poured the contents into the toilet, checking first to see that it was not left over brandy. Her nose twitched.

'He's disgusting,' I said.

'He's your father,' she said, and bent over to press the flush button. Her pink, quilted dressing gown was stretched tight against her bum. Underneath, my mother wore a skin-coloured girdle that covered her from above the knee to her shoulder straps. She had lost her stomach muscles, she said. That was why she was so round in the middle. From all the babies she had carried.

In the smallest hours of the morning, when my father had finally succumbed to a deeper sleep than all his daily catnapping allowed, I snuck into the lounge room and studied his absence. The chair behind which he hid his bottles was now empty. I avoided this chair by day, particularly when he was in it. And no one else dared occupy it when my father was not there. The chair, a Jacobean reproduction in oak, was propped in the darkest corner of the room. The tapestry cushions bore the imprint of his flat, almost invisible bottom.

My father was bottomless through his clothes. His over-pressed shiny trousers dribbled down his legs and his body was like cardboard. What he lacked in bulk he made up for in height. His huge black shoes, dulled by walking and age, were spread before my feet like open boats. I tried them on for size, careful to place my toes in such a way that no part of my body touched the leather. It was both exciting and terrifying to breach the man's territory, all the while hovering on the edge of being caught.

I sensed my father's absence more than his presence. When he was there, time stood still. At night when everyone slept and my father visited us girls, I waited for him, expecting at any minute to brush up against his cold, clammy skin, rib-tight and tense. There was no flab on my father, just the thin white crepe of his skin tightly stretched over his bones. I waited for him and wished myself paper-thin, light as a feather and easy to overlook.

The next week as we watched television early Saturday night, Henry was furious with me. 'Get out of the way,' he said. 'You're not made of glass.' Whenever anyone interfered with his view of the television he bellowed. I hadn't meant to block his view. I'd needed to use the toilet. I only stood up for a second. I hadn't wanted to be visible; to get in Henry's way, or anyone else's for that matter.

We were watching Brian Henderson's *Bandstand*. Maria was singing, her thick top lip moved up and down like a sliding garage door to reveal perfect white teeth. I imagined myself the possessor of such a mouth. I practised rolling my top lip up slowly along the surface of my teeth. It never worked. My mouth was too small, my lips were thin and my teeth, crooked and patchy, bore no resemblance to the broad, milk white, marble keys in Maria's mouth. Instead, my lip curled up under my nose and on the odd occasion when I'd been caught out practising by one of my brothers, I was left feeling ridiculous.

'*Kom, Lisbeth. Kom jij hier.*'

My father was asking me to sit on his knee. I dared not refuse, besides Juliana was already up there perched on the other knee. I was wearing Hannah's old, Sunday best dress, turquoise and waisted, a pale turquoise more like a mint with white braiding across the sleeves and neckline. It just fitted me though lately it had been a struggle to do up the zip. I always managed to squeeze in but it was a tight squeeze and a reminder that I was growing up and out. Hannah had outgrown this dress years ago and I'd only recently started to wear it myself. My body was sneaking up on me. I was getting taller and wider and bigger and now it seemed, even Hannah's dress was too tight for me.

STRANGE THINGS had been happening to my body. I almost dared not look. I knew I would grow breasts like my mother's one day. I just never knew how. Would I simply wake up one morning and they'd be there, round, pink bulges with a dark nipple on top? Or would I feel it happening gradually, as if I was wearing two balloons that were slowly inflated. My nipples popped out now, and were textured around the edges, darker too maybe, not just pale pink buttons like those of my brother's. I'd taken to changing from my bathers after swimming in the closed off cubicles at the pool. I was mortified. As much as I'd wanted breasts for years, I did not want anyone else to notice.

Saturday night and we were gathered together in the lounge room as if for Mass but watching television and waiting for a volcano to explode. Worse still, I feared I was sitting at the mouth of the volcano, beside Juliana perched on my father's knee. His hand rested on my shoulder. It felt like it was burning through to my skin.

My mother was smoking a cigarette. She leaned back in the chair, which was set diagonally in the corner beside my father's chair. The glass on the gas heater between them reflected back the images from the TV. There were no warm flames from the heater that night. It had been turned off for the summer. My mother seemed to live in another world, oblivious to my discomfort, sitting there on my father's knee. She was absorbed, lost, consumed by the singing on the television, and the deep drafts of her cigarette.

I could not reach her by telepathy or simply wanting her to notice. She must have realised there was danger. It was bad enough that Hannah sat on my father's knee as often as she did, especially on Saturdays when our mother was not there. But I was not ready for it, not yet, not ever.

My father started to play with my zip. The dress had a full-length neck to waist zipper. Access, a gash, an opening. If I had worn a cardigan I could have sealed off the entrance but it was not cold enough that day, though I felt freezing then, numb at the centre. What was my father doing to me here in full view of my family, mother, brothers and sisters? No one noticed.

Tears rolled down my cheeks. My mother did not see? Eventually I thought she would rescue me but still her eyes were riveted on the television and this unspoken, unseen game went on as my father played with my zipper, up and down, up and down, repeatedly as though tantalising himself, while torturing me.

Up and down, a rush of air on my naked back and I could only wish myself into a numb state beyond which he could not reach me. There was nothing to say because it was not supposed to be happening. At least, I thought it was not supposed to be happening. Fathers did not play strip games with their daughters, did they? But no one noticed and I did not tell.

Camping

'**DIG YOURSELF** a hip hole,' Gerard said as he pulled out the tent pegs in readiness for our next school holiday adventure in the backyard. The ground was hard and as Gerard tugged the tent into shape, the huge khaki coloured canvas thing that we took with us on family holidays, I scraped away at the surface of the grass. It was dried out through the summer sun and I needed to scratch it out with my hands. Then I reached for Gerard's trowel. The soil below was compacted as though someone had driven over it with a steamroller.

We pitched the tent to one side of the garden near the fence to give it shelter from any winds that might spring up during the night, not that there were winds predicted, only clear skies ahead. I had wanted to sleep without a tent in my sleeping bag on the grass as we had done months before in the cold of winter. But my mother said under canvas we'd be safer from mosquitoes and any other prowling insects at that time of year and Gerard liked the exercise.

He was practising for his school cadets. He had started that year and already had his uniform on standby. He polished his shoes daily even when he had no cause to wear them. They seemed to give him a sense of order and it was like he needed that, more than me. He was a boy and older. He must have felt the strains of our father's drinking. Although my father picked on the girls most, he provoked the boys into fights.

At fourteen Gerard was not yet big enough to tackle my father but I could sense his temper flare whenever my father tried to interest him in a conversation about what he was doing at school, a conversation that my father inevitably turned into a competition and one he needed to win.

Gerard was the genius of the family, smarter even than Dirk and Ferdi and maybe even smarter than our dad, whom everyone knew was also a genius. My father spoke five languages, Dutch, German, French, Latin and Portuguese, and although his English was not so good, it was passable for him to get a job as an accountant. He could count in any language.

Gerard was smart at languages, too, but he was good at physics and chemistry as well. My father had always wanted to be a chemist while he was growing up but the war got in the way. Then after he migrated, he needed to work at anything he could find for the money. He could only study at university in the evenings. Accountancy was a sure way of guaranteeing a good enough job and an income high enough to feed all his children.

Gerard tightened the straps to hold the tent in place and with a hammer he found in the garage he banged down on the pegs which yielded, finally, despite the hard soil. We ate our dinner inside with the others but could not wait to get outside for our night of camping. Gerard had set up two tents, the other one for Henry and Juliana. They too would camp out, but I was the lucky one who could share a tent with my genius brother while my less than genius brother shared the tent with my younger sister, even though he was the oldest of us all. Henry was only interested in exploring the natural world. He was a dreamer most of the time but he had a fiery temper and he did not do so well at school. He could share with Juliana and the two might fall asleep while Gerard and I talked.

Gerard had been reading the stories of the ancient Greeks and Romans and he told me the story of Ulysses who travelled the seas and met with strange creatures on his way to Hades, the dogs with eyes like saucers at the gates of Hades, the River Styx and the ferryman. He told me about the Cyclops with one eye who guarded the sheep that Jason wanted to steal. He told me of all these imaginary creatures from centuries ago and I fell into a sleep of imagination fit to burst with the magic of it all.

My father's rage was nothing compared to that of Zeus, the god of thunder. My mother's beauty was nothing to compare with that of Diana with her bow and arrow. The gods that reigned from on high were able to wreak havoc and create order. They offered an escape from the trouble inside the house while Gerard and I slept underneath the stars, the thin line of canvas protection against mosquitoes and being seen.

One Saturday afternoon, weeks after our camping adventure, we hung around in the lounge room. Gerard and Henry were stooped over a chessboard in one corner, Juliana and I dressed and undressed our dolls, and the two little ones, Becca and Jacob, scribbled on butcher's paper in another corner. My father who had been studying from his books had taken himself off to bed. My mother was reading her newspaper in her armchair when my father called for us one after the other from his bedroom. He began by calling for our mother, and then for Hannah — but she was away at choir practice. When no one answered him, he called for me, then for Juliana and once more for our mother. No one moved, but my mother looked up, sighed, and then went back to her newspaper.

Earlier that morning we had gone to the Maytime Fair at Xavier College with only enough money to buy a sticky toffee each and when we came home bursting through the kitchen door it was clear we had upset our father who had again been preparing for his next set of accountancy exams. We had not meant to upset him. We had not meant to be noisy, but it was hard to tip-toe past the open door of the lounge room in silence and as we filed past to go to our bedrooms, our father threw his books onto the floor, picked up his car keys and drove off to the local hotel.

Unlike other fathers who drank on weekends, my father did not drink at the bar in company. My father had no friends. He brought his brandy home to drink alone. By mid afternoon he had shifted from being a man studying for his chartered accountancy exams, from a man who was interested in what a microscope might show up, from a man intent on winning his game of bridge, to a man demanding attention.

He called for my mother again and this time she went to him. She stood up and walked through the double glass doors of the lounge room across the hall way and into their bedroom and then closed the door behind her. She had done this for us, we knew, to give us peace, to let us play, and be free of our father. But we were not at peace.

No one said a word, but I sensed that Gerard and Henry, like Juliana, were listening, too. From the lounge room and from behind the door of my parents' bedroom we heard the sounds of their muffled voices, the clink of something small falling onto the ground, the cars in the background on Canterbury Road.

The silence when it came was scarier than all the noises put together. We could not read silence. We knew only that we needed to listen for sounds that might tell us our mother was in trouble and needed help. We listened and time ticked by.

After the length of time it took to play a hand of bridge, my mother yelled out something, a word like 'Don't' or 'Stop' in Dutch, and there was a crash, as if a chair had fallen over or a curtain crashed to the ground. We were up, we four older ones, and out of the lounge to our parents' bedroom, Gerard at the lead. He threw open the door. I was a step behind him but could not see into the bedroom.

'Get out of here,' my mother yelled at Gerard. 'Get out.' And I watched my brother in slow motion back out of the room, as we all backed away and went back into the lounge. My mother slammed the door behind her.

She had not wanted Gerard to see. She had not wanted any of us to see. But I did not know what. Something told me later, I should not ask Gerard what he saw in our parents' bedroom. Whatever it was, it made him different. I saw it in his eyes. A hollow look, as if he had decided to move out from his body. As if he had decided to move away from all of us in his mind. And worse than me, he continued to grow more and more silent and invisible with each passing year.

Not a dancer, scientist or gardener

AT PRIMARY school on Mayday, the day on which we commemorated the Blessed Virgin Mary, the teachers converted one of the moveable basketball rings into a Maypole and tied a series of ribbons around the hole, twice over. Each girl in grade six was to take a ribbon and then pull it outwards as if lifting the hem of a skirt. We stood still until the music started and slowly each stepped one place ahead, then another, weaving in and out with our ribbon.

Mine was pink. Other girls held onto blue, green or yellow ribbons. It was meant to be a graceful dance around the Maypole but I could not get the hang of moving in and out of the girls who stood ahead of me. My ribbon kept twisting.

We needed to begin again and again before Mother Mary John was happy. I dreaded the day we would go around the Maypole in front of our parents. Mine would not be there as it was a middle of weekday event but it was almost as bad to have other people watch flat footed me hobble around in what Mother Mary John told us was meant to be a graceful event in honour of the Blessed Virgin's ascent into Heaven.

The nuns loved Mary. They modelled themselves on her and we girls could well do the same. What better model for womanly behaviour, Mother Mary John told us. She did not mean in outward appearance. She meant only as far as our souls were concerned.

A short and plump, bespectacled woman in a long black dress had nothing on the slim beautiful woman who stood in statue form in the grade six classroom in one corner and also another likeness at the side of the altar in church. Always at the side or in the corners.

We girls were not to get ahead of ourselves. Mary was the mother of God, a good woman, a woman who worked hard to raise her son, and keep house for her husband but she did not demand attention or make a show of herself. Mary was modest.

The least modest thing I could do was fall out of step during the Maypole dance but I couldn't help it. I had no sense of rhythm when it came to my feet. I needed to watch them all the time to see they did not trip on the heels of the girl in front, but Mother Mary John told us repeatedly, 'Eyes up to Heaven, girls. We are honouring Our Lady.'

To look up was to see the tangled mess of ribbons twisted over one another around the basketball ring. Mother Mary John had said if we got it right then there would be a neat plait from which the last of our ribbons could dangle.

On the day, I longed to reach the end of my ribbon. To let it fall away, step back and bow to the audience, a scattering of other people's parents and the rest of the school. There was nothing worse than stuffing something up, but to do it in front of other people was worst of all.

The audience clapped and Mother Mary John scowled. She made the worst of the dancers stay back to untangle the mess of ribbons once one of the fathers had laid the Maypole on its side. The ribbons had lost their shine. Some were dirty, most of them crushed but the three other girls allocated to this task and I pulled the ribbons apart, untied them and then rolled them into neat reels, the way mother Mary John had taught us to do.

This was something I could manage. This was easy. Why didn't she give me easy jobs, things I could manage? Why did she always ask me to do things that I could not get my mind around, like pulling the pot plants from the mantel on the veranda and giving them water?

The pots were high up and heavy. I needed to stand on a chair to reach them, carry them down onto the bench below, and rest them there. Then I needed to dust around the edge of each pot, careful not to disturb the soil. Mother Mary John wanted her feather duster to stay clean. Then I had to water them from the watering can under the sink in the cloakroom. She never told me how much water to put into the watering can, nor how much to sprinkle over each plant. She told me only to water them.

Mother Mary John put questions in such a way as to suggest you should already know the answer. Your mother should have taught you, your sisters and brothers, your father maybe, some-one from your family. Good families prepared their children for the world and Mother Mary John's job was to implement this knowledge in the running of her classroom. And for the rest, she educated us.

'You're as senseless as a wet hen,' Mother Mary John said once after a pot plant fell and cracked open. I had never seen a wet hen. I did not understand what this might mean but the words stung. The year was coming to an end, and after all those months of pot plant duty, never once did I dirty her feather duster or give too much or two little water to her plants. I had not even asked her about this. I had used my intuition, which I knew was not good as I made many mistakes, especially the things to do with numbers, but never before had I broken a pot.

This was the last mistake I ever made at our Lady of Good Counsel, my primary school, which took such pride in coun-selling children on how to be good, following Mary's advice. Things would change, I hoped, when I moved to the convent school Vaucluse, in Richmond with my older sister. But I was wrong.

In science one day, after I had started at Vaucluse, Mother Mary Paul gave us the job of measuring the Azimuth of the moon. To this day I still do not know what this means, but at the time I took it to mean the distance of the earth from the moon. We were meant to measure the distance with our hands. Mother Mary Paul showed us at the front of the classroom. She held out her arm straight as a rod. Then she held her fingers tight together, lifted her thumb to the ceiling and held all four fingers straight in front. She pointed her arm to the window, which overlooked the veranda upstairs and although it allowed only a tiny view of the sky she pretended that the moon was out there high up and that she had the flat of the horizon in front of her.

'Remember, girls,' she said. 'Point your hand out to the horizon, with your thumb parallel to the moon, and then measure the Azimuth.' We should have known by now how to measure angles, ninety-degree angles, one hundred and eighty degree angles and all those in between. Our thumb and the line of our index finger was the best way to measure.

'Keep a record of these measures in your notebook,' Mother Mary Paul said, 'and at the end of the month you will be able to measure the earth's movement around the sun, the sky, the moon.'

I did not understand which planet moved where. All this stuff about planets orbiting the galaxy made no sense to me. The earth moved, Mother Mary Paul told us, and I believed her, even though I could not feel this movement. The Earth rotated around the sun and somehow, the moon dangled nearby and must do its best not to shrivel up. The moon had its own orbit and we could measure that by getting the angles of the Azimuth.

Every night for a month I went out into the back yard of our house. I could hear the television inside blaring, but I had been

busy in the kitchen doing my homework at the kitchen table
alongside my brothers and sisters, only the bigger ones, the ones
old enough for homework.

When I reached the science part of my project I took myself
away. I did not tell the others what I was doing. I had always
thought of the horizon as in the distance but the only horizon
I could see from the back veranda was the line of the fence that
separated our house from the one behind.

I placed my hand at my eye, the way Mother Mary Paul had
shown us and I levelled it parallel with the fence line, the near
horizon as it had become. Then I raised my thumb upwards to
where I thought I could see a thin sliver of moon. It was hard
to see, too many clouds, but I gave it a stab. Fingers to thumb,
about 145 degrees Azimuth. It sounded okay and so I logged in
the figure in the column I had lined up for results in my notebook and took myself back inside to finish my homework.

As the days progressed, with each new measure of the Azimuth,
I thought of the mess of the Maypole ring. My Azimuth did not
ascend or descend as I figured it must. My figures were scattered
all over the place and when I handed in the results to Mother
Mary Paul she asked what I had done to achieve such results.

'I did as you said,' I said, polite as a thirteen-year-old girl should
be in front of a nun whose wiry eyebrows curled upwards like
a man's.

'I'm not sure you have the makings of a scientist,' was all she
said.

Not a dancer, not a scientist, not a gardener. My future
looked grim.

The Facts of Life

HANNAH DECIDED it was time for me to know the facts just as I was turning fourteen. She had learned them from our father, curled up on his lap each Saturday morning. There was something about the way they sat together, something about the way he held her—my sister Hannah was sprawled across my father's lap and he was whispering in her ear. I tried to ignore it.

In between sitting on our father's lap, on most Saturday mornings while our mother was at work at the children's home, Hannah went about tidying the house. She washed clothes, then hung them from the Hill's Hoist in the backyard, which had grown lopsided after we swung on it once too often, and took instructions from our father. Meanwhile Juliana and I, our swimmers hidden underneath our dresses, went off to the local baths to escape.

Hannah did not like swimming or so it seemed to me. She came with us once or twice but she was not much fun. She spread out her towel on the concrete near the edge of the pool and spent the afternoon on her stomach asleep. The dimples on her thighs grew redder by the minute.

Hannah was a hypocrite, I thought then. She'd told me I should suntan slowly, ten minutes a day, five on each side then into the shade but she never took her own advice.

It was three whole summers before I had dared to stand at the end of the pool where the sign, "9 feet", marked the deep end.

Three whole summers before I dared to jump. As I plummeted to the bottom I had time to wonder whether I would ever reach it. When the tips of my toes finally touched the slippery tiles I needed to push myself up fast in order to reach the surface and still have air in my lungs. Hannah never joined me in the water. I learned to swim alone.

ONE AFTERNOON when I came home from swimming, Hannah was standing in the middle of the kitchen.

'Baking a cake, Hannah?' I asked. Hannah nodded. There was a line of flour down her cheek like the sign of Zorro and white hand marks on the dark skirt covering her bum. She pushed the cake into the oven and stood at the door staring after it, as if she were waiting for it to cook. She shoved her thumb into her mouth and sucked on it, while with the next two fingers she stroked her face.

'Can I help ice it?'

Hannah pulled her thumb from her mouth. 'No. I don't need help with the cake. You can do some ironing instead.'

'I don't know how.'

'I can teach you.' Hannah went to fetch the iron from the closet.

'I don't want to learn,' I said. 'If I learn to iron, I'll have to do it all the time.'

'You'll never grow up then,' Hannah said.

'I don't want to.'

Hannah came back, iron in hand, the cord snaking behind her. 'Sooner or later you have to learn.' She bent to plug in the iron then flicked on the switch. 'We start with the collar.' She laid the shirt out flat against the white sheet that was fixed on top of a grey army blanket and spread over the coffee table. 'You test the iron is hot enough by licking your finger like this and putting it against the metal.' She pulled her finger away and the iron let out a hiss. 'That's hot enough,' she said. 'Be careful to iron the underside of the collar. That way you won't clump the edges.' Then she took the cuffs in turn and laid each one out flat. She unbuttoned the cuffs and pulled them apart, pressing down the iron on each one in turn.

'Then we do the sleeves.' She laid them out, one at a time, making sure there was a straight line down the middle and ironed them one after the other. 'Then we do the body. This is the hardest bit.' She pulled the shirt over one corner of the coffee table so that one sleeve hung down loose and worked her way across the entire shirt from one side through the back across to the other side taking special care to poke the pointy bit of the iron between each button so that the shirt was finally stiff. She shook it out to smooth it and put the arms across a coat hanger. Then she hung the shirt behind her with all the other shirts she'd already ironed, my father's shirts, at least five of them floating from their hangers like ghosts.

'Now you try,' she said propping up the iron. She squeezed out from behind the table to make room for me.

'I'll do the hankies first' I said, 'for practice.'

'Suit yourself,' Hannah said. 'But one day you'll have learn to do the hard stuff.' She started to hum, not the words, just the music. She measured out more flour and sugar for a batch of butter biscuits, two cups of flour, one cup of sugar, and a pinch of salt from the *Saxa* box, wedged between her thumb and index finger

I could not understand my sister's pinch of salt, nor her sprinkle of sugar. Hannah put sugar and salt in with the boiling carrots; she put sugar and salt in with the boiling peas and beans; she put salt in with the porridge and then we covered it with golden syrup, which was just another form of sugar. I did not understand why my sister liked to put these two things together. To me they were opposites; they cancelled one another out, but Hannah put them together, she said because 'they sharpen the taste.' Our father had told her so.

'I think it's time I told you the facts of life,' Hannah said. 'I think you're old enough now.' I pressed the iron down on one of my father's handkerchiefs as hard as I could. The hankie had the letters JC, my father's first initials, embroidered in one corner. The stitching bunched up with the embroidery so I could not get it to fold into a perfect square.

'The man puts his penis into the woman and leaves his seed,' Hannah said.

I wanted to block my ears. I did not like the word 'penis.' It was a foreign word, an ugly word, a secret word.

'The man puts his penis into the woman's hole, which is called a vagina,' my sister said.

I screwed up my face. 'Yuck.'

'I thought you'd be more mature than that,' Hannah said. 'I thought you were ready.'

I remembered then the green football oval beside the children's playground near Dennis motors, where the black and grey Holdens and Falcons were lined up for sale. I remembered, as if it was a dream, that on the wide verge of grass at the end of the oval where it rose up to meet the road, there was a blanket. The blanket moved. There were people underneath the blanket. That was why the blanket moved up and down, as if a kitten had curled up inside underneath and was looking for a comfortable spot in which to sleep. The kitten was pawing at the ground, digging with its claws, scratching and clawing at the earth to make itself comfortable.

I thought of myself in bed at night when I first crawled under the blankets and curled myself into a tight ball because the sheets were too cold to stretch onto. I curled up and straightened until I felt warm enough to stretch out and finally roll over to sleep. The kitten body under the blanket was not yet ready to sleep. The kitten body under the blanket was still pawing and rubbing itself up and down. Henry, who was walking with me that day, said, 'They're doing it. There are people under that blanket and they're doing it.'

Hannah made a hole in the middle of the flour and sugar, which she had mixed together so well you could barely see the sugar crystals anymore, although the flour looked coarser, more like the sparkly bits on the asphalt footpath outside. She took a small saucepan off the stove. She had heated the butter over the stove where she kept the kettle full of boiling water. The butter had turned into a golden river, which she poured into the well of flour and sugar. A puff of steam floated across the surface. She set the saucepan aside and then took up her wooden spoon to stir. The mixture started off lumpy. Bits of white stuck to lumps of golden rocks of flour and sugar. She had to stir with all her effort. She worked her mouth up and down. The dough sat in the middle of the cracked pudding bowl.

'I'm only telling you because you're old enough,' Hannah said. 'Better I should tell you, than someone else.' I tried to straighten out my face, to wipe off the look of disgust that had landed there. I piled the handkerchiefs one on top of the other and left them on the bench.

'Can I stop ironing now?'

'You'll have to do better next time,' my sister said. She bent to switch off the iron. 'You'll never make a man happy, if you can only do hankies.'

A Birthday, a dressmaker and some cake

MY FEET hurt and blisters had formed at the back of my heels. Those dainty shoes, white with a small rosette in the centre, were Olga's choice for her bridesmaids. Olga was the yellow-haired, broad shouldered girl from Germany whom Ferdi had chosen to marry and I had been chosen as her second bridesmaid, second to a girl named Julie who was two years older than me and like Olga, lived in the country, in Moe near Yallourn. Moe was an electricity town shrouded beneath a tapestry of metal grids woven across the sky and supported below by rows of slender poles that once carried the branches and leaves of eucalypts.

Hannah should have been bridesmaid. She was the oldest girl; such privileges should belong to her. The year I was born, Hannah was the flower girl at our Auntie Joan and Uncle George's wedding. Our mother still talked about how sweet she looked in her white satin dress with matching party shoes. She carried a basket of rose petals.

But this time was different. This time, I was chosen.

Olga said I had to be bridesmaid because Julie was closer to Hannah's age and Julie was her choice as senior bridesmaid to represent the bride's family. Olga was an only child. You couldn't have two seniors and so our family had to be represented by the assistant, an appropriately aged bridesmaid, and at just fourteen I fitted in perfectly.

Hannah was miserable, and tried hard not to hold it against me. It was not my fault, she said, but underneath I wondered; was it because I was prettier and thinner? My brothers rubbished Hannah for being fat. They called her compost heap. At meal times, Hannah served herself smaller portions than she served the rest of us. She worried about getting fatter but could not bear to go hungry. During one Sunday dinner, after our father had left the table and I was enjoying the last few mouthfuls of my Neapolitan ice-cream, Hannah reached lengthways across the table to steal from my plate.

I thumped down my hand, splat into the middle of the bowl of ice cream, which Hannah had doled out to me earlier. She reeled back in horror. As long as she insisted on depriving herself—she called it dieting—she could not stop herself stealing food from the rest of us. She said sorry later but I stayed angry for a long time.

It was hard to stay pretty for the wedding. I was worried about my next cold sore. Cold sores erupted every few months and I could never tell when one was on its way. A tingle, then the hot throbbing of my lip as a blister burst out and open. It took days to heal. For weeks I agonised in bed at night about the possibility of the next eruption before the wedding but it never happened.

Three times before the big day I went with Olga for fittings to a dressmaker in Springvale. On the first visit, she measured me up for size, her tape held across my chest, my waist, my hips and all these disapproving grunts and sighs, as if my shape was impossible to accommodate. I hated taking my clothes off in front of anyone. The dressmaker would not let me escape to the toilet. She did not care about modesty.

My mother had said all her children were slow to develop. Maybe that was a good thing. I did not have pimples yet and my period, that dreadful thing that still did not make sense to me, had not yet arrived. I was tired of waiting for it, ever sensitive to any sense of wetness below and terrified that others would see a dark red stain on the back of my dress that I had not noticed myself.

One night I woke up from a bad dream and looked into the crotch of my pyjamas where I saw the stain. At first I cried, not knowing what to do. When I finally plucked the courage to turn on the light, I saw there was nothing there. What a fool. I should have remembered like all my siblings, I was a slow developer.

On the morning of the wedding, I woke up in a strange bed. Outside the birds were stirring and for a minute I could not place myself. The bed was foreign and fresh smelling with a hint of mothballs. Then I remembered I was in Moe. Ferdi had driven me there the night before in his new car, a Volkswagon. The Vespa had to go. Olga refused to be dinked.

We had travelled late into the night. Ferdi had simply dropped me there. He told Olga's mother he'd stay with friends. So on the morning of what happened to be my fourteenth birthday I woke up in a strange bed in an even stranger room surrounded by cakes. They lined the top of the wardrobe and sat cheek by jowl on the dressing table and across the chairs. There was not a surface that did not hold at least two cakes and even in spaces on the floor' Mrs Horvat had stashed a plate filled with iced meringues.

It did not take me long to recognise that the cakes in this room were not in honour of my birthday but for the wedding. Mrs Horvat must have cooked for days. I climbed out of bed. The floor was covered with a circular coiled rug whose ridges rubbed against my soles. I lifted the covering from one of the cakes. Surely no one would notice one missing flower. But one was not enough. I looked around for more, from cake to cake, undressing each from its wrapper and scratching at the raised chunks of icing. Then I flopped back onto the bed, guilty. I wanted someone to come and collect me. It was my birthday. I did not want to eat cake alone.

AFTER WHAT seemed like hours, I braved the outside corridor where Mrs Horvat greeted me. She was waving a ten-shilling note in front of her.

'I wondered when you'd wake up. Here, for you. Happy birthday,' she said.

I took the money and thanked her.

'Come now. Breakfast.' Mrs Horvat led me down the hallway and into the stink of fish.

'We have kippers to eat,' she said.

I had never heard of kippers before but the smell told me I would hate eating them, more so with a stomach full of icing. I stared at my plate.

My brother arrived clattering at the back door. He took one look at my face, another at the plate and said to his soon-to-be mother-in-law,

'*Mutti*. Don't force her.'

Mrs Horvat lifted my plate and passed it over to him. My brother soon emptied the kipper onto his own and then reached for more.

On the afternoon of the wedding, I stood on the steps of the church, my arm hooked into that of a man who was a stranger to me. My feet ached and my blisters throbbed. My partner was one of Ferdi's friends and assistant to his best man, Dirk. We stood along the steps to be photographed, Olga and Ferdi in front, Dirk linking arms with Julie on the next step and one step above them all I stood supported by this strange man whose name I had trouble remembering.

AT LAST, on my fourteenth birthday, there was no mistaking it; I had breasts.

During that first fitting for the bright yellow dress — Olga chose the colour — the dressmaker told her how much she hated making dresses for my age group.

'They're in between,' she said. 'Buy her a padded bra, 32 A, and I'll make up the dress to fit those measurements.'

The day before when Ferdi had arrived to collect me, I'd laid all my clothes out on the table, ready for packing. When Ferdi noticed the new white padded bra among my otherwise fading underwear, knickers and socks, he seized upon it and held it against his chest.

'My little sister's titties?'

I did not want anyone to notice and tried to hide my face behind my hands, which made Ferdi even more determined. It reminded me of the way my father zeroed in on women and their breasts.

At the wedding, I was secretly proud of my new bra, despite Ferdi's ridicule, but every time I tried it on I was aware of the halls of air that stood between the hard peaks of the bras' reinforced lining and my own body. You could poke your finger into the bra and the indent would stay.

Although he got drunk at the reception, my father said nothing about my sudden rise to womanhood. And if my other brothers noticed, they did not admit to it either.

When we came home, I hung my yellow dress in the wardrobe and pushed the bra into the back of my drawer. I wanted to wear it again under Hannah's hand me down green jumper but feared it would be too obvious, especially to Juliana. We took to sharing a bedroom now that Ferdi had left home. Hannah had started at the Teacher's college in Chadstone and could have a room to herself.

'You're not living up to our standards,' I said to Juliana as we walked together to school soon after the wedding, up Cox Street through Robross and onto Centre Dandenong Road. The traffic whizzed past.

Juliana's school bag flapped at her side, but with her free hand she reached out and grabbed my hat. Up and over the fence into the nearest yard it flew. I could see it through the fence slats caught in the branches of a rose bush.

'Look what you've done,' I wailed. 'Go and get it.'

'No way,' she said. 'Get it yourself.'

'But it's trespassing.' I said, as though Juliana had no regard for the law.

Juliana was lawless. She had written on the central blackboard at school, two letters that defaced Mother Xavier's orderly list headed by the single word MARKS.

Marks for order, for punctuality, for application and the big one, worth five points, marks for deportment.

Juliana had added the two letters 're' to the word 'marks,' creating the word 'remarks' and Mother Xavier had summoned the entire school to find the culprit.

Can you imagine my shame when Juliana finally put up her hand? She lost her shield: two full marks for deportment, ten points, and took a letter home to our mother. Our poor mother overburdened with trying to find the money to pay our school fees, and here was Juliana abusing the privilege.

'You go and get my hat,' I said again, but Juliana had shot off ahead.

'You'll miss the train,' she called back.

I had no choice then but to break the law, too. I slipped the latch on the gate, fearful of every creak. I slid up the pathway and hunched my shoulders. I had a plan. If anyone came out I would apologise and tell them the wind had blown my hat over their fence. No matter there was no wind. I could see a television screen flickering through the scrim curtains in the front room. I heard the rumble of noise.

I snatched my hat off the bush and ran for it.

'Don't you ever do that again, or I'll report you to the prefects,' I said to Juliana when I caught up with her.

'And I'll report you for not wearing your hat. And tell Mum about your teeth.'

For all her insolence, Juliana cared about her teeth. She was not going to let them rot in her mouth and she had nagged at our mother until she agreed to let Juliana go to a private dentist, one who worked nearby in Cheltenham. My mother could not refuse, despite the expense, because Juliana told her again and again, she needed to look after her teeth.

'You should go to the dentist, too.' Juliana said to me again and again, given the nights I spent rocking myself to sleep. But I did not complain to my mother about the pain in my mouth. Not simply because I did not want her to think she should spend any money on my teeth. More than that I could not bear the thought of the dentist's words when he would gasp and tell me my teeth were the worst he had ever seen. I hoped only the pain would go away and that my dreams might come true and one day some magical dentist might take them all from me.

Eventually, Juliana could not bear to listen to my moans at night and she told our mother who said, despite everything, I must go. Once Juliana's teeth were checked and two holes filled, my mother made an appointment for me.

All day long at school I trembled at the thought of the dentist opening my mouth to take a look. After a day of torment in the build-up to my appointment, I took the train from Richmond, got off at the Cheltenham railway station over the way from the graveyard, and arrived at the dentist's rooms to find I had missed my appointment. I had written down the wrong date. I could come back the following week.

I walked home relieved but also distressed that I had wasted all that worry time on something I should then have to worry about again the following week. Halfway home I walked into our new parish church, Our Lady of the Assumption, and sat at the front, full of prayers. *Could God please arrange the surgery of my dreams? Could he please arrange some way in which someone might bypass the agony and complete the work without my noticing?*

For months I had felt bits crumble away in the back of my mouth. For months I had suffered the throb of one tooth then another, especially at night when the only relief was to rub toothpaste into the cracked hole and hope somehow the mint might do something to stop the pain.

On nights like these when my tooth ached and throbbed and swelled, I floated off into dreams where the dentist, a man in white whose face I could not see behind his mask, put another mask over my mouth and left me to drift off into the sleep of the dead only to wake up with a mouth full of blood. No more jagged edges.

I had taken to talking to people with one hand across my mouth to hide the stain on my front teeth. By now both my incisors had turned a purple yellow from decay and it was only a matter of time before my front teeth went the same way.

When the dentist's secretary offered me another time, I told her I needed to speak first to my mother. After I walked home, I threw my school bag onto the floor, and joined my younger sisters and brothers to watch Kimba the White Lion on television. Even the whiteness of the lion reminded me of the yellow state of my teeth. And during an advertisement for MacLean's toothpaste with a teacher encouraging the children to brush up big, I imagined all my sisters and brothers—the older ones had joined us by then—pointing their fingers at me for not brushing my teeth as I should have done when I was little.

It took another two years before any dentist looked inside my mouth and by then even I had decided I could not bear to go on with the pain.

EARLIER THAT year the money from the sale of the Greensborough property, held up for all those years, had finally come through and my parents could at last afford to buy their own

Australian house. They visited an endless array of display houses and eventually settled for one in Cheltenham.

When we moved in, the air was thick with the smell of fresh paint but I didn't complain. If anything, I enjoyed the newness that came with white walls and the chemical pong of freshly-laid lino. The floor boards gleamed with varnish enough to act as mirrors and I thought for the first time ever I might be able to invite one of my school friends into this house, if only during the day when our father was not drinking.

Memories of the Camberwell house and all its mess fell away and I began to take pride in wiping down the benches after breakfast each morning. At night I looked out of the window above my bed and tried to imagine I was living in some foreign country closer to the equator, than here in Cheltenham on a busy main road in the new AV Jennings estate where every house matched its partner in all but number.

So I had first choice of bed. I took the one closest to the window and Juliana was happy to look across to the sky from her bed on the other side. The two of us took turns to be the last to say goodnight in an interminable game of who'd be the last to speak, and, although our father had told us to leave the Venetian blinds alone, only to open them in the morning and to close them at night using the cord that adjusted the light, ever since our arrival I'd pulled the blind up to the top of the window frame so that Juliana and I could both get a complete view of the night sky from this large window that was nothing like the windows from the houses in which we'd lived in the past.

Those old houses blocked out the light with tiny windows that were designed to minimise heat loss, but here in Cheltenham, when people no longer feared the cold and heat so much as they did when our parents first arrived from Europe, we could have windows that took up whole half walls and more.

For weeks, the ritual of going to bed, of raising the blinds, of staring at the night sky until my eyes grew heavy and I fell asleep, was one of my favourite activities until one morning at breakfast when my father decided to check on our room. Not so much to see whether we had made our beds — our father never seemed troubled by such things — but to see whether our room was a mess.

Most mornings, I remembered to put the blind to rights before I left our bedroom for breakfast, but on this morning, an autumn morning when the weather was beginning to turn, my father asked, 'Which one of you pulled up the blind last night?'

His face was frozen over as if just a few inches under the surface of his skin, an army of soldiers were gearing up for attack. My tongue stuck to the roof of my mouth.

'Why shouldn't we fix our blind any way we want?' Juliana said in a voice that stunned me for its audacity. Without a word, my father grabbed her by the head and threw her against the wall with all the force of his arm and she let out a cry. He let her loose then and she slumped into a chair while he turned and walked back to the lounge room to his favourite seat by the fire. I looked at my sister and worried about brain damage from the force of the blow. Juliana began to cry quiet tears and I felt like a criminal, and worse still, because I dared not take responsibility for my crime.

From then on, we left the blinds alone and I missed my full view of the night sky, especially as the year wore on and the daylight lasted longer. At last the school year ended and we set about preparing ourselves for Christmas. My brothers found a tree on the Melbourne Metropolitan Board of Works estate four blocks down the road from our new house in Cheltenham and dragged it home in such a way that its underside had sheared off and the tree looked crooked. They propped it up in a pot filled with dirt in the lounge room, the bald side facing the wall.

'Come and help us decorate,' Henry said. The tree smelled of pine, the smell of Christmas and the baubles tinkled in their sectioned boxes. The special balls that had come all the way from Holland were wrapped separately. The tear-drop shaped bauble with a sunken centre in blood red with sparkles scattered on top was my favourite. I lifted it carefully from its tissue paper bed and untwisted the wires.

'Put that one here,' Gerard said. 'It's better to have all the good baubles spread across the front.'

'I want to put the angel on,' Jacob called from the hallway. He'd just come in from playing outside.

'You can't. You're not tall enough,' Henry said.

'Then let him put something else on.' I found another bauble, the one shaped like a toadstool, red with white spots and a fat white stalk.

'Here you can have this one.' Jacob took it into his hands.

'Gentle,' I said. He managed to attach the toadstool such that it stayed put. We covered the tree first with baubles then Henry wound layers of tinsel round and round in cascading circles. Gerard uncoiled the lights and we all helped to wind them through the tree. Finally, Henry put the angel on top and we were set.

On Christmas Eve we went to bed early, in readiness for midnight Mass.

'I don't think I'll be able to sleep tonight,' I said at dinner.

'I won't either,' Juliana said.

'Just read for a bit,' my mother spooned *nasi goreng* onto plates.

'Pass these around,' she said. We handed the plates around, chain style. I was not interested in dinner. Too excited. Through the double glass doors I could see the lights of the Christmas tree flash. They blended in with the headlights from cars that raced by in front of our house. The part I liked best in *nasi goreng* was the fried egg, which my mother sliced into strips and spread on top.

When all our plates were set on the table, she took another plate and piled on the mashed potatoes, boiled beans and steak she had cooked separately to take to my father who ate alone in the lounge room. With the door closed between the lounge and the dining room we could almost pretend he was not here. The television flickered through the glass door along with the Christmas lights.

There was silence around the kitchen table as we took in forkfuls of rice and my mother ferried in my father's plate.

'I wouldn't feed that to a dog.'

'Maybe you'll want it later,' my mother said.

'Never. You make me sick. Go back to your children. Go back and pray with them. I'm just an old drunk. Just kill me off.'

I could hear the scraping of the double glass doors that led into the hallway, then my mother's footstep. She came back into the kitchen through the second door and put the plate of food down on the bench. The kitchen in this new house formed a long rectangle; the end beyond a central bench where we sat became the dining area. The lounge room next door was visible through the glazed lines of the single sliding door.

My mother took her place at the end of the table and started to eat.

My father called out for her.

'What is it?' she called back.

'You feed your bloody children. What's there for me? I'm starving.'

My mother shuffled on the spot. This time she did not go the long way round. She dragged open the sliding door that stood between our father and us. From my position at the table I could see him face the room, still seated in his chair across the way from the television set.

'I just gave you your dinner and you didn't want it.'

'You call that food?' He lurched up from his chair.

'You can have *nasi goreng*, too, if you like,' my mother said, 'but it's not right for your diabetes.'

My father stood in the doorway and towered over my mother. He was swaying. 'Bloody stupid whore.' It was not clear whether he leaned towards the Christmas tree in the corner near the door for support, or whether he intended to tip it over, but as he reached towards it my father shoved his fist through the branches, took hold of the trunk, and dragged the tree onto its side. It smashed onto the floor beside him. We leapt from the table.

'There now,' my father said. 'I hope you're happy. Happy bloody Christmas to you all.' He staggered from the room, out past the sliding glass doors, up through the hallway and into his bedroom. The Christmas tree rested on its front, the bald side visible. The lights continued to flash but were dimmer as they shone through the branches, muted by the tree's bulk.

'Come, help me get it back up,' our mother said. Gerard and Henry pushed the tree back into place. Dirt from the pot holding the tree spread over the floor and mingled with loose pine needles and the shattered silver glass of the broken baubles.

'Don't come in here without shoes,' our mother said. 'I'll get the dustpan and broom.'

The others hopped around the room gathering up broken baubles. The toadstool was still in one piece but my mother's beloved tear-drop, the one she bought years ago for her first Christmas after marrying in Holland, had caved in. The metal wire that held it to the tree had popped open and there was a hole in the middle. I picked it up and rested the pieces, as many as I could find, on top of the dresser, next to the nativity scene.

The manger was still empty. That night when we arrived home from midnight Mass we would put the porcelain baby Jesus in its place in the stable and everything would feel complete.

But not this Christmas.

When school began after the holidays and life took back its usual pattern, every night we four older kids sat around the kitchen to do our homework after dinner. I had begun to study biology and opened my *Web of Life* to take down notes on the life cycle of a dung beetle. Dung beetles fed off decaying matter. They broke down the cowpats that littered the green fields. The book started off by talking about photosynthesis, the process whereby the grass started to grow. The cows ate the grass, and then shat it out. The dung beetle broke down the cow manure into the soil and the cycle began again. Lots of diagrams of cartoon animals leading to arrows that went around in circles, grass to cow, cow to dung, dung to beetle.

I tried to take this in over the hullabaloo of my father's voice and the television blaring in the next room.

'You're such a wonderful woman.' My father shouted at my mother above the drone of the news. The newsreader's voice had a steady hypnotic flow. 'Two children died in a house fire in Maribyrnong this afternoon. There are no suspicious circumstances.' I had some sheets of paper and onto these I wrote down my father's words. On small pink squares of paper I wrote down everything he said.

'Kill him off, Liesje, you just kill him off.' My mother did not respond. In the silence I could almost see her as she sat out of sight in front of the television, her eyes ahead, refusing to be drawn in.

'Why don't you go back to your family?' my father said. 'Go back to your mother and father. You're a stupid bloody whore. And I? I have to sit here, night and day. I have to sit here and eat the muck you serve. I work all day. I work bloody hard, Liesje. You don't believe that, of course, do you?'

On the other side of the kitchen, I could see the plate of food my mother had made earlier resting on a pan on the stove. Mashed potatoes and carrots, peas that had turned a turquoise colour from sitting out of the can for too long and the congealed fat of a piece of steak, brown as dung, with white streaks of fat bordering its edges.

'You're such a good woman, Liesje. Nine bloody children. I should have used a *capotje* (a condom). All those bloody children. But God loves you. You'll go to Heaven, you and your bloody children.'

I wrote as fast as I could to keep up with him. All the words, like a newspaper reporter. I wrote and wrote. It kept me sane. That was my thought as I wrote on and on and on. This writing keeps me sane. If I listened to my father's words, if I tried to decipher their meaning, I would go mad. My father was mad. Not just drunk. He was mad. My mother said he was an alcoholic. A-L-C-O-H-O-L-I-C, she said it like that, spelled out the word. He could not help himself. She had joined Al-Anon. She went to weekly group meetings. She came home from these meetings full of praise for the wonders of serenity. My mother was serene as she watched the television while my father blasted her from all angles.

My mother's serenity seemed to impel him further. His voice grew louder and louder. I wrote faster and faster. I would keep these sheets of paper forever. One day when I was older I would bring them out and let others read my father's words.

I heard him lurch out of his chair. The heavy thump of his bare feet on the lounge room carpet. What next? I stopped writing. Waited. The click of the television knob and it was silent.

'I'm going to bed,' my father said as he staggered across the carpet to his room. I heard the slide of the double glass doors and my father's footsteps up the hall. The slam of his bedroom door.

I closed my *Web of Life* over the top of my notes and tiptoed to the lounge room door. My mother was sitting in her chair, opposite my father's now empty chair. She had her eyes fixed on the television, as if it was still on. Her eyes were glazed with that far-away look she got more and more these days when she was practising her serenity.

'We do as if nothing is wrong,' she said and turned to look at me as I stood in the doorway. I wanted to tell her about my notes. I wanted to show her the evidence. My father was mad. My father was a crazy lunatic drunk.

'Best you go to bed now,' she said, a smile spreading across her face. 'God grant me the serenity,' she recited the Al-Anon prayer.

Now I felt like my father. Rage, red and hot. How could she ignore him so? How could she just let him go on and on and on, like that? He was like a wild animal chained to a post and left out in the hot sun waiting till the birds came down to peck out his eyes.

Night after night it went on like this. The *Web of Life*. I could draw arrows in a circle leading from one to another, from him to her, from her to him, and to us, my brothers and sisters, clustered in the middle. We were the products of this marriage, like so many pieces of cow dung left for the dung beetles to break down and send back into the earth.

IN THE middle of winter on a Sunday evening after another crazy weekend, we huddled together behind my mother at the front door and waited. Cars streaked by on Warrigal Road. There were only seven of us left at home now and I was the tallest, even taller than my mother. She stood hunched over in her green mohair coat, while the rest of us shivered in the cold. The liquidambar tree in the front yard stripped of its autumn leaves rose like a skeleton against the glare of headlights, while our new house, an AV Jennings special in cream brick veneer, was in darkness. My mother tried the door handle and sighed.

'He's locked us out again.'

The day before, my father had gone on a drinking binge. He threw the radiator at my mother because the porridge was lumpy and then fell asleep on the couch. My mother took her coat and purse then and waited with us on the nature strip for the blue Ventura bus, which took us to Ivanhoe. We spent the weekend there with my uncle and his family in their double-storey house. But with school the next day, we needed to come home, to return for books and uniforms and our ordinary lives.

My mother tapped on the door. I hoped it would stay shut and we could walk away. She tapped again. My father, sober by then but surly, stepped aside to let us back into the house. I half hid behind my mother, ready to run again. That night in the shadow of my fear, I made up my mind to rescue people like me from families like mine. I would become a social worker. I would work with the families of alcoholics.

Every year from this time until the year I turned eighteen I sent out letters to universities asking when I could apply to study social work. What did I need to do to get in? What were the alternatives? I wrote letters to the technical colleges. What did I need to do to become a welfare officer? I was frustrated by their suggestions that I wait, wait until I had finished my schooling and then apply.

But I was determined. I would become a social worker, or if I did not get high enough grades, I would work as a welfare officer. I would do things differently from my mother. For one thing, if I was married to a man such as my father, I would leave him, and not just temporarily but for good.

Alateen

IT HAPPENED like this. On Friday nights my father drank himself into oblivion. Most times he fell asleep in his chair in front of the television. He left us in peace, but sometimes the drinking started earlier, before Friday. It might have even begun on a Thursday. On days like these, my father did not go to work. Instead he drank and slept and in between times he looked to us for company and for fights.

He looked first to my mother, but given her serenity she pretended she didn't notice him and the more she pretended the more angry he became until in an explosion of rage he threw his shoe at her, as he had that morning, or he ripped off her dress as he had the week before, or he tore out her hair.

One weekend we stayed with my older brother and his new wife where they rented a half house in Hawthorn but we could not overdo such visits. They had a new baby and didn't need another seven children in the mix. So the next weekend we visited a friend of my mother who let my mother and the two little ones spend the night with her. This friend had no more room, so we older kids needed to fend for ourselves. We went back home alone without our mother, but not to stay. We aimed to find somewhere else nearby where, as if we were homeless, we could spend the night.

The bus dropped us off two stops before our house. We walked around the block and approached our house from behind. We did not want our father to see us from his front seat in the lounge room. Even from behind, our house did not feel safe. There was a vacant block behind the back paling fence that divided our house off from the next as yet unbuilt property. We decided to sleep there, but it was not like camping.

My brothers climbed the fence and snuck into the backyard to collect three towels off the washing line. We had left them there the day before, after we had been swimming. We used the towels as blankets.

Mine was a yellow towel. It was summertime. I did not need a blanket. I used the towel as a mattress, a thin mattress that could not cushion me from the rocks and rough bits that stuck into my body every time I tried to turn over, but it was a comfort nevertheless. Henry and Gerard offered the towels to us three girls as an act of gallantry. They were strong boys. They could do without.

I looked at the stars and imagined myself far away even as I marvelled at the idea of my fifteen-year-old self as this homeless person. How shocked they would be at my school. Families from my school did not sleep out of doors at night because their father was drunk.

In the morning we gathered together in the garage to wait till it was time to go to Mass. My mother, and the little ones would join us later. Henry had rolled himself up into an old sleeping bag he'd found pitched in the corner from the last time the boys went camping.

Juliana and I needed to pee. But where? We couldn't pee into the bushes like our brothers and it didn't feel safe going to the outside toilet but we had no choice. We crept along the garden path to the back steps. They were incomplete. The builders had left before they fixed the metal guardrail. It wobbled when I brushed against it.

By the time we reached the top of the steps, I could see our father through the kitchen window looking out at us. My heart skipped a beat. I could not go forward. I could not go back. Juliana was right behind me. She slipped on the step and grabbed hold of the metal rail, which fell over under her weight. Our father opened the back door.

'What are you doing here?'

'We need the toilet,' I said. He said nothing, turned back inside and closed the door behind him. I heard the key turn in the lock. Good. If he locked us out, he locked himself in.

I told Juliana to hurry and we each stood guard at the toilet door. My pee came out the dark yellow of early morning and even though I was desperate for it, it came slowly and only in a trickle. The pile of *Reader's Digests* were still there in the corner. My favourite reading during the day when no one came, given we had two toilets by then, one inside, and one out.

I did not dare to look back at the kitchen windows as we scurried back to our hideout in the garage. We closed the metal door behind us and sat down on sheets of newspaper to wait for our mother. The floor of the garage like the step railing was not finished. There was no actual floor; instead the ground was made up of fine dust, like grey talcum powder, which got between the toes of my sandals.

Out of nowhere there was a glare of sunlight through the darkness and my father was at the door. He stared at us then looked down at the rolled out sleeping bag. He lifted his foot and kicked it right where Henry's head was resting. Henry had hidden himself in the bag.

'You focking whore,' my father said to the body in the sleeping bag as if he thought it was our mother. We held our breaths. There was a faint yelp from inside the sleeping bag and my father walked back inside the house through the kitchen door.

We helped Henry up. He was not dead. The layers of sleeping bag must have cushioned him from our father's shoe. Henry was not even winded.

We stopped waiting for our mother then and walked along the road to meet her. At Mass the priest in white and gold vestments droned on about the need to give generously to the School's Provident Fund and I looked down at my dirty fingernails, dirtier than usual for all the grit of my stony dirt bed the night before, and I marvelled at the way life could seem so very different from the outside.

THE NEXT Friday after school, Hannah, Henry, Gerard and I took a train into the city. Hannah told me I was old enough to come, too. I could not understand what we were doing there in those draughty halls, which you entered through dark corridors, where the windows were covered with thick drapes that scarcely let in any light from the setting sun. We had gone straight from school and were still in our uniforms. We had no time beforehand to do anything other than drop our bags at the door at home before Hannah had us back on the bus, onto the train and into the city.

'Room 6A,' Hannah said over to herself as she led us through corridor after corridor checking at each door for the right number. I knew we must have found it when we came to a room whose door was wide open such that we could not even see the number behind the door. It was full of people seated in chairs, mostly young people around my age, lined up in rows, each with their backs to us as we walked in behind them and took our places in the last few chairs still vacant.

I could not understand what I was doing there, the youngest of my four siblings to come along. I had not thought to ask Hannah why we were there and what we had come for. We would be safe with her and my brothers sat on either side of me, their knobbly knees white at each bend.

'Welcome,' a woman said to the room and people stopped their chatter and looked to her expectantly. 'I see we have a few newcomers.' All eyes turned to the back to look at us. They looked at us with inquisitive eyes, no smiles, more curiosity as if to say, and what brings you here?

I would not have answered such a question if anyone had directed it to me. At that moment I could not understand what I was doing there.

'We have quite a deal of business to get through tonight,' the woman said. All eyes turned back to face her and we were left once again facing a montage of backs, hunched shoulders, cardigans draped over chairs, and the hush of expectation. 'We might start with your stories. Damien, would you like to begin?'

There was the scraping of a chair against the parquetry and a boy not much older than Hannah stood beside the woman in front and looked at us with a nervous expression on his face. He looked as though he had been caught unawares, as though he was wholly unprepared for this position, which he had now taken up in front of us in the draughty room above the clocks at Flinders Street Station, but he cleared his throat to speak.

'My name is Damien,' he said. 'My mother is an alcoholic.' Damien told us then about his life as one of three children, born to different fathers and each living every day with a mother who drank all day long and in between drinking she slept or ranted. 'Sometimes she hits us,' Damien said, 'but it doesn't bother me much any more. She's not strong, and now I'm bigger I just push her away. But the two little ones get scared. And she used to hurt me bad when I was little. She used to make me cry.'

And so I discovered, just like Damian, we were there on business. We were there to deal with the alcoholism of a parent, a friend or a relative. We were there to develop detachment.

As I looked around at the women in this strange place, I could see something of my mother's eyes in theirs. No wonder the woman who sat behind me, clutching her black handbag on her lap, tugging at her skirt, no wonder this woman did not turn to introduce herself. She had developed detachment, or so I imagined. But then it was possible this was her first visit, too.

Lost opportunities

GERARD AND Henry built a cubby house underground in the Farm Road estate. The builders had cleared the area of trees and all signs of the market gardens that once spread for miles across this flat landscape.

The boys used shovels and picks, which they had pinched from our father's garage and risked getting into serious trouble if he had known, and then for weeks over the school holidays they dug a hole deep enough and wide enough to occupy two of us at a time.

To my mind this was not good enough. It was no fun being down there underground when you knew there were two others on top waiting for their turn. I wanted to stay in this hole for hours, because the hole was the closest I could imagine to really being below the earth, underground in caves like I had read about in books.

So we took it in turns, one girl with one boy because my brothers who were older believed we girls needed a boy to protect us. When my turn came, Gerard showed the way.

'Get down on your belly,' he said. 'Then slide like a snake. Try not to let your back touch the roof, otherwise you'll dislodge the lot.'

This was tricky. To make myself as skinny as a lizard, to make myself slide in, without ever once letting my bum stick up in the air even while I needed to bend my knees to get momentum.

'Could you maybe hold the roof up just a tiny bit till I get through,' I asked. Gerard obliged and then I shimmied into the hole as slippery as a fish. My brother followed. Beyond the opening the boys had dug a pit, deep enough for two of us to sit in as long as you hunched your shoulders a tiny bit. It was almost pitch black inside, but, at the edges of the hole around the roof line, which were made of old doors and bark and planks pinched from our father's garage, I could see chinks of light, especially through the round keyhole on the door. But when Gerard lit the candle they'd left down there for future visits, the place lit up like a grotto. Like the grotto at school, a place carved out of rock in the side of one wall to house the statue of the Blessed Virgin. On special occasions the nuns turned on a light in the grotto so that it made Mary's halo shine.

Gerard and I sat in silence, breathing in the smell of dirt and tree roots, kneading the crumbling soil under our heels, and I imagined what it was like to be a soldier in battle hiding from the enemy. For me the enemy was still outside, Henry and Juliana waiting their turn. I could hear them pacing about, their feet catching on fallen branches, rustling leaves. Their impatience percolated down through the bits of wood the boys had used to support the walls of their house and I decided I would need to return to this place alone.

'It's our turn now,' Juliana called and her words sounded muffled, but clear enough for us not to ignore them any longer. Once again the belly flopping wriggle out of the rabbit hole and back into the daylight but only after Gerard had snuffed out the candle and left us once again in darkness. Then we were like blind people, inching our way forward with our hands in the dark.

I took my turn to hold up the roof ever so slightly so that Juliana could wriggle her way through and then waited. The ten minutes seemed a long time before Henry called out they'd had enough and it was time to go home.

I did not tell them I had a plan. One I had tucked away in the corner of my mind.

My family always travelled in twos or threes and fours.

'Never go out alone,' my mother had said. 'It's always safer to travel together. That way, if one gets hurt, the other can call for help.' But even when we travelled in groups of three, four or five, we were never able to get help on the nights my father drank too much and began to yell at my mother and wished us all dead. The cubby-hole would not be big enough to fit us all, and it was a long way away. Besides, my mother would never be able to get through the entrance, nor Hannah. The only safety for them was to say nothing, and if things got really bad to make an escape through the back door and out into the night to wait some more until morning or until our father had fallen asleep and forgotten his threats.

On the last day of the school holidays when my brothers had gone off on their paper rounds and Juliana had decided she wanted to stay home and read another one of her female heroines of war books, I took my pencil and note pad, an extra jumper for warmth and snuck out the back door. It was mid-afternoon and no one noticed me disappear, at least no one called out to me after I had scaled the back fence and began my walk across the vacant blocks of the Farm Road Estate.

There were half-built houses everywhere, in some places only the holes in the ground for the concrete and stumps. In other places whole wooden frames, frames that reminded me of the insides of beehives for their orangey colour and the smell they gave off, of turpentine or some other chemical that made me want to move past them quickly. There were other houses that had reached lock-up stage and I peered through their sealed windows to see empty lemonade bottles strewn about on the floor. The workers had left them there. On good days, they'd leave the empties outside and my bothers and sisters and I collected them for the deposit offered at the milk bar. Sometimes we could raise as much as two shillings or more.

I tried not to trouble myself with the possibility of money for empties and walked on to the area beyond the estate where work had not yet begun, the area surrounded by a row of Lombardy poplars. I worried that my brother had not left the candle and matches in place or that the matches might have gone soggy through recent rains. I worried that I might not find the hole. That it might have gotten swallowed up by the shifting leaves and twigs over the last several weeks since we had visited. I worried about how I might get down to the hole all by myself without disturbing the roof.

And then I saw it, the hint of red from the old door speckled with the undergrowth. I knew to lift the edge ever so slowly but I was not strong enough. I could see myself already safe underground but without my brothers I could not raise the opening wide enough.

I sat on the edge of the hole with my notebook and pencil and decided to write a poem about lost opportunities, about life's disappointments. Lofty themes, I knew, but wasn't that what poetry was all about? I used the longest words I could find to contrast the grandeur of the trees with my predicament, a small urchin. I liked the word "urchin". It meant a vagabond child, an orphan or a poor soul but to me it conjured up a creature of the sea as well, a sea urchin, but that did not fit my poem one bit so I tried to find another word that might reflect the sorrow of my story, the sadness of my situation.

Words were like that. They could make the worst of things better if only I could find the right ones.

On Saturday I took my notebook and pencil in my pocket and scaled the back fence. My mother was at work down the road at her new job in the old people's home and my father sat alone in front of the television. My sisters and brothers were scattered throughout their rooms and a voice in my head called out to me:

'You must find nature.'

I hankered to go out in someone's car to the countryside, to be among the green hills, the trees and the sheep, but all I could manage was a long walk down Farm Road to the as yet built housing estate. I had given up on our underground hut, which some other boys had caved in for fun.

There was a point along the way where the concrete on the road stopped and the path was made of gravel. At that point I knew I could turn my back on the houses and streets filled with cars and people. The Lombardy poplars and pines in front forced my eyes upwards to the clouds and the sky. I was priming myself for the life of a poet.

On one side of Farm Road a cyclone fence protected passers-by from the golf balls that flew overhead in the Cheltenham golf range. On the other side, a long line of dilapidated sheds gave off the stench of long dead chickens. These, too, I saw as a last line of humanity, after which the countryside, once row upon row of market gardens now abandoned in readiness for the housing estates, prevailed. I was free to find a spot, a tree against which I might rest, take out my notebook and, with pencil in hand, write down my lofty thoughts.

The very act of writing down the words, inspired by the skyline, the lapping of leaves on the Lombardy poplars, the thought these trees once came from Italy, their forebears a sign that the world outside was vast and immeasurable, turned me into an important someone. I was a poet who could write down words in my notebook and the hours and hours of wasted time, spent during the summer holidays doing nothing but killing time would come to measure something of worth.

'Hi,' a voice called to me across the fence. A man in a cap with a caddy and golf stick. He called through the wire, and I wondered: had he lost his ball?

My brothers came here, too, but not to write poetry. They came to crawl through the stubby grass on the edge of the road to look for stray golf balls that had somehow managed to get over the cyclone fence. They took them to the golf course manager at the clubrooms in the centre of the golf course where they could trade the balls for money.

I looked at this man and felt a flicker of annoyance. I did not want him here. I did not want anyone here. People interfered with the flow of my thoughts. I was like Wordsworth, a man worthy of words. I was the creator of glorious scenes from nature and brought their beauty alive on the page.

'What are you writing?'

None of his business. But I had been brought up well. Not so much that I did not speak to strangers but that I would offer something of my polite self without interfering with my intentions.

'Poetry,' I said and turned back to my page by way of dismissal. Wordsworth never had to put up with interruptions like these.

A Trip to the Beach

THERE WERE days when the sun bore down so heavily all you could do was lie flat on top of your bed. Legs widespread on top of the sheet. Arms outspread like a star. On those days the bitumen on the road was soft underfoot. In places where someone had kicked it with a stick or sharp stiletto heel, it peeled open like an orange, the tar oozing out, sticky as gum.

On one such day the doorbell chimed. I was too exhausted to get up to see who was there. But, long trained in the art of politeness, I could not ignore the summons of the doorbell, the summons of a telephone, the summons of my little brother calling in the night for attention.

My room stood opposite the front door. But Hannah beat me to it. Her voice rose with the singsong sound of greeting.

'Hello, Father.'

The drone of Father Walsh's Irish voice lilted down the hall way and all thought of heat ran out the door as he stepped in. I rushed up to them.

'Would you girls like a trip to the beach?' Father Walsh — we called him Father Willie — looked at my sister and me with eager eyes, flitting from one face to the other but invariably his gaze landed on Hannah's face, up and down her body for an instant, then back at her face waiting for the answer. I gave it.

'We'd love to come.'

A trip to the beach, in a car, Father Willie's sticky vinyl-seated grey Valiant, was better than the bus, better than walking and far better than staying spread out on hot sheets in the late afternoon.

Father Willie, the young curate at our old church, was especially friendly to Hannah. He had travelled all the way from Deepdene to take us to the beach. To take us included all of us, as well as my mother when she was home.

Today my mother was away. She was at work down the road at the Old People's Home, where she was responsible for clearing up after each old person who died. She had drawers full of spectacles and razors, things the family of the dead person did not want but that my mother considered too valuable to throw away. I did not like these spectacles. They had a musty smell. I did not like the idea of looking through someone else's glasses, almost like looking through their eyes, especially the eyes of dead people. I thought these things should be destroyed but my mother would not hear of it.

'Where are the little ones?' Father Willie asked, meaning to include them on our trip. He always included them, he included all of us on trips to the beach but on days when Hannah was out, when he called unexpectedly, he never stayed. He was friendly at the doorway, if my mother was home, he might have stopped for a cup of tea but we only ever went to the beach when Hannah came too.

I sat in the back of Father Willie's Valiant with the three little ones. Hannah sat in front. We wound down the windows to let the air blow through as Father Willie drove the car away from home, along Warrigal Road. One end of the road formed a T-intersection with Canterbury Road near where we used to live, the other ended at the beach past the Mentone Bowling Club. The idea of all these miles between on one long stretch of road thrilled me. That you could be at one point in a road and still hours away from some other destination on the same road. I considered these things in the back seat of Father Willie's Valiant pressed up tight against Juliana's legs. She practically sat on top of me because there were only three seat belts in the back of this car and not enough room for four. Her legs pinched on the skin on one side of my thighs in a way that made me want to scream but I could only shift a little so as to rearrange her weight. I did not want to be impolite when Father Willie took us to the beach.

Father Willie in the front seat of his car talked to Hannah. She was eighteen years old and would soon leave home. She used to be the fat one in our family but lately she had been on a diet. Now it was my turn to be the fat one. It happened without my noticing. One day I was beanpole thin like my little sisters and then another my clothes no longer fitted.

I first saw the black hairs above my pubic bone in the change rooms at the public baths when we lived in the old house in Camberwell. They would not stop growing, these hairs, even as I tried to cut them off with scissors. It was funny how breasts and hair went together. Not long before we left the house in Camberwell, I decided it was time to cut the hair on my head short. The hair on my head hung to my waist. Hannah plaited it for school. During the holidays it grew tangled and messy because I could not be bothered to comb it through. Hannah had said, 'You'll look older with short hair.'

My mother had said, quietly when no one was listening, 'It might be time for you to wear a bra.'

I decided then to leave the hairs on my pubic bone alone. They were black and ugly even though the hair on my head was fair. I let them grow thick and only changed in the change room cubicles. No longer did I change in public, like my little sisters, in the swimming pool change rooms, where you hung your clothes and towel on a peg that ran in a long line of other pegs. We could never have afforded to pay the booking fee for a locker, even as I longed to be one of the swimmers who wore the big silver locker key attached to a silver pin, on the strap of their bathing suits.

We drove to the beach past the post office on Warrigal Road, past the fish and chip shop, past the kiosk. Father Willie parked his car on an angle alongside all the other cars that were parked at the beach for the day. Too many cars, when you considered it was only a weekday and not the weekend when everyone travelled to the beach. Jammed tight in the car and then jammed tight in the parking lot I needed to open the door carefully and squeeze myself out onto the hot spiky gravel underfoot. Because it was summer, I had not bothered with my sandals.

I could not stop to help the little ones out of the car. They at least were wearing shoes. I hotfooted it across the gravel to the nearest tuft of grass up against one of the posts that divided the car park from the beach. As soon as my feet were cool enough I raced across the white sand as fast as I could to reach the point where the sand grew darker in colour from the water off the sea. Only then could I stop. Conscious all the time of my body in my bathing suit, I had draped a towel around my waist to cover up my bottom. Hannah had told me my bottom was too big.

I stood now on the slushy sand at the edge of the beach and waited for the others. Together we looked for the widest space of sand not already occupied by people or towels. I wanted to sit. I wanted to squat on the sand to get down low. Not only was I growing fat, I was growing tall. I was taller now than Hannah. I was taller than my mother, even. If I was not careful I would grow as tall as my four tall big brothers, maybe even as tall as my father and then no one would ever want to marry me.

I wanted to take off my towel, to take the long walk across the wet sand into the sea but this was the worst walk of all. Once upon a time I had thought nothing of running around the beach in my bathers as the three little ones did then. Once upon a time I had thought nothing of splashing into the sea, proud and tall. Now I needed to figure out how I could get from there to there without anyone seeing me. How to be invisible?

I could not take my towel with me into the sea, yet I could not bear to leave it behind. It was my cover, my way of making the bottom half, that part of me, which Hannah had said was too fat, invisible.

Father Willie and Hannah sat on towels side by side. He wore dark blue swimming trunks, the type my father owned. His skin was freckled and pale as if it never saw the sun. My sister's skin was olive tanned. She spent hours in the backyard at home building up her tan. She started at the beginning of summer. She coated herself with coconut oil and allowed herself ten minutes of the sun on day one, turning herself around every two minutes like basting a chook in the oven. On day two she increased her time to twenty minutes, day after day until she had reached the two-hour mark. She would not sit in the sun for longer than two hours she said, because then she might have burned, but this way her body adjusted to the sun and by the middle of the summer her body was a beautiful chocolate brown. She had a beauty freckle in the middle of her cleavage that I thought was ugly. It was all I could see as I looked across at Hannah and Father Willie who chatted together on their towels, spread out on the sand.

The three little ones were in the water.

'Why don't you come in?' Gerard called out to me. I had wanted to join them. But I was too big and fat and hairy to move. Tufts of pubic hair sprouted between my legs where my bathers ended. I tried to pull my bathers down to cover them while making a tent of my towel.

'Why not go for a swim?' Hannah said. I could have asked her the same thing. Years ago I used to ask her why she never went into the water, why she only ever sun-baked on the edge of the swimming pool back at our other house so far from the beach, as if she had been frightened of getting wet. But today I did not ask.

In one sweeping movement I threw off my towel, pulled at my bathers in front and behind, then I strode as gracefully as I could towards the water. Not until the sea had reached my waist did I relax. By then I was safe. I could have fun, my body hidden by the water's folds and for a moment I could forget that at the other end of this swim, I would need to make the return trip across the sand and this time it would be worse because I would look straight into their eyes.

Revolution

THEY WERE looking for workers at a small transistor factory in Moorabbin. Under-eighteens could apply and no education or prior experience was necessary. A friend had told me about the position. I could apply with her if I wanted.

I took the train from Cheltenham on the first morning of the school holidays. If I could get this job and earn money every week I could buy everyone in my family a proper Christmas present and I could buy myself new clothes instead of having to rely on Hannah for hand-me-downs. The train rattled as it slipped through the three stations from Cheltenham to Moorabbin and to my friend.

We walked down Chesterville Road alongside the factories and offices that lined the main road and spread into each side street. The transistor factory was tucked into a cul-de-sac behind a paint distributor and a coat hanger manufacturer. The woman in the tiny office out front took our names and introduced us to the foreman who led us to the back of the factory and to the manager who would decide our fate.

'We only need one worker,' he told us. 'I'll take you,' he said pointing to me. I did not see the look on my friend's face, but I sensed her shame. I thought I knew why the manager had chosen me. My friend was smart, the smartest girl in our class. She even studied maths and chemistry, but her hair stood on top of her head like a dried out mop and there were large wet patches under her arms from the perspiration that soaked into her clothes, irrespective of the weather. She had a moon face, white with freckles, and wore wire-rimmed glasses. I was not a beauty, but I was better looking than her. I watched her as she walked through the factory into the sunlight that shone through the front door. Her silhouette passed into the street and she was gone.

'You can start straight away', the manager said. 'I'll fix the paperwork later.'

Several women sat in two lines on opposite ends of a series of trestle tables that took up the entire factory floor. The foreman stood at one end and passed down transistor parts to the two women at the front. They tweaked at the small metal plates with tweezers and pulled through wires and then sent them along to the next women who performed their set tasks, on and on down the line until the parts came to me. The foreman showed me how to pull two thick wires through holes set at the base of each panel. Then I had to twist the wires together on the back to hold them in place.

It seemed simple enough but when it came my turn my fingers froze and I found it almost impossible first to thread the wires through the right holes and next to twist them into tight plaits.

'You'll get the hang of it soon', the foreman said and then went back to his place at the other head of the table. There was a pile of panels waiting for my attention beside me. I took up the first and fiddled with it. By the time I had finished my first panel five minutes had passed and another four panels sat on top of my as yet to be completed pile. I tried not to panic. I tried to ignore the buzz of voices from the women along the table who chatted to one another as they worked. The woman opposite, who sat waiting patiently for me to hand over the next panel, took to helping me with mine.

'You'll get the hang of it soon,' she said, but my fingers were beginning to ache with the effort. I had managed to puncture my skin with the sharp wires in the process of trying to thread them through. Drips of blood fell onto the table. After what seemed hours, an alarm rang out to announce morning tea. The women put down their pieces and moved through a door into a room on the side, which I assumed was the tearoom. I stayed behind. A back door at the end of the factory stood wide open. I could see out and across a stubby carpet of grass onto the back fence with its wire gate, which stood ajar.

I knew then I could not stay in this place. I took myself out into the yard as if I were looking for fresh air and made my way through the gate and out onto the street beyond. I cut through several side streets until I found Chesterville Road again and could work out my direction home.

It was a long walk, but I took as many side streets as I could find that led away from the factory. I feared turning back. All the way along I could feel the manager at my heels. I could imagine him enraged and indignant. How dare you, he would say, how dare you walk out on me like this? Why do you think I gave you the job? I needed a worker, not a wimp.

The sky ahead was crystal blue. Every step I took led me further away from the factory and the manager and foreman. Every step I took drew me closer to the safety of my home.

When I got there I telephoned my friend. I heard the surprise in her voice. 'It's a good thing you didn't get the job,' I said. 'It was terrible.' I told her about my bloodied fingers and the pile of panels unfinished at my side. 'I just couldn't stay.' My friend was silent at the other end of the phone. I did not want to hear what she was thinking and she did not say a word. That was the way with my friend. She kept herself to herself and so I could only imagine that she might feel, as I would have felt, resentful and bitter that her opportunity had been taken from her by the likes of me. I stole it from her and then threw it away

'I'll have to go,' my friend said. 'I start work at the newsagents down the road. I saw an ad in the window on my way home from the factory and applied. They want me to start this afternoon.'

Now it was my turn to feel bitter. How did she do it?

'I'm so pleased for you,' I said, holding back my bile. 'I knew you'd get a job sooner or later.' I did not tell her about the nagging fear in the back of my mind that, had the manager chosen her, she might have managed and proved me even more of a failure.

With no holiday job to speak of and no school to occupy my time, I had to settle for reading books and hanging around after Hannah whenever she would let me. Hannah had left school and mingled with people who seemed so much older. Still I preferred them to Juliana who despite only two years between us seemed so much younger. The day Hannah said I could join her with the others from the Catholic Younger Set I jumped at the chance.

'so you want to start a revolution ...' the words came through the speaker in Chris Willee's car and I began to reconsider my take on music. I had not heard this song before. Beatles or Rolling Stones, it did not much matter to me. I was sitting in the back and Chris Willee had the radio volume up high. Hannah was in the front. She had told me since I had turned fifteen I could come along to this gathering but only if I behaved myself.

What could she mean, 'behave myself'? I always behaved myself; though I had a sneaking suspicion by 'behave yourself' she meant, don't say anything that might have embarrassed her. She was easily embarrassed. Like the time I told Julian Stamp that Hannah had spent the night before trying to make her hair curl. She had not wanted him to know that and I should have realised as much, because I was not sure if I too had been trying to impress a boy that I would want him to know anything about the lengths to which I had gone to look good for him. Hannah looked good when Julian took her to the school ball in her low cut dress. Not too low cut to stir up the nuns' disapproval but low enough to please our father who liked cleavage. A funny word, I thought to myself from the back of Chris Willee's car.

The song was over by the time we arrived at the church hall. Chris Willee let Hannah out in a sweeping gesture. He got out of the driver's seat and walked all the way around the front to open it for her and she stepped out slowly like a princess exiting her carriage. I made my own way out, not that Chris Willee would not have done the same for me had I waited, at least I hoped he would. But I disliked this game of mothers and fathers that I saw my sister play whenever she went out with Chris Willee and his friends.

Someone had set up a table in one corner of the church hall and laid out cups of orange cordial. On another trestle there were cakes and sandwiches. At the entrance to the room, Beebe McCallister handed out name-tags, which we needed to attach to our tops, careful not to put holes into the fabric. Chris Willee helped Hannah with hers and I could see that he too wanted to get close to her cleavage, not that there was much showing in her black polo jumper, but the outline was still there.

Someone put on a record of pop music, the music I tried to take no interest in, because I was more sophisticated than the other girls in my class who spent hours at lunchtimes examining their signed copies of the Rolling Stones and Beatles, trying to decide which one they loved the most. Such folly, I thought. These musicians would never have taken an interest in the girls at school. Why waste energy on unrequited love. Why not go for Beethoven's music, or Brahms's or Bach's? They were all dead. There was no need to fall in love with them, no need to have become that most horrible of entities, a fan. No need to have wasted your energy on imagining someone else to love when he would never have loved you in return.

It was awkward standing there at the door not knowing what to say or do next. Hannah looked across at me with dagger eyes that said, 'piss off, you', not that she would ever have used those words. Go away and fend for yourself. 'I'm busy', she would have said. I imagined she was worried if I stuck around her for too much longer I would say something embarrassing.

Chris Willee took her by the hand and they walked across the hall to the side where a group of their friends had gathered, orange cordial cups in hand. I was not sure I wanted to start a revolution, but I didn't know what to do with myself. All the sophisticated older people from the Younger Set looked at me as though I was a nuisance and there was only so long I could take fiddling to get my name-tag right.

No revolution, just a quick exit back out the door, my best strategy at times like these. It was cool outside, though not really cold, and just cold enough for me to pull my cardigan closer around my shoulders. I could not stand there forever hovering at the front door of the Younger Set hall. I sat on a lump of wood near the fence; wood they used for fires when it was really cold and looked up at the stars. The Southern Cross, Alpha, Beta, Gamma, Delta and Epsilon. I had learned the names in Girl Guides where they made a fuss of things like stars because they reckoned the stars could help you not to get lost.

The stars were not helping me that night. Besides, I was not lost, not really. I knew exactly where I was but I did not belong there with this revolutionary bunch. Nor did I belong to the girls from my class who carried on over the Beatles as though they were about to marry one.

Home seemed the best place to go, away from the hall down Corrigan Road and onto Warrigal, then a straight walk along the highway till I got to the section where they'd concreted the pathway. After that it was easy.

I was walking along the grassy path when a car slowed down behind me. My heart seized. I'd seen this happen in movies. A young woman on the side of the road snatched into a car and carried away forever. Terrible things happened to this young woman; only I could not let my imagination take me that far.

Father Costigan in his black soutane wound down his window.

'Now what are you doing here on your own? Shouldn't you be somewhere else?'

I climbed into the back of Father Costigan's car and thanked my lucky stars that I was now with one of my favourite people, although that was a secret. I would not tell a soul.

'I'll take you back to the hall,' Father Costigan said after I told him I'd just been there. 'Your sister will be worried.' And then it hit me.

Hannah again. Everyone wanted my sister, including Father Costigan. Something about her sophistication and her cleavage, even under black polo necks, something about her allure, led them to her like butterflies to a lily and even though Father Costigan was a man of God, he could daydream, couldn't he? Though I knew he was not supposed to.

'I'd rather go home,' I said. 'If that's okay?' And I could sense the disappointment in Father Costigan's voice when I had deprived him of an extra chance to speak to my sister. He'd have to make his own excuses now.

Foster care

IN THE summer of 1968, when I was at my fattest and the rest of the world was in turmoil—Prague Spring, civil rights unrest in America, fights over apartheid in Africa, and everywhere felt more revolution in the air—my oldest brother Dirk had hatched a plan that we four youngest children should be sent away from home so that our parents would be free to sort out their affairs without the added pressure of children. That makes it sound like it was an act of kindness to my parents. For my father it might have been. We were a burden to him, but I prefer to think that it saddened my mother. That she found life without any of her children difficult, as much as it might have freed her up to sort out her husband's alcoholism. However she might have done that, I do not know.

But Dirk's plan was fixed, and based on his knowledge of what had gone on between my father and Hannah, he had the upper hand. He found homes for all of us. Years earlier, when he was eighteen, Dirk had run away from home. Just like that, one day at the dinner table arguing with our dad who kept picking on him to eat up, 'Hup, hup hup.' Three years later, as suddenly as Dirk had left home, he reappeared. I'd almost given up hope of ever seeing him again. How could a big brother abandon all his sisters and brothers without protection, without a word? But unbeknown to me he had been in contact with our mother and with Ferdi. And unbeknown to me, too, Dirk had travelled to the top of Australia, and across the ocean to New Guinea where he became a lay missionary, studying, teaching and preaching, with an eye to the priesthood.

Now in his mid-twenties, Dirk was not frightened of our father, and along with Ferdi, who was visiting our house, they wanted to punish our father for what he had done to Hannah. Until then they'd had no idea what had been going on. No idea until one day Hannah told them. Just like that. And the sky did not fall in as I had expected it would. But other things happened, like a snowball gathering speed.

In the lounge room, in the middle of the house, Dirk dragged our father out of his chair and pushed him up against the fireplace. I cowered in the kitchen with Juliana and the little ones, amazed and relieved that our "Old Man" had finally been defeated, or so it seemed this time. Dirk told our parents that he and Ferdi, the two oldest children in our family, would take away all responsibility from them as parents in the form of fostering out the younger children to give them space to sort themselves out. With the knowledge exposed, our father's hold was broken.

My mother agreed. My father had no say, and one by one, we were farmed out. Hannah had already left home. Gerard and Henry (at 17 and 18 years of age) were old enough to live independently. Henry found a job and moved into a bed-sitter. Gerard went to live in college at the Australian National University. Jacob and Bec moved in with Ferdi, his wife and their two daughters, while Juliana and I went to board with a Dutch family in Camberwell.

I told Dirk I was pleased when he and Father Maas, the Dutch priest, who had placed a number of children with Catholic families willing to help out, arranged for us to stay with this family.

'Away from home, I can study better,' I said to Dirk. As if my study were the only thing that mattered. Leaving home had felt like a miracle then, not one of my mother's many miracles but a miracle all the same. I had never gone away before, at least not for more than a few days at a time. But I had an uneasy feeling when Mrs Dijkstra greeted us for the first time at her front door that she saw us as her new daughters. I did not want another mother. I wanted my mother. But I was glad to be free from my father.

THE FIRST time we arrived at our new home, this time in Pleasant Road in Camberwell, we were two awkward schoolgirls. We came there directly from school. We had taken the train from Richmond to the Camberwell Railway Station, dawdled down the long shop fronted Burke Road, staggered up the other side beyond the junction and rapped at the brass knocker. Mrs Dijkstra welcomed us in.

My uniform pulled tightly against my breasts and waist. I had been trying to ignore it, till Hannah had warned me yet again about eating less.

I hoped the Dijkstras would not notice. Mrs Dijkstra was a large woman, with a pasty complexion. Her hands were broad like a man's and she dressed more like a countrywoman than a Camberwell matron.

'Come inside. I'll show you your room,' she said with her thick Dutch accent. There was a spinning wheel in the entrance hall that reminded me of witches. I was conscious of my size. With one heavy case each, we struggled up the stairs.

The bed in the room at the top of the stairs was clean, crisp and white. It almost shimmered.

'You'll have to share a bed,' Mrs Dijkstra said. There was no time for settling in. She led us back down the steep staircase, along the corridor, back through the house into the kitchen and to the meal table. Everything was set in the Dutch way, but it was unfamiliar. Already I missed my mother, yet I could not let myself dwell on thoughts of her. I was too busy holding myself together.

At the table, with heads bowed, we said grace before meals, led by Mrs Dijkstra. She headed the family in everything. Mr

Dijkstra, seemingly half the size of his wife, deferred to her from his place at the opposite head of the table.

We arrived on a Thursday, family day at the Dijkstras. All the children with the exception of the one married son, Hank, sat at the table, which was covered in a hand-embroidered table-cloth. The little cornflowers, poppies and roses tucked into tight stitched bouquets at each end of the table were faded and flattened by too much ironing.

Mrs Dijkstra cut up and served each of us a piece of meat pie, her specialty. This was my introduction to puff pastry, golden and flaking. It melted on my tongue. Mrs Dijkstra had a strict regime of meals. For breakfast and lunch we ate *boterhammen*, bread with different spreads, including *hagel*-chocolate sprinkles, jam and honey and cheese. Lots of cheese, cut thin with a special knife that you slid over the top. A blade like a razor peeled off slices in thin or thicker wedges, as you liked.

Every night of the week Mrs Dijkstra cooked a particular meal. On Sunday she shifted the hot food from dinner to lunch and it was always a roast with baked potatoes and gravy, roast tongue, silverside, chicken. Roasts reminded me of my mother's cooking but Mrs Dijkstra never burned the food. My favourite night was Thursday, when she baked her meat pies.

For a while we played at being dutiful daughters, each trying to outdo the other in cheerfulness. At breakfast, we chatted about school, our subjects, French, History, Latin, Literature. We did not notice Mrs Dijkstra's hints that we help more in the kitchen, with the washing, with the ironing. She was not interested in our schooling, and frowned when Juliana walked into the kitchen one Saturday morning dressed in trousers.

'Can I have trousers, too?' Mrs Dijkstra's youngest child and only daughter, Maddie asked.

'Trousers are for men.' Mrs Dijkstra glared at Juliana and went on about the need to behave like a lady, sound like a lady and dress as one. We said nothing.

As the days rolled into weeks, the weeks into months, I sensed Mrs Dijkstra's growing displeasure. She lowered her head to avoid eye contact and said very little, but her silence screamed out her discontent. She spoke in monosyllables, did not engage with us any more, took no further interest in our daily lives and appeared to be freezing us out of hers, if only by blocking us out of her line of vision. Baffled and wounded, it seemed she could not make sense of us at all.

In turn, we were secretive. We closed the door to our room, trying to conceal our underwear and stockings, which we washed by hand and hung from the bars on the brass bed. I could not bear to hand over my underpants to Mrs Dijkstra for washing. I had started menstruating. She would see that my underpants were ready for the rubbish bin. We needed to wash our underwear everyday. My mother did not visit but she sent a small supply of sanitary pads through the nuns. By now Juliana had also started her period. We were both desperate to invent ways of mopping up and hiding the blood.

The house was crowded. Although the two oldest boys no longer lived at home, they visited often. Juliana fell in love with them. She was fourteen now and flirtatious. I, on the other hand, kept my distance, feigned indifference and adopted a superior attitude. But I was in love, too.

Jealousy burned.

The second son, Willem, studied medicine. He liked to experiment on his family. He was interested in teeth. He wanted to look at mine for practice. I hid, while Juliana, whose teeth were cavity-free, opened her mouth wide to Will's gentle fingers. I hid in the park nearby, swinging up and down on a rubber tyre for hours on end. Jealousy burned and I wished my sister dead.

ONE AUTUMN day, we watched the oldest son, Jon, the soon to be ordained priest, play in a football match with his fellow seminarians. These young men in white shorts and brightly coloured

T-shirts, greens, blues and yellows, jostled with one another across the oval, which was pock-marked with mud holes and gashes. As they slipped and slid in their footy boots I marvelled at the sight of all these cheerful young men, wasted, as far as I was concerned. How could they do it? How could they give it all up, even for God?

Jon visited on Thursday evenings for the family dinner. He was only months away from ordination. Juliana and I had become his friends. He took us on jaunts to the Seminary in Glen Waverly on special visiting days when outsiders were welcome.

We had been living at Pleasant Road for a lifetime of four months when Hannah invited us to her apartment for Friday night dinner.

'Can we invite Jon?' I asked. 'I'd love you to meet him.'

ON THE train ride home after the dinner at Hannah's, Jon sat on the green vinyl seat between us. Juliana's head tilted forward onto her chin and she began to snore. Jon and I exchanged smiles. He would be ordained in less than six months and wore the black uniform of a seminarian. His skin was olive. His eyes were brown with lashes that curled round and upwards almost to his eyebrows. He folded his hands in his lap; his fingernails were perfect with white half moons above the cuticle, each nail the same length as its partner. Through the corner of my eye, I could see Jon's eyes slip closed, too. We needed to change trains at Richmond. If I were not careful we would sleep through.

I thought back over the evening. Hannah now lived in a flat with a friend from school. Both were in training to become teachers. Hannah could prepare a dinner party for six people for fewer than ten dollars. She had a list of recipes stuck on the wall of her kitchen, which she divided into a series of menus, each with the ingredients for three courses listed, with exact costs and where to buy the cheapest and best quality. Most of her recipes did not

include much meat. Meat was expensive. She chose things that
could be bought cheaply and fresh, though she sometimes used
canned pineapple and frozen peas. She had a recipe for pavlova,
topped with passionfruit pulp from a tin, when she could not
pick passionfruit off the neighbour's side fence.

'Your tunic needs hemming,' Hannah had said to me that
night before we sat down to dinner. The edge of my skirt had
folded up and you could see the silver safety pin holding it in
place. I shrugged my shoulders. I did not care about these things.
When we were living at home together Hannah might have
hemmed my skirt for me. More likely she would have made me
sit down beside her and taught me yet again how to sew a hem.
I knew hemstitch. I could do it then, even without Hannah's
help. But it was easier to keep up my tunic with a pin.

'It'll do,' I said and then remembered Mrs Dijkstra back in
Camberwell.

'Does she know you're here for dinner?' Hannah asked.

'I told her we were visiting you after school. I didn't say for
dinner.'

'Then ring her now.'

'I already have your food on the table,' Mrs Dijkstra said, when
I told her we had been held up at Hannah's. 'What a waste,' she
said in her thick Dutch accent.

For our dinner Hannah cooked roasted chicken with baby
carrots, beans and potatoes. She was in a bossy mood and the
way she talked to Jon was troubling, as if she disliked him. I'd
looked forward to their meeting. Hannah was good with priests.
She knew how to talk to them but somehow with Jon it was
different. He would say something, offer an opinion and she
would jump in. 'No, that's not right,' to almost everything he
said. Later when we were leaving, when I went back to the
bedroom with Hannah to get our coats, I asked her what she
thought of Jon.

'A bit too conceited,' she said.

I listened to the rattle of the train and counted every beat when it went over a hump. I listened to the steady murmur of Juliana's breathing on the other side of Jon. His eyes were closed now. He breathed through his nose, his mouth sealed like a zipper. We were coming up to Richmond. Soon I would nudge them awake. By the time we caught the second train, I could not keep my eyes open anymore, and Jon took my place as the watcher.

Once off the train at Camberwell, we found the platform deserted, with not even a guard to check our tickets. We walked out onto Burke Road, down and up the hill, through the closed shops past the church to Pleasant Road. It was autumn now, and the plane trees on the side streets were empty of leaves. Their branches stuck out like gnarled old ladies' elbows, twisted and bare from too much pruning. They cradled the lines of electricity that hung between. The trams were still running, but the shops were closed. We decided to walk.

Jon left us at the front gate of the house. 'Must rush,' he said. 'I've still got an hour before I reach the seminary. At this rate I'll miss my curfew.'

He kissed each of us on the cheek and my heart gave a little skip. All the girls at school were jealous of me. Never before had I been the one to have something special in my possession. Jon had told us he wanted one day to assist at Mass and maybe even say Mass in our school chapel after he was ordained. A few months later he kept his promise and came to the school. It was as if the Beatles had come to town, all the girls wanting to say hello, all of them milling around Jon and he smiling back and showing off his perfect white teeth against the black of his hair and his sleek, tailored cassock. I felt so proud because he was mine.

But now we waved at Jon's retreating back. He turned and waved one last time before disappearing around the corner. Then we turned towards the blackness of the house, down the gravel path. Not a light to be seen. We must have broken our unspoken curfew. Mrs Dijkstra had sounded angry, when I rang earlier.

All evening the thought of Mrs Dijkstra had been flicking across my mind like a black crow. Every time she flashed those great wings she blocked out the light. I had tried to shoo her away but now she was back in my mind and everything was in shadow. The crow had landed on my shoulder.

We bypassed the front door where she had greeted us that first day four months ago. Juliana and I walked on tiptoes down the side path to the back door. We were careful not to crunch the gravel. We had made a plan. We would slip open the back door and make our way through the hallway to the stairs. We would creep past Mr and Mrs Dijkstra's bedroom. We would not disturb them. Then we would tiptoe up stairs. We would not use the bathroom. We would not wash our underwear. The next day was a Saturday so it did not matter. We would slide into bed and tomorrow we would say we were sorry to be so late.

I turned the handle on the fly screen door. Snibbed tight. I tried several times thinking it might have been stuck but it was rigid. I looked at Juliana. She looked back at me. I knocked and knocked again. We waited a few minutes, the polite amount of time to wait after you have knocked at a door. No one came, so I tried again. 'Hello,' I called out. 'Hello,' I said. 'We're home. It's just us, hello.' My voice sounded tinny in the night air. Our breaths came out in puffs of white.

Maybe Mrs Dijkstra had misunderstood. Maybe she thought we had planned to stay at Hannah's for the night. We could not go back there now. We had no money. The trains had stopped. I knocked again and called at the same time.

We heard the shuffle of slippers along the kitchen lino, and then a key turned in the lock. Mr Dijkstra stood behind the screen door. He flicked on the light. He was wearing his pyjamas and a striped dressing gown. I smiled at him. He did not smile back.

'You'll have to leave,' he said. 'We don't want you here anymore. You can stay until morning but then you must go.' He turned back into the kitchen and waited as we moved through the screen door and past him into the hallway. He locked the door behind us, and gestured with his eyes that we should go upstairs. His bedroom door was shut as we walked past but I could almost hear Mrs Dijkstra breathing rage behind her door. She did not want us anymore.

In the bedroom we did not speak. Juliana took off her blazer, tunic and blouse and crawled into bed in her underwear. I could not undo a button. I sat on the edge of the bed, in uniform. I sat and sat till I could sit no more. Juliana was asleep by then. I could hear her slow breathing. I could not sleep. I stayed awake all night. I needed to solve this problem and fell back on top of the blankets at an angle from Juliana. My school blazer bunched behind my back and I stretched out to loosen it. I watched myself from another place, lying still, stiff like a mummy.

In the morning I planned to get out of bed early before anyone else and walk to the top of the street, across the road to the presbytery at Our Lady of Victories. I planned to knock on the door of the Parish priest's house. I would tell the priest what had happened. I did not know this priest. I only saw him from a distance in the pulpit on Sundays. But I would talk to him and he would talk to the Dijkstras. He would tell them they must change their minds. He would say they were being harsh and unreasonable. These children have nowhere else to go, he would say. These children have no home. These children cannot return to their mother.

And Mrs Dijkstra would tell the priest she was sorry and Mr Dijkstra would understand. And I would say I was sorry, too. I would never be so rude again. I would always let Mrs Dijkstra know beforehand when we could not be home for dinner. We would not waste her food. We would be polite and grateful.

By the time the light of the morning crept under the door I had fallen asleep. Later, still in my uniform, I woke to the smell of coffee. It was too late to sneak out to tell the priest. Mrs Dijkstra did not look at me when I walked into the kitchen. Mr Dijkstra looked up from his newspaper. 'You had better ring your sister now and ask her to come and get you,' he said. 'Stay in your bedroom, please, until she comes.'

I made the call and went back to Juliana, who had waited in the bedroom, too scared to go downstairs. Hannah took a long time to arrive. She came with Jon. She said that she and Jon would have a talk with the Dijkstras. We waited in our room. The hope that the Dijkstras might let us stay was fading. An hour passed. You could tell it was mid-afternoon by the way the sun cast a long shadow across the wall of the house next door. I should have been hungry but I was too scared to think about anything other than what was going to happen.

A tap at the door and Hannah stuck her head around. 'I've rung the school. The nuns say you can go there. You can board. They'll take you at least till the end of term. You can stay with me tonight and for the rest of the weekend. The Dijkstras don't want you here anymore.'

Boarding school

IN MY most sorrowful moments, I thought it outrageous that any self-respecting sixteen-year-old should be sent away from home, first to live with another family and then forced to go to board at her school. No longer a day scholar who could leave each afternoon and take the train home, I was in essence locked behind the school walls day after day.

The other boarders came from country Victoria and, although some were given leave on weekends to visit family in Melbourne, by and large they spent the entire school term at the convent, chafing for the freedom of life outside, though no one ever said as much. Boarders were used to the life of a student confined to a convent, where they formed close bonds with one another.

Day scrags were an inferior lot from within the boarders' circle and so it came to pass that Juliana and I moved my status from a day scrag to a boarder and the boarders were unsure as to how they might treat us. To begin there was the problem of clothes. Not just the school uniform, which we already wore, though we did not run to multiple pairs of stockings and blouses and tunics and dresses. We had always managed with only one of each, and we washed them overnight as needed, at home. But at boarding school, the nuns sent around a laundry basket every few days in which the boarders threw their underpants and stockings, all clearly marked. It was tricky holding back my stockings to wear several days over given I had only two pairs of each, which was more than I had at home. Tricky to retrieve the one in readiness for the next time I needed to wear them, which happened every day.

Boarders stayed in uniform all week long even on weekends. It was tricky, too, as our labelling system, a permanent marker of our initials on the tags, let us down and before long it was hard to identify which stockings were mine, and which not. The underpants problem was worse still as boarders had to wear regulation underwear, a pale brown colour, which my mother could not afford. We went for the closest and cheapest possible and our non-regulation underwear stood out in the pile of clean washing that returned to the dormitory every third afternoon in readiness for the next few days.

This was one of the tricks of that year, 1968, when I became adept at hiding my need for clothing, the limited amount of my clothes, the regular sense of being inadequately dressed and the arrival of the dreaded periods. My mother visited the convent a couple of times in the eight months during which we boarded and both times she carried with her a pack of Modess, a ten pack, which lasted only the length of one period per each. She hid this packet in her basket in brown paper. You could only buy sanitary napkins from the chemist and they were stored in brown paper so that no one would be reminded of the fact that women had periods. When we ran out of pads we used rags from the science building, which I could send through the freshly installed machine in the newly built science block, but it was hard to find my way there in the middle of the day when I should have been elsewhere and on weekends too, whenever the need arose.

We had spun a yarn to the other students as to why we had to board, something about our parents needing to make a trip back home to Holland. It would not do to tell them that our parents were in trouble and needed time out to clear up their differences, their differences being my father's drinking. So we pretended to be a wealthy family whose parents could afford a trip overseas where they stayed for several months, leaving all their children home and in various states of care.

Becca and Jacob wrote me letters from Ferdi's house, full of spelling mistakes about how sad they were. Jacob, then eight, took to wetting his bed again and the shame screamed at me from the pages of his notes about missing home. I had no time to think about the others in my family given my own desperation to get by.

The list of things I needed to hide included my teeth, rotting in my mouth, and the occasional outbursts of excruciating pain when one of the nerves behind each rotten tooth decided to throb. All the toothpaste in the world on the open hole in my mouth could not stop the pain. Only time could stop it. I lay in bed at night and counted the throbs as I prayed to the Blessed Virgin to bring me relief, which came often enough so that I could go on as a boarder without any need to report my pain to anyone.

The nuns loaned us dressing gowns as we did not own them at home but they could not find any spare slippers in their store cupboard, left over from previous careless boarders, so, in the evenings after we had dressed for bed, we walked around to visit the toilet for the last time and to brush our teeth in bare feet. It did not trouble me in and of itself, the cold tiles underfoot, but I sensed the other boarders' disgust at my bare toes.

Who did we think we were, masquerading as proper persons among the neat and respectable country girls from wealthy farming families whose parents could afford the fees necessary so their daughters could attend boarding school? We should have been day scholars. We wanted to be day scholars; at least, I wanted to be a day scholar. I wanted to go home, however horrible home may have been. I wanted to be free to be my own miserable self, away from the need to pretend to be someone I was not.

By then, my thighs were the size of tree trunks. But I had managed not to notice it much. In boarding school we hid in our uniforms by day and at night we slept in dormitories. One bed ran alongside another in a long row, two long rows in the Immaculate Conception Dormitory. There were no mirrors, the windows were set high up because the ceilings were tall and there was no way you could reach the window ledge without standing on a chair or fetching a step ladder. The windows were never open. You could never reach high enough to see your reflection. So I didn't notice my size until it was too late.

Then the holidays came and I needed clothes. Hannah took us shopping, to the Myer store in town and we looked through the racks of trousers.

'Try these on. Dark blue jeans, size fourteen. Should fit.' She was horrified when they did not.

'God, you've gotten really fat.' So we went from shop to shop. I had wanted plain blue jeans, flared legs. I tried them on and saw myself in the mirror. My feet were like pins on which the rest of my torso rested. I was okay from my head to my waist but then I ballooned out like a hippopotamus, huge hips, broad hips and legs like bollards.

Back at school, I could not wait till afternoon teatime. At the last bell, the day scholars went home as I once used to do and the boarders filed into the refectory for hot chocolate and sticky buns, heated, plump with sultanas and spread in the middle with rich yellow butter. Once back at school I did not care about my weight. I could be fat. Who cared? I'd become a nun, hide under my habit. No one needed to see.

At breakfast, the kitchen staff, Sisters Anne and Julia re-heated bread rolls that the local bakery donated. They tossed them into a bowl of water then slid them into the oven on long racks. The rolls came out steaming. They were crusty hard on the outside and like soft marshmallow within. I could smell them as we left the chapel after mass. All the way down the long corridor to the refectory my mouth watered. Fresh hot bread rolls for breakfast with butter that started melting the moment it met the roll and golden honey swimming on top.

Sister Frances read stories from the bible and for the first half of breakfast we ate in silence. It pleased me the opportunity to eat uninterrupted. Did the others notice me when I reached for my third roll? No matter. I was still starving.

At lunchtime, we ate roasts, hot baked potatoes with thick brown gravy, squishy green peas and sautéed carrots, alongside slices of corned beef, or lamb. Sometimes there was chicken as a treat. Once a week we ate fish, great fat pieces that had been filleted from some huge fish or bright yellow cod from Scotland. Salty and smooth on the tongue, cod blended well with the fluffy white mashed potatoes piled to one side. The other girls turned up their noses. Especially when the puddings arrived, spotted dick, blancmange, tapioca or bread and butter pudding, studded with raisins and again brimming with melted butter. I loved them all, except the sago, with its lumpy texture, which the other boarders called frogs' eyes.

Once a month it was my turn to help clear the dishes, take them to the kitchen, clean, wash and put them away. The kitchen was like a metal cage, stainless steel benches, a huge *Bain Marie* on one side, wall-to-wall ovens and great troughs for washing up. Sister Anne was proud of her kitchen. Here there were plenty of reflecting surfaces like mirrors. Sister Anne insisted it stayed so. Here I could see myself. No optical illusion, like looking into those mirrors at Luna Park. I was wide and rippled along the surface of the oven door like a roly-poly doll I once saw at the Royal Melbourne Show. A kewpie doll with golden hair formed in plastic on top of a body that was all of a piece. The legs and arms were not jointed. The doll was perched on the end of a long balsa wood stick, held firm by a shiny silver ribbon. She had a painted mouth in bright pink and red spots for cheeks, blue dots for eyes. No ears. They were hidden underneath the

gold/red hair and she wore a net tutu that stuck out like a balle-
rina's. Her thighs fitted together as if joined and ended in tiny
fixed feet with toes etched in, and not enough toes. They only
ever gave her four toes. They left out the middle one.

I looked so big in those shiny mirrors in the refectory that
I came to hate my duty day even when there were left overs on
offer and Sister Anne offered us all the treat of a cream biscuit as
we left for the last of playtime till school went back in.

One morning I found a swelling in the side of my mouth
that seemed to be growing by the minute. I had first noticed
it during early Mass as I sat in front of the altar watching the
priest raise the host in the Hosanna chorus and felt it with my
hand. It was warm and throbbing. I could not use both hands
to hide my mouth and eating the soft bread rolls at breakfast,
much as I loved them, was a torture. Every time I moved my jaw,
my cheek ached.

I did not know what this could be. It must have had to do
with my teeth and therefore I could not report it to the nuns.
Still it needed attention soon or else my mouth would explode.

Some instinct led me to the toilet where I took out the safety
pin that held one part of my hem in place and opened it to
reveal the shiny point. I took the pointy pin and pressed it into
the side of my mouth inside my cheek and pushed it till a hot
liquid squirted out.

I did not know of abscesses then but I had burst mine and
the swelling in my mouth went down. I used toilet paper to sop
up the muck and then went off to class with cheeks the size of
every other girl in the school, no longer red, and with only a
dull ache in its wake.

Nuns and Biology

DURING SECOND term of boarding, my relationship with my favourite nun, Sister Mary Vincent, blossomed. I took every opportunity to be with her, which was not easy, given she took me for English and Latin only, but once I was boarding the chances to meet increased. I offered to help her in her role in charge of decorating the altar in the school chapel. And so we met in the sacristy on a Thursday night as planned.

She wore her black apron over her nun's skirt and the ties fell loosely behind. A wisp of dark hair flecked with grey peeked out from under her veil. She had taken off her glasses and rested them on the edge of the table. She took care not to let the lenses hit the surface. Sister Mary Vincent then tried to read instructions from the label on the *Brasso* bottle close up to her nose. Her forehead, what little I could see of it under the line of white plastic-like fabric that tucked into the black of her veil, was freckled. She scrunched up her nose as if to open her eyes wider to read better.

'Don't creep up on me like that,' Sister Mary Vincent said. 'You might at least knock.' There was one light globe, uncovered, hanging from the centre of the room and no windows at all. Her shadow flickered on the wall behind her like a dark ghost.

'I'm sorry,' I said. 'I didn't want to disturb you.'

'You're not disturbing me but you needn't walk around as though I'm about to hit you.' Mary Vincent's oval face in the faded light looked as beautiful to me at this moment as a saint's. She twisted open the lid from the *Brasso* bottle, poured on some liquid and rubbed it onto a vase.

'You smear the *Brasso* like this. No need to rub too hard. You don't want to rub off the gold.' She demonstrated by holding out the vase close to me and then added more *Brasso* to her cloth.

'Don't be wasteful. Once you've covered all of them,' she pointed in the direction of a row of vases along the bench on the far side of the room, 'you can leave them to dry. Then start on the candelabra. I'm going out to get the flowers.' Sister Mary Vincent untied her apron and flung it on the table beside me. 'I'll be about ten minutes.' I heard her footsteps clatter away as she passed from the sacristy, past the chapel and off to the nuns' dormitory, which was off limits to the boarders.

I did not add more *Brasso* to the cloth. It was already wet enough. I smeared the cloth over each vase in turn, eking out every drop till they were all covered in a grey sludge that turned white as it dried.

I sang to myself. Not too loud for fear one of the other nuns might have found me. It was okay for me to be there in the sacristy at six o'clock on a Thursday evening, I knew. Sister Mary Vincent had asked me to help her but, without her presence in the room, one of the other nuns might not have believed me. I should have been in the study with the other boarders, doing needlework or silent reading.

Some time later, Sister Mary Vincent returned, her arms filled with flowers. I could smell them even before she came into the room. The smell of the *Brasso*, the perfume from the liliums mixed in with the stale wood smells from the sacristy filled me with joy.

'Hurry up now. We haven't got all day. It's nearly supper time.'

Who cared about supper? Sister Mary Vincent chased away my hunger. I could have been with her all day, all night and forever and never ever need to eat again.

'Right. You're up to the candelabra. Good. But you won't be able to do them now. The nuns will be onto me if you're late for supper.'

'Can I come again on Saturday?' I asked, a lump in my throat.

'Check it out with me first thing Saturday morning. I may need to go to Monash to get some books.'

I scurried off, my heart full to brimming over with the prospect of another time with Sister Mary Vincent, alone together in the cool air of the sacristy.

By the year's end, as I sat one day in the chapel up early for Mass, good girl that I was, I found myself the only boarder in the first three rows. The nuns, like a flock of black birds, knelt behind me their heads bent in prayer. And so it fell to me to ring the bells for communion. I had never done this before and I could not find my way into the order in which I should have rung them. The Latin Mass offered few clues. Before the *sanctus*, before the communion, three times, a fast jiggle of the bells, and if I got it wrong, would the priest stop hoisting the white host into the air and tell that girl in the front to get her bell ringing right?

I could feel the nuns' eyes bearing down on my back but I did not reckon on Sister Mary Vincent's taking note of my bodily proportions. After Mass she came to me.

'Your suspender belt is cutting into your skin. You need a bigger dress.'

I smiled and took my leave. Alone in the vacant block next to the school that would soon be worked over to become a tennis court I kicked at loose stones. How could I ever go back?

I HAD two options in my mind during this time. The first was to become a nun. This way I could be close to Sister Mary Vincent forever and although she had shamed me for my increased weight and things like body size seemed to matter to her, even though she was a nun hidden under folds of material, her best friend also a nun, a friend she was not meant to have she once told me because nuns were meant to abstain from wanting anything, especially from wanting friends. Her best nun friend was tall and big, not so much fat but there were other nuns who were round and roly-poly and so it seemed I could get that way, too, as a nun. My shape would not matter. But if I went the other way and began to take an interest in boys then I would need to do something about my body. No one would ever want to marry me looking like I did. But I had decided too that the most important thing in my life at that time were my studies. I needed to get good results so that in time I could go to university and study social work.

I could decide on a convent life or boys later, but the boys became an increasing problem once we began preparations for the senior school dance, the year I turned seventeen. For months, the girls in my class talked about little else. Our term at boarding school stretched into another year, and although the other year ten boarders already had their dresses which they had carried separately on coat hangers and kept with them the whole time on their respective trains from many country destinations to Richmond, I still had no idea what I could wear.

Hannah came to the rescue. She sent me a letter in response to mine after I had told her about my problem, how I could not go to this dance without a proper dress and I could not stay away from the dance either, the shame would be unbearable. She wrote to let me know she had arranged with the nuns that I might meet her in the city late one afternoon after school and before the shops closed.

A week later we met at Flinders Street Station under the clocks after her day at teachers college and together we walked down Flinders Street and a short way along Elizabeth Street until we came to an entranceway that led up pokey stairs to

Adele's Formal Hire. There were dresses pushed one against the other along the four walls of this room with scarcely space for a desk. There was dust all over the bare floorboards but each of the dresses was cocooned in plastic. The woman in charge, not an Adele but a Karen, helped us peel out dress after dress from under the plastic, first in catalogue form and then from around the walls.

'It's better to choose your dress from these, so I can be sure I have the one you want available,' Karen said. Most of the dresses were for brides, white and shimmering and there were matching collections in bright colours for bridesmaids, but these too would be suitable for school dances Karen told us.

'Choose a dress that gives you room to move,' Hannah said. A waisted one would not do and so together we found a dress, navy blue almost black, with a chiffon overlay of spotted material that gave it a shimmery feel despite the black.

'Dark colours are flattering,' Hannah said.

Only one difficulty remained besides the cost, which Hannah told me not to worry about. She had brought the deposit and our mother had agreed to cover the rest. How, I had no idea, but I was more concerned with the other problem, the fact this dress was sleeveless. Such a dress left me with the issue of what to do with my underarm hair.

I had not shaved since the February when I first left home. It did not matter hidden under my school uniform day after day but in a dress like this I would not be able to move my arms without hair showing. To speak about this to anyone, even Hannah, was mortifying. It was a problem I needed to solve on my own.

For a week before the dance every night before lights out I took off into one of the toilet cubicles and although the light was poor there was just enough to be able to take it in turns one arm pit after the other and with nail scissors clip my underarm hair as close as possible to the skin. It was tricky with skin folds and bones located in awkward places. More than once I nicked myself. I could not get my arm hair shorter than stubble, and it was uneven but at least there were no long hairs sneaking out below the line of my armpit. It would do.

I survived the dance, survived the wallflower feel of standing around and hoping against hope that someone would ask to be my partner. And after it was over and we trundled back to the dormitory, that first flush of pleasure at being held in a young man's arms soon faded and I decided yet again, a nun's life was for me, a life of prayer and sacrifice, to make up for past sins perhaps but also to protect me from the agonies of my body.

IN MY final years at school, biology became compulsory to offset my almost total immersion in the humanities. Useless at maths, chemistry and physics, I settled for what seemed the easiest option. Twice a week we sat on stools in the new science block alongside pinewood benches where the copper taps, shaped like swans' necks, sloped into sinks below the bench line.

'Take a glass, girls,' Mrs Raj, our biology teacher, said one day. She had put out a line of tall glasses along each bench top, one per girl. Mrs Raj wore a red sari over her cropped bodice. I could see the line of dark flesh between the waist of her sari and the edge of her top and I wondered two things: Why wasn't she cold and what did the nuns think?

'I want you to spit into your glass,' Mrs Raj said.

Murmurs bounced off the walls.

'Spit into your glass, girls, as much saliva as you can get.'

We looked at her face, the set of her jaw. I hesitated. My mouth was dry but I puckered up enough saliva to collect a series of tiny dams on the end of my tongue. I shot them out from behind my lips.

'Now set the glass in front of you and wait.'

The puddle in the bottom of my glass was thick and sticky. My stomach roiled.

'Now,' Mrs Raj said. 'I want you to drink it back again. Do as I say, girls. It won't hurt.' The saliva was cold on my tongue, worse to swallow than cough syrup but I got it down.

'Now can you see the difference between your inside and your outside?' Mrs Raj's voice did not falter against our bemused stares. 'When the saliva is in your mouth, as it is every minute of every day, you don't notice it. Your saliva is you.' The red henna spot on Mrs Raj's forehead jogged up and down as she spoke. 'Spit it out and it becomes not you. Drink it back and it's like something foreign to you, when only minutes ago it was yours, a part of you.'

Mrs Raj beamed a smile that showed her straight teeth, white against the gleam of her skin. The red smudge on her forehead matched the redness of her lips and the faint blush in her cheeks.

Mrs Raj was different from our other lay teachers. Not just her nationality, but also her attitude. She helped us to understand our bodies as physical entities and not just temples to be preserved for God or for our husbands when we finally married. For these were our two choices in the late sixties, the convent or marriage. And we needed to prepare our bodies accordingly. Being beautiful, which goes without saying included being thin, was necessary to attract a man, or else we had to be invisible to please God.

Mrs Raj invited a few of us into her Richmond apartment near the school one weekend to help with extra tutorials before the exams. Only a few of us showed up, but her sitting room was crowded. Mrs Raj offered to let us try on her saris. I was embarrassed to let my pale skin show underneath the bodice. I could not fit into the red and gold sari Mrs Raj had spread out on her bed, not without it bunching under my arms, as if my insides now showed on the outside.

Lay Low

AFTER A year of boarding school, we went back home again, with promises from my father that he would not drink any more, but his promises did not last, despite my mother's certainty in yet another miracle. Within a month he began to drink again and so there were many nights when the best thing anyone could do was lay low. Go to your room and lay low. That's what I did. I crawled into my bed and read my book. As soon as it was dark, I slipped into my nightie and stretched under the sheet with my exercise book to make another summary. I was reading *The Scarlet Pimpernel* for school. I was reading about the guillotine, all those crazy women sitting around knitting, waiting for the heads of the aristocrats to fall at their feet.

There were noises up the hallway, raised voices. My father must have woken up.

'You call this food?' I heard him yell and the murmur of my mother's usually easy-going voice in reply. It was not easy going then though. Her voice, even as I could not make out the words had a high-pitched sound, like a baby bird fallen from its nest. The way the aristocrats must have felt before they went to the guillotine.

My father's words chopped through the air and then suddenly there was silence. I stayed put, and did not want to investigate. Soon there was the shuffle of footsteps up the hallway, the line of light under my door cut out and I imagined they'd all finally gone to bed.

The house was silent for a while, long enough to read the next chapter. It was getting exciting; the Scarlet Pimpernel was about to save another aristocrat. I was drowsy. This chapter summary would need to wait till the next day. I flicked off the light, watched the stars through the open slats of the Venetian blinds and drifted into the beginnings of sleep.

Not for long. There were noises up the hall way again. Slammed doors, slaps and bangs and grunts.

My mother opened the door. 'I'm sleeping in here,' she said. 'I can't stay with him.'

There were two beds in my bedroom jammed in side by side. Hannah used to sleep in this room but she'd left home when our brothers decided we must all leave and so I had the room to myself. I had made the bed into king size to give myself more room. As well, I liked having two beds to sleep on. I could spread my legs without worrying about them falling over the edge of the bed where anyone lurking underneath could grab at them.

My mother slid into the bed beside me. She was hot and panting. I could feel the fleshy swell of her breasts as they pushed out under her nightie. She smelt sweaty, scared, and sticky hot. I did not like her there beside me but I said nothing.

'Try to sleep,' she said to me, as she plumped up the pillow under her head.

My father was in the hallway again. I could hear the thud of his bare feet on the floorboards. His thuds were not even, more like a shuffle, thud, shuffle and thud. He was opening and shutting doors, one door after another. He was looking for her.

All the lying low in the world was of no use now. The band of light under the door well lit up and the door opened. My father stood silhouetted against the light. He leaned against the piano for support.

'You focking whore,' he yelled at my mother. 'What are you doing here?'

I squeezed my eyes shut and waited for him to go. He would go eventually if we said nothing, if we laid low.

'I'm staying here tonight. The way you behave. It's disgusting.' My mother was not laying low. She was speaking to him, saying too much if you asked me. I thought she should be quiet, hold her breath and be quiet and soon he would get tired of standing there like that, standing and leaning against the piano, soon he would get tired and he would leave us alone.

'If that's the case I'll join you.' My father came into the room and crawled over the top of my mother's body onto my side of the bed. If I had thought my mother's body beside me felt awful, my father's felt worse. He had taken off all his clothes. His wrinkly skin pressed against my arms, which I had closed around my front like a saint's dead body for protection. I could smell his winey breath and the stink of cigarettes. I squeezed as far back into the wall as I could, right up against the window ledge. If I had been little I could have slipped through the gap between the wall and the bed and slid down onto the floor, under the bed and out into the safety of the hallway. But I was not small and the space was not wide enough.

It was hot there beside him but I kept the sheet pulled up to my chin. I was laying low. I was holding my breath. If I spoke, he might notice me and then? I did not know what then, except I was waiting for my turn, my turn after Hannah had her turn, after Hannah who had left home in such a hurry after Dirk came back into the house and told our father he was a filthy alcoholic and a pervert and that he would never be allowed to see Hannah again. After she had left I knew it was just a matter of time.

'If he touches you, scream,' she had said. He was nearly touching me now. Not quite, if I kept squeezing myself up tight like a sheet of paper, thin enough to blow away, he might not have touched me.

He was touching my mother, putting his hand onto her body under her nightie and she told him to let her go. He was nuzzling into her back, while she pretended to sleep and I was pretending that I was not there. Jacob called out in what sounded like a bad dream and my mother pulled herself out of my father's grip and tottered to the door. It was still open the way my father had left it but for some reason that I did not understand my mother decided to close it behind her. She closed it fast with a thump as though she was blocking my father out for good. But what about me? Had she forgotten me?

I could feel the warmth of my father's thigh through my nightie. He was on his back and his breathing, which had at first sounded heavy, began to slow. I hoped he'd fallen asleep or better still that he was dead but I knew he was none of these things. I held my own breath steady as if I was dead, or at least no longer there. And waited. I feared this might be my turn at last to take Hannah's place and I squeezed my eyes shut to block my father out.

Minutes passed. Endless minutes before my mother opened the door. My father rolled over towards the light.

'Go back to bed,' my mother said. 'Leave her alone.'

She'd come in the nick of time. Any longer and my head would have burst with the fear of what was to come. A fear that stays with me still.

Without a ticket

DIRK BEGAN to train for the priesthood with the Missionaries of the Sacred Heart in NSW, so Ferdi took over organising our family. This time, rather than taking the last four children still at home out of home, as Dirk had done two years earlier, Ferdi arranged for our mother to move into a place of her own. He rented it through a real estate agent and we four youngest moved in with her. After a few weeks, Henry joined us. He had been lonely in his bed-sitter and slept in an outside bungalow on the property.

The Parkdale house, which was once a shack, had a holiday house feel. It creaked when the wind blew in from the sea. Its rooms were a series of add-ons to its centre, a kitchen, a living area and two bedrooms, which had been extended to four, with the bungalow out the back. Made of Masonite and weatherboard, the house sat on a slope of grass, two streets from the beach on Royal Parade. The street name may have been Royal but the house was anything but. Its greatest advantage was its proximity to the sea, alongside the absence of my father.

This was my final year at school. This was the year in which I wanted to do well enough to get into social work. This was the year when I wanted to make my mark on the world. But my mother was unhappy.

In the mornings she went back to Cheltenham to her job at the old people's home. On winter days, she set a pot filled with water and dried split peas on the stove. She added a ham bone and put it on the stove to simmer all day until we came home from school and stirred up the soup, scraped off what had stuck to the bottom, turned off the flame and let it sit till she returned. Pea soup with its bacon taste — my mother added butter for richness when she could afford it — filled us up on cold winter nights. My mother was pleased to be able to provide for us in this way but her heart was elsewhere.

One Saturday, I was sitting in my bedroom taking notes on Chaucer. I studied the personality types Chaucer lists in his *Canterbury Tales*, trying to figure out where I belonged. I liked to think of myself as sanguine: even-tempered, warm-blooded, and good-natured. Just like my mother. But then again the tragic image of the melancholic also held some appeal. Sister Mary Vincent told us we must be careful how we read Chaucer because he wrote centuries earlier when life was different. She liked to skim over the bawdy bits, the bits where Chaucer talked about priests and nuns as though they were ordinary people and not chaste at all.

Juliana, a grade lower than me, despite being almost two years younger, was going out with a boy to see the movie *MASH*. She didn't choose the movie, the boy did, and our mother disapproved. Still Juliana was determined to go.

'War is bloody,' Juliana said after the movie, and regretted her decision to fill her mind with all that blood, even for the sake of a boy. I wished I'd had the courage to go out with a boy, too, but I had convinced myself to get on with my studies and do so without the distraction. Besides I'd have to find a way of looking the part, instead of frumpy and undesirable. The idea of boys kept creeping into my mind as something I wanted to explore more, but school was more important and other issues like getting there when we had very little money to spare and now even less since my parents were living apart.

My concession card had long expired but I kept it tucked inside my uniform top pocket in the hope that every time I flashed it to the stationmaster at the gate, he would not notice and I could pass through. For a year we travelled like this, Juliana and I. From Parkdale Railway Station beside the sea to Richmond and its factories in the middle of which in a green oasis of gardens and trees sat our school.

It had become something of an art this business of concealment, with many different strands and possibilities beyond my expired concession card. Every day as we stood on the platform waiting for the train we looked to the ground for cast off tickets. There were some, which were useless. They had a pink stripe or a bold print declaration that marked them as tickets once used by someone in a special category, different from ours. We needed tickets that belonged to concession eligible students and there were plenty of those around if only we were lucky. I had a store of these tickets in my blazer pocket, which I used at the other end of my journey. I had become adept at walking past the station man with a cool air. I tossed the ticket into his open hand along with all the other people who did likewise. It was important to get into the middle of a large bunch of people. This way the station man did not have time to look too closely at out tickets when they fell into his hand.

My anxiety was at its height at these times. That climactic moment as if in a movie when the ticket man might have looked down at our ticket, dragged it out from the pile and looked at its past-its-use-by date, or the fact that it was a ticket for a journey that had stopped four stations before in Malvern, or seen that it was a ticket that should have been used last year, seen that we were frauds and called to us to stop within the crowd of strangers, and then selected us out as non-persons, people who were not worthy of such travel.

It could get worse. In my imagination we were held hostage in the stationmaster's office until the police arrived. I was not so young and foolish these days as to imagine that we would be sent to prison for our crime, nor was I worried about what our mother would say. She did not have money to give us to buy our tickets. She knew we travelled on imaginary ones. She never said a word about this to us and we knew not to ask. She had worries enough about finding money for food and rent.

Nor did I worry about what the nuns might say. The nuns were more tolerant of poverty than many and since we had started to travel to school from Parkdale, (since our parents had separated and the nuns knew the story from Hannah, who had once planned to be a nun herself but they would not take her on the grounds of possible insanity, given her link to our father) the nuns had been kind. They turned a blind eye to my partial uniform, to the fact that my indoor shoes were worn out and should have been replaced, to the fact that I held my pinafore together with a safety pin. They turned a blind eye, especially, after we had stopped as school boarders after a year and a half and moved back home.

Still it was my fellow students who tormented me with their stares, like the anonymous throng of people scurrying from the train. I saw them in my mind's eye when the ticket man called to us to stop—'That's not a proper ticket.' When he grabbed me by the wrist as if he imagined I would attempt a quick getaway, then it became the single eye of the anonymous crowd like a giant eye blinking down from the sky that stared with accusation and criticism. It was a look I had seen in my mother's eyes when she disapproved.

For that year we travelled on trains twice a day. We sat in the middle carriage, hands on our laps, our bags at our feet. We shared the bag of lollies that Maureen from my class, who lived in Bentleigh, had bought at the shop in the tunnel of the Richmond Railway Station on our way home. We did not have money to buy any in turn. Still we sat together in a huddle, white gloves in summer, brown in winter, demure schoolgirls and chattered about the day's events over Maureen's shared lollies.

I watched the doors at every platform when the train came to a halt. I watched for the men in grey — the ticket inspectors. I had a plan laid out in my mind. The ticket men would prepare to walk into our carriage. We would see them as the train pulled into the station. As soon as we saw them we would stand up, make an excuse to our friends; grab our school bags and leave. Then we would take ourselves to the toilets in the middle of the platform, well away from the exit and the stationmaster at his gate and wait for the next train, but we would not take the next train or the train after that. We knew that ticket inspectors got on and off from one station to the next and it would take at least five or six more trains before the inspectors had exhausted all the stations when we would be able to complete our journey without detection.

In that same year, Hannah had left for Tasmania to teach. Her leaving came as a surprise, but I imagined she had gone so far away because she wanted to be free of our father. After Dirk and Ferdi had learned about what had happened between Hannah and our father, the new priest at our Lady of the Assumption Church arranged for Hannah to live with an old lady from the parish who needed help with her diabetes, but the arrangement fell through so Hannah moved in with a family in South Yarra free of charge in exchange for looking after their children. That arrangement fell through, too, because the family expected too much of Hannah and did not pay her well enough. Finally, Hannah rented a flat in Mentone with a school friend for only a few months before she decided to go to Tasmania. I was so busy struggling with my own life, I almost forgot her.

One Saturday, Ferdi arrived unannounced in his car, a Volvo sedan, a prestige car that told the world this brother had done well. Only in his mid-twenties, he was a successful businessman now with a carpet shop, a wife and daughter and another one on the way.

'Can you come and babysit?' Ferdi asked me. I was sitting at the kitchen table surrounded by Latin verbs and French clauses, which I had written onto scraps of paper in readiness for my exams. The idea was to rote-learn as many of them as possible and so impress my examiners with my superior knowledge. I knew these words from the dictionary but the longer ones made little sense, other than as sounds I could make, or as letters that fitted together on a page. I rote-learned them all like a parrot, over and again, bored but happy to be stuffing my head full of knowledge.

'You want me now?' I asked Ferdi who stood over me as if he were my father but his tone was kind enough. He smelt of Amphora tobacco, the stuff my grandfather smoked. The smell came through the fibres of his jacket, which Ferdi kept on even on the hottest days because he was a businessman and needed to look the part. He tapped his pipe on the edge of the table to dislodge a wad of spent tobacco, and then took out his plastic folder to start up a fresh batch.

'Now, if you can,' he said. Olga and I need to go shopping.'

Ferdi had never asked me to babysit during the day before. Only ever did he ask me to go over some weekend evenings when he and his wife went out for dinner or to a party.

'I'm off to babysit,' I told my mother as Ferdi and I walked to his car. She had overheard the conversation from her chair in the sitting room, with her newspaper spread over her lap. She looked up to wave goodbye.

We drove along the Beach Road from Parkdale then up the freeway to Ferdi's house in Moorabbin. He liked to give his address as East Brighton because of the prestige associated with that address, but we all knew he lived in Moorabbin. At the same time, he was building a new two-storey house in Highett, even closer to Brighton, and soon he would be richer than the rest of my family combined.

The seats in his car were made of leather and the back of my legs stuck to them in the heat. Ferdi was frugal, for all his wealth. He only used air-conditioning on the hottest days. Open windows were good enough. I could smell the sea mixed in with car fumes from the traffic on the highway, and sat back in the front passenger seat, a young woman of substance now seated beside her big brother. For all I knew, people might think I was his wife, a young wife perhaps, but old enough to play the part.

Ferdi let us in at the front door. Olga was nowhere to be seen but the minute we stepped into the front room Hannah looked up to greet us from her place on the couch. How did she get there?

No one had told me she was coming home. She stood up to give me a hug and then I saw her belly, big and round and ever so pregnant. I had only then learned to use the word pregnant in biology classes. Otherwise I would have said she was expecting. How could she have been expecting? She was not married. She had no boyfriend the last time I saw her.

'Can you guess the father?' Hannah asked before I had much of a chance to say anything.

My only thought it must have been one of the boys from the Catholic Younger Set. Hannah had been in the choir, too. She went on excursions with many young men.

'Chris Willee?' I said.

'No,' she said. 'Guess again.' I did not enjoy this guessing game. I could not see the point of it but there was something in the way Hannah drew me out that seemed a distraction.

'Jon Dijkstra,' Hannah said and my head swam. How could it be him? He was a priest. He had been ordained only the year before. He was a man of God. He belonged to God. Priests did not become real fathers, only spiritual fathers, to guide us. My mother had told me once when there had been talk of priests being able to get married, that she preferred her priests to remain celibate, otherwise how could she have felt safe in confession? What if she had said something in the confessional she wanted only God and the priest to hear? If priests were married they might want to say things to their wives. Things they should not tell them.

I tried then to readjust my thinking. Hannah knew more than me about the ways of the world. Only two years earlier she had told me the facts of life after she had learned them from our father. He had taught her, he told her, or so she told me, because he needed to educate her in a way our mother could not. He had taught her to stretch open her vagina to make it large enough and warm enough to welcome in a man's penis. He had taught her this so she would be ready for marriage.

'What will you do?' I asked her. Olga walked in before Hannah had given me an answer and then we four sat down on chairs around the room while Olga's baby slept and the two pregnant women argued over what was the best thing to do.

'I came home to Melbourne,' Hannah said, 'because I couldn't bear to give up this baby, and I missed Jon.'

'But he's still hearing confession, doing baptisms and holding Masses on Sunday,' Olga said. Olga was like my mother and me. We all knew that priests belonged to God not to people, not to women like my sister who should have found herself a husband from the Catholic Younger Set.

'I've met with the Archbishop,' Hannah said. 'He blames me for it. He told me I should leave Jon alone. That I should give up the baby for adoption and let Jon get on with his vocation. I can't do this. Jon told me he only became a priest because his parents wanted him to. He'll write to Rome to ask for a dispensation.'

The porcelain figures on the mantelpiece, a bowl, a vase of flowers and a terracotta cow looked down on us and seemed to disapprove. Olga scowled and Ferdi tapped his pipe against an ashtray in readiness for another smoke. Hannah was crying now, a slow trickle of tears down her face. I could not understand why Ferdi and his wife needed to be so stern, but I knew there was worse to come.

'Don't tell a soul,' Hannah said, when Ferdi went to drive me home. I had stayed only a couple of hours, long enough to give the impression that I had been babysitting.

It was early evening three days later when I heard a car pull up in the drive way. I had been forewarned, my mother had not. I watched as she went to answer the knock at the door. I watched through an open window as she walked to the car. My sister sat inside and I could see the shock of surprise run through my mother's body as she came near enough to see. Then doors slammed and for a while there was silence until a few minutes later. My mother let out a wail so loud and so deep I thought the mirror on our mantelpiece might crack.

SOON AFTER, Ferdi and my mother decided that Hannah needed a home and so they shifted Henry out of the bungalow and moved Hannah in. She was seven months pregnant by then and spent a lot of her time in the bungalow alone or with Jon who visited often. No one predicted the eclampsia that took Hannah's baby and almost cost Hannah her life. I heard about these events second hand, at home with my sisters and youngest brother, unable to feel much other than a strange sense of awe at the thought my sister might die.

When she came back to the bungalow Hannah was subdued. She did not stay long before she found a home with Jon. My mother saw it as a sign from God that Jon and Hannah could now go into a normal relationship, once the dispensation came through. But Hannah's next pregnancy came sooner than my mother would have liked before even the year had ended. And I buried myself in my books, oblivious to all the fuss around me.

DURING THE final months of my school life, the pain in my mouth reached fever pitch. I walked the streets of Parkdale day after day during the school break before my mid-year exams. I carried a notebook filled with relevant facts on whichever subject I had chosen to study that day. Walking helped to drum the information into my head as long as I repeated it over and over.

I walked down Rosella Road and onto the beach trying to take in all the knowledge I needed to absorb to get the desired mark. The sand scrunched under my running shoes and the waves crashed in unison with my repetitions.

As I walked, I could not predict when the next burst of pain might erupt but at one point I had to stop, hold my head in my arms and sway. I decided that day to take up Juliana's stance and begged my mother to take me to a dentist.

Despite her concern about the costs, my mother, too, decided we could put it off no longer. This new dentist worked from a room attached to his house on a side street off the Nepean Highway and he worked alone, apart from his young assistant, who went by the name of Carol.

Carol held the suction hose as Dr Trevelyan first examined and then went to work on my teeth. He could not save my top molars or my incisors and talked to my mother about taking these out first. He could replace them with a partial denture and for the rest he would scrape out the muck from the smaller holes in the salvageable teeth and then seal them.

The whole procedure took six weeks, once a week, but after I had gone that first time into his room, I felt like a small animal who had been wounded and, although I dreaded the work, I knew it was for my own good and that soon I would be free of pain and able to walk around like other people without the need to hide my teeth or to wait in terror for the next assault.

Dr Trevelyan agreed to let my mother pay the costs in small instalments on a month-by-month basis over the next two years and so I entered a new world of normal teeth. Even though some were no longer my own, they were clean and white and I vowed never to let my teeth go to rot again.

At the end of that year, I sat for my final exams. One day stands out. The sliding doors of the Exhibition Building peeled open and I felt the pressure of countless bodies urging me forward. The inside of the building was broken into open halls filled with single desks and chairs, lined up in rows. In between desks there were large letters of the alphabet that signified subjects and names.

I sat in the row marked E for European history. My desk rattled. I shifted it to get a better balance, but it wobbled even more. I looked down and saw that I had dislodged the cardboard wad someone had put down before me to keep the desk stable. I fiddled with it. I tore it in half; rolled it into a thicker piece and stuck the bits in two places under the legs to fix my desk in place.

'Do not touch your paper until you are given the signal,' a voice called over a microphone.

I could not see where the voice came from, but I did as I was told like all the other students. I was bursting with facts and figures and all the dates I had piled into my mind.

'You may begin.'

The rustle of a thousand sheets of paper turned in unison. I looked at the pages of questions, one after the other.

'Do not lift your pens until reading time is over.'

For fifteen minutes I looked at the pages in front of me. I read through the questions. I could not write yet, I would not write yet or I would be disqualified. I could not hear the other students read the questions on the page. I could only hear the murmurs and grunts of a thousand sighs as they read over the questions and prepared to answer them.

But I could not think. I had opened the page and each question swam in front of me, the letters formed words, and the words formed sentences but none of it made sense and I was gripped with a terror more terrible than any terror that I had known before.

My mind was empty. There was nothing there. I tried to hold myself steady by reading over the questions again. One after the other beginning with the first: "A series of events led to the First World War. Discuss." My father was born in 1917, the year of that war and memories trickled back into my mind, dates and memories and all the arguments I had read in my history books.

I picked up my pen and began to write and as I wrote more ideas came. Ideas enough to fill more than the one notebook provided with words that answered all five questions and I left the Exhibition Building, in the same state of mind as after my father had closed the door on my bedroom in the Cheltenham house.

ONE DAY soon after my exams were all finished, my mother called me aside. 'I saw your father in the front yard watering the plants,' she said. She had been out to shop at Southland and saw him from the bus. 'He looked so thin.'

She had grown thinner too. I could not understand that she might still love my father. I could not understand that she should have so much concern for the man who had treated her so badly. She wanted us to go back home, she told me. Our father had stopped drinking again and he promised her it would be forever.

I thought of that year, my final year at school as the best year of my life. We had lived away from our father, so things were predictable. We had next to no money; I was used to that. But we could sit up late at night in the kitchen or living area and read or talk or listen to music without any fear.

Years earlier my mother had told me she married our father because he looked marvellous in his uniform, as if these things mattered to her. She mattered to him more, it seemed, in so far as he had agreed to become a Catholic to marry her and went through hours of religious instruction to pass the tests necessary before baptism.

He proved himself that way at least, but even in their early days, my mother described times when he would become moody, when he refused to speak to her for days. She'd done something wrong, she could tell, but he did not say what and she had no idea what caused the distance and cruelty.

I have no memories of my father speaking to my mother in anything other than the negative. She was dumb and stupid, a whore, a terrible cook, a worthless piece of junk. His insults were endless and predictable to the point my mother believed them.

Perhaps that's why she went back to my father time and again. Perhaps that's all she thought she was worth. Perhaps even after we had lived in the house by the sea for many months and she saw our father in the front garden she forgot his past cruelties and her heart rushed out to him.

The two of them, slowly disappearing without one another and yet we all knew and perhaps she did too. If she went back to our father and dragged the rest of us with her it would only be a matter of time before his benders began again.

A miracle she said, whenever our father was able to stop drinking for more than a week or two, a miracle and sign from God that all would be well now. A week before Christmas in 1970 and I sat in the kitchen at Parkdale, alone in the house except for Juliana. The others had gone back to Cheltenham and Juliana and I had stayed on for the final tidy up, after which, we too would return home. I sat at the laminated kitchen table and listened to the radio play songs like Frank Sinatra's "My Way".

I was just eighteen years old. I had finished school and was waiting for the results of my final year exams. The future lay before me as an unknown. I knew though what my mother's miracle meant. My father was once again in charge. I did not expect my mother's miracle to last any longer than my own childhood attempt at miracles had lasted. But I was high on the dream of a better future.

I wrote a letter that night, and addressed it to my twenty-one-year-old self. My pen scratched into the paper. I tried to fill every space on the two foolscap sheets of paper I had pulled out for the occasion. I asked myself question after question about what I would be doing and pleaded with my future self to keep my innocence and idealism alive. That was before I went to university and before I had encountered a different version of life, one that included the thrill of sex and the joy of being free of my father, if not metaphorically then at least literally. But a whole year of living under my father's roof would take place before I was finally able to move away from all these failed miracles.

Student revolt

I HAD taken a job at the post office in the city to help clear the excess Christmas mail. Before they set us to sorting letters, the bosses asked us to fill out forms and swear allegiance to the queen. We were sworn in as public servants and required to obey codes of confidentiality, integrity and honesty. We might see things in the mail that we were not meant to see, or that might unsettle us or that could be dangerous. We were to report to our superiors anything that looked suspicious and to sort the rest.

Thousands of envelopes, all shapes and sizes, spat at us from different directions to be sorted by postcodes. People then did not routinely include their postcode with each address so we had to learn the area codes of each suburb and sort accordingly.

I dreamed numbers at night in my sleep and my fingers dried out for the spreading of envelopes. I was shy. I did not speak to any of my fellow workers. All that allegiance for only two weeks. Then came Christmas.

With my job ended, I walked out to Flinders Street station with my first ever pay packet, a wad of cash in a rectangular yellow envelope with a pay slip that detailed my hours and status, casual and temporary.

We still lived in Parkdale near the sea but I could at last pay for a proper ticket when I travelled to and from the city by train.

I came home one night and called out to whichever of my sisters or brothers were in, but there was no one there.

I went outside then to catch the last of the sun. As soon as it brought with it a hint of heat I made it my business to spend at least ten minutes a day almost naked under its warm glow. It played on my mind. If there was ever a day when I could not get outside into the back garden hidden from view or later to a nearby swimming pool then I became anxious. I would not be able to appear on the street in summer unless my skin was tanned. Unlike Hannah whose skin, like our mother's, held an olive glow, my skin took after my father's, pale and prone to freckles.

Every summer I was determined to spend more hours in the sun than was possible. Even as my mother went on about our aunt who spent her entire holidays on the beach, 'Her skin will go wrinkly.' Even as I could not fathom the right amount of time to spend in the sun, to grow into an ideal brown, not too brown or I might be mistaken for an aboriginal and my skin would wrinkle as much as if I were an eighty-year-old. I knew I still needed to get to that optimal colour.

That evening as I sat in the back garden soaking up the last of the sun, I wondered about the sense of loneliness that had hit me. My first pay cheque ever and there was no one to tell. I could never live alone, I decided then. I needed people around me to keep me safe; otherwise the feeling of my father's fingers might creep against my skin again. In my imagination perhaps, but in those days my imagination felt real, as if my fantasies had substance and if they were bad, I needed to avoid them.

AFTER CHRISTMAS I joined a group of other students to take our positions behind the counter at Hall's bookstore for the remainder of the holidays. The store needed a large casual labour force to deal with the influx of orders, especially of second hand schoolbooks, at the beginning of the school year. Our job was to fill the orders that came in from schools and to deal with customers who arrived on foot with orders in hand.

When our shifts finished, groups of us came together to socialise, mostly in one another's houses, but never at mine. I became good friends with two sisters, Helen and Johanna, who taught me how to get thin. They were the oldest girls in a family of eleven kids, Irish Catholics, who lived on the other side of town, in Newport. Every weekend their father, a hard-working wharfie, who, unlike my father, was devout and did not drink, went to the market to buy weekly food for his children. He bought fruit by the kilo, and in summer came home with trays filled with apricots, peaches and other stone fruit.

'If you eat only apricots all day long, it'll give you the runs and before long you'll lose weight,' Helen who was beanpole thin, told me. This way of getting control of my appetite, of filling myself with only one type of food each day, something loaded with roughage, something that was easy to get rid of down the toilet, became my introduction to a different body, one I could control through rigid limits I had not ever been able to contemplate before.

Jo was my age and in her first year and Teacher's college and Helen a year older in her second year of teacher training. They took me out to parties in Newport and let me stay over-night and I met their friends, including boys, whom Helen had befriended at college. They also had an older brother who asked me out one day. He was short and gentle and did not appeal to me other than as the brother of my friends, but the idea that he might have been drawn to me was thrilling.

I began to let go of the idea of life in a convent and to lust after something else, even as it terrified me.

One day towards the end of the holidays, I met Paul, who worked downstairs. He saw something in me I did not see myself, something attached to my foreign name perhaps, because he called me 'Frenchy'. The exotic ring of this name left me tipsy with excitement.

I took to sneaking off downstairs on the pretext of needing a book we'd run out of upstairs in the hope I might see Paul, that we might catch one another in some unspoken hold.

'How about we go to the movies?' Paul asked me one day, seemingly out of nowhere, just as I was leaving work.

'I'd like that,' I said.

'How about we go see the *Satirycon*?' he said.

I told him I'd ask my mother, as if I had forgotten that I was now eighteen and an adult.

'By all means go to the movies with this man,' my mother said later when I told her about this older man's request, 'but not to that film.'

'I can't say no.' I said.

'If you can't say no now, when will you ever be able to say no?' My mother was stirring soup on the stove. I did not tell her, although I could not say 'no' to this man, I could at last say 'no' to her.

Paul and I watched the *Satyricon* in a darkened picture theatre, my heart thumping as he reached out to hold my hand. He kept holding my hand as we crossed the road on the way back to his car after the movie. Kris Kristofferson was singing on the radio, 'take the ribbon from my hair' and I was floating through the words.

Paul parked his car in a parking lot abutting the beach and held my hand as we walked through the tree-lined walkway that led to the top of the sand dunes at Edithvale. A cloudless night and stars studded the sky like so many twinkling eyes but I did not sense there was anyone there to look over us as he settled himself down on the sand and beckoned to me to join him.

I did not want my dress, one I'd borrowed from Hannah, to get creased or littered with sand. But I was fuzzy in my head with pleasure at being with this man at last, filled with a sense that I had finally reached an age where I could call myself a woman. I needed to behave like one and so I decided that the sand would not matter as long as I kept the back of my dress flat. As long as I let my heels slide over the sand carefully, they did not dig into or loosen the surface.

I needed to go down like a feather and, even as Paul leaned over to scoop me into his arms, I needed to position myself on top of the sand, to stop any stray grains from getting inside my person. It was not easy to keep my mind within the sensations of being held and at the same time of keeping out sand but Paul did not notice, or at least it seemed to me, he was intent on his part of this dance, his part as the man in the piece, and it seemed to me he knew his part well; whereas I was operating on instinct alone, that and what I'd seen in the movies.

When I felt something hard against my thigh, after Paul had rolled over on top of me, I decided I need not worry any more about the sand, but concentrate instead on this strange experience, in which I felt both hot with fear and at the same time heady with desire.

We wouldn't do it out here on the sand, would we? We couldn't. All that sand and open space everywhere. We could not take off clothes to make it possible and so I wriggled my way back onto my own side where the sand was still well-compressed and tried to break the spell.

'I think I should get back home now,' I said and heard Paul's deep inrush of breath. I hoped it was not disappointment or frustration and that he might decide it was okay for us to start talking now, which is what I had hoped to take up in the first place, heady words of pleasure and flirtation, a Jane Eyre sense of passion, as she was with Mr Rochester, and not this display of physical affection.

'You're right,' Paul said. 'It's late. I start work at nine. Let's go.' No conversation now, just the steady swish swish of the traffic on Beach Road and Paul drove alongside the flash of waves

behind the casuarinas on the coast. Maybe this first venture into
our bodies had taken it out of him because our conversation
flagged and I began to worry that I had blown it.

When he pulled up in front of my house and leaned in for
that last goodnight kiss, I wanted to ask when we might meet
again, but this was far too forward for a man of Paul's uncertainty, so I let the words catch in the back of my throat and
affected a nonchalance that bore no relation to my actual state
of mind. I stepped out of his car and moved towards the house.

'I'll give you a call,' Paul called through the open car window
and then wound it up to seal himself back inside and he was gone.

Once more, a long wait began, the hours that dawdled into
days, even weeks before I might hear from him again and I had
to soothe myself with the knowledge that I had spent a night,
not only at the movies with a man who held my hand, but
several minutes at the beach in the dark on the sand, filled with
a promise of union that would leave any woman shuddering
with excitement.

The words of another song on the radio stayed with me: 'I
don't know how to love him, what to do how to move him ...' I
had become Mary Magdalene in my mind, in love with a man
so much more sophisticated but like all good things it ended
almost as soon as it had begun, and Paul was gone. He left the
bookstore almost at the same time as my casual position expired
and he moved to the country.

BY THE time I began at university the following March Juliana
had asked our mother to ask the nuns if she could go back to
board so that her final year at school might be less troublesome.
But I had no choice other than to stay at home in Cheltenham,
the oldest now with only the two little ones, Bec and Jacob,
below me for comfort.

At university when I took myself to the Medical Library
and looked up books on the human sexual response, I figured I

would find books about the body. But the ones on procreation were so dense with jargon I came away with an added layer of unfathomable words in my already overwhelmed head. Words like orgasm, coitus, clitoris. Basic words to me now but then they were unimaginable, unmentionable.

I was the only one from my school who went to Melbourne University that year. I knew no one. In Orientation week I went to the Catholic Students' Youth Camp at Mt Evelyn. I wore my new white jeans. I was still fat but at least my jeans made me look more like the rest of the students. We met at Spencer Street Station and took the bus to the gum trees of Mt Evelyn. We shared rooms, in groups of four, girls separate from the boys. We stayed up all night, as if by requirement. I jumped up and down on the trampoline in the gym to keep me awake. I walked to the top of the mountain with a boy I had never met before, a boy named Peter. At the top I was breathless with anticipation. Would he kiss me?

He did not. We did not even hold hands. We simply walked and talked. But my mind was overwhelmed with a burden of desire. I wanted more. I wanted less. I do not think I experienced Peter's failure to touch me as rejection. He, too, was a good Catholic. You do not do things like that. He, too, was shy. Perhaps that is why he chose me to share the climb.

On the final afternoon the priest in charge of the camp called us together for prayers.

'If any of you has anything you'd like to discuss with me of a personal nature,' he paused as if to scan his mind for words, 'about your experience here, or your future at the university, please find me later for a chat.'

A chat. I heard it as a call to confession. I wanted to confess. My sin of desire, my sin of lust, impure thoughts. I wanted to tell him, too, about my father. The very wanting seemed wicked. Others milled about the priest, a young Dominican in flowing white cassock, and fresh out of the seminary. I kept away.

During my early months at university I sometimes visited Sister Mary Vincent, but over time my connection to her and to my school thinned under the weight of these other allurements.

At lunchtime when I walked up to the mezzanine in the Union Building and into the cafeteria filled with tables and chairs in row upon row, I looked to right and left hoping I might see a familiar face. No one from my social work course was there and in the end I squeezed myself onto a table with a group of men from another faculty.

They all knew one another and were welcoming to this strange and, to my mind, big, tall and gawky girl from Cheltenham. They were Saint Bernard's boys; a group of them with connections that ran back to early childhood and most were studying engineering or commerce. Apart from the Catholic connection, we had little in common, but they included me in their conversations and I began to feel like their female mascot.

One, in particular, took me under his wing. Taller than me, thinner, and with crooked teeth and a jutting chin, Alex from Preston was an only child. His mother made him sandwiches on thick white slices of bread, which she filled with double layers of cheddar cheese and ham or salami. His father ran a concrete business. Alex drove his own car, a second hand Falcon, into the university every day and complained about the cost of parking. In those days it was still possible to find a park nearby the university. The fact that Alex had a car meant that he and I could go out driving alone and begin to experiment with intimacy.

How else could I describe those first furtive forays into fondling? He stroking my back and inching around ever so slowly toward my cleavage, the tip of his fingers into my bra, towards my nipple, but I wriggled if he ever advanced below the waist. Alex was a good Catholic boy and respectful of my prudishness. It matched his own. And something of the hot excitement of my time with him came to override all my desires for Sister Mary Vincent.

Every day during that first university term, I walked from Warrigal Road to the Cheltenham railway station and took the train into the city. I carried a hardboard clipboard with a silver fastener on top to which I attached my loose-leaf sheets. I carried a cloth calico bag. I scuttled away from the Psychology pracs on the tenth floor of the Redmond Barry Building where we studied such things as how many people could roll their tongues to demonstrate innate genetic ability. Some could roll their tongues. Others could not. We experimented with memory, how many words in a group we could remember.

We were meant to complete these prac labs like scientists but my work was sloppy. This was not the psychology I wanted to study. This was not an exploration of people. In the corridor, I walked past a black-framed picture of Oscar Oeser and other former dignitaries from psychology in Melbourne. I heard mutterings about the death of psychoanalysis. The real stuff, then, was in behavioural cognition. No point in delving into the past, the past was like so much dry grass, nothing to chew on, but present behaviour was all that mattered. Gestalt principles, the here-and-now. Get on with it. Existentialism was all the go.

One autumn day, in my first year, radical students gathered to confront the government over conscription to the Vietnam War outside the Admin buildings. They wore rough and ready clothes from the opportunity shop, the girls in long granny skirts in velvet and calico, and the men and boys with long hair and jeans, chanting and waving banners.

I wore my tight woollen skirt, a hand me down from Hannah, with stockings and sensible walking shoes. The only pair I possessed. On Mondays, Wednesdays and Fridays I wore my white jeans. I washed them each alternate night and hung them in front of the lounge room heater after everyone had gone to bed. The skirt I wore on the other two days.

Although I told myself I did not want to be like these hippie students, those making the noise down near the union building,

I hated to see myself as old-fashioned. In my mind, I was still horribly fat. Most of the weight I took on in boarding school had stayed with me, despite my efforts to eat the way Helen and Jo had advised, and my white jeans made my legs wider than they would have been had I hid them under a dark skirt, but I had wanted to wear jeans like these ever since I was twelve. My mother had given me the money reluctantly.

One day, I slipped past the dangerous group of students. The police had arrived with batons and shields. Such rebellion frightened me. I needed to escape. I had no more lectures. I left the university for home, not the safety of home but its familiarity. The university was still a place of strangeness. And so I had worked hard to keep a smile on my face and confidence in my step.

When I arrived home and walked through the front door I could see my father through the window. He had the crumpled look of too much to drink. As soon as I walked past the double glass doors of the lounge room, doors of opaque glass that were kept open except in winter, my father called out to me.

Most other times like this, I said as little as possible and moved past quickly, but this evening my father called me into the lounge room. He was affable, not yet completely drunk.

'How's university?' he asked. 'What are you reading?' He did not wait for an answer. 'Have you read Nietzsche yet?'

I froze. The name had a ring of significance I could not fathom. Maybe it signified brilliance. I knew Nietzsche was a philosopher but I could not tell my father I did not study philosophy.

'Yes,' I said and ran from the room.

For years afterwards I could not consider the idea of reading Nietzsche without a shudder. Nietzsche had become as dangerous as sex. By the time I hit second year and was having sex with a real boyfriend, I rebelled against my father's insistence on such old men of ideas.

The sinking feeling of my ignorance crawled round my feet up my knees into the pit of my stomach. I could not profess ignorance or curiosity. My father filled me with a sense of impending danger, greater than the police outside the university with their truncheons, greater even than the anger-fuelled rabble of students hell-bent on getting inside the admin building.

Come out to play

I WAS nineteen years old, home alone, cramming for my first year exams. I had the run of the house but I stayed at my desk for as long as I could. If I moved to the kitchen I'd eat, if I moved to the lounge room, I'd watch TV. If I moved outside I might be tempted to strip off and sit in the sun as it struggled to get hot. I could not possibly concentrate then. I'd wind up plucking out pubic hairs. I hated the way they ran below my panty line. I used tweezers and in the process gouged out lumps of skin. So I stayed put listening to the loud tick-tock of my *Opa*'s clock in the hallway. The clock was like the one in the nursery rhyme. The one the mouse ran up. It had a gold chain with a brass weight that moved slowly around whenever the clock chimed the hour. There was a hole cut into the clock face above the hands that showed the sun and moon in motion. At that time of day it was meant to show only sun but somehow the moving picture on the clock had gotten stuck on a half-moon surrounded by billowing clouds.

The traffic outside roared past. It was late October but the house inside felt cold. The early morning sunshine could not get through the windows and walls to warm me. I was wearing my thick red jumper and navy tracksuit pants. The only heating in the house was in the lounge room and I would not go there. The lounge reeked of cigarettes. Besides, my father might

222

have come home at any minute and find me there. My father still worked in the city. He travelled to town first on the blue Ventura bus then on the train. He wore his dark suit and blue tie. He carried a brief case. His tie was too tight. He pulled it into a lumpy knot around his throat. It was in a dull navy with no pattern, no stripes or swirls — just plain old navy. He kept his shoes well enough polished though. But they were so worn in places the leather had peeled away.

My mother still worked at the old people's home down the road. The only joy in the job, she said, was that she could help make the lives of these sad old people a little more cheerful.

The telephone rang and my heart skipped. It was Paul. He had written me letters soon after he left Melbourne, from a pub in Tocumwal where he'd taken the job of barman. Tocumwal because there was a job on offer and because it was close enough to the nearest racetrack. Paul was preparing for life as a professional gambler, he wrote to me and I tingled at the thought of his amazing life. Now he was back.

'What are you up to?'

'I'm studying,' I said. 'I have exams next week.'

'Why don't you come down here?' he said. 'Come and play with me.'

'I can't. I have to study.'

'One day off won't hurt. Come on.'

Why not, I thought. No one needed to know. I could do these things now. I could visit a friend in the middle of the day.

I took the train to Edithvale. I sat close by the window and stared out at the silver-blue sea. It spread beyond the line of backyards behind rickety houses with red roofs and grey paling fences. I had borrowed Juliana's new burgundy dress. The one she loved. She'd only worn it twice. I had to be careful. The dress was tight over my hips. It rode up my thighs as I slid along the train's green vinyl seat. The day was heating up. I was glad I chose not to wear stockings.

Paul lived in a street off the Nepean Highway where all the houses were painted in the same pastel colours with long side driveways and rows of hedge plants like diosma, box and tea tree. Waist high cyclone fences divided each house from the other. There was a jacaranda set in the centre of each nature strip.

My sandals, also Juliana's, made a click-clack sound on the footpath. There was no one else around. Everyone was at work or school. I needed to get back home before four before everyone else, so they didn't realise I'd borrowed her stuff.

Paul answered the doorbell in his shorts without a top. He was not much taller than me, round faced and chubby. I melted at the sight of him.

'I took a sickie today,' he said, by way of greeting. 'Wanted to go to the Derby at Sandown but if I went I'd probably lose more than if I stayed home.' I could hear the drone of the race caller in the background. Paul led me through his kitchen to the back of the house. The sporting section of the newspaper was spread out along the kitchen table. There were lines marked in red along the small print on the race page.

'I'm just in here.' I followed Paul into his bedroom. I'd never been in his house before. The other times we spent together he took me to the movies or the races. His parents were at work, he told me. His father pulled beers at the RSL and his mother managed the delicatessen at Safeway.

Paul's bedroom had all the signs of a boy growing up. Two model aeroplanes set on top of the wardrobe under a thin layer of dust, a row of miniature soldiers along the window ledge and the skeleton of a miniature dinosaur enclosed in a glass frame on the dresser. Paul closed the door behind me, took off his shorts and leapt into bed.

'Come on,' he urged.

I sat on the edge of the bed, my hands in my lap eyeing my sister's sandals. They were pretty. I did not want to take them off. Still I slid out the pin, unbuckled the clasp and slipped out each foot, putting the sandals carefully side by side near the door. I had never taken off my clothes in front of a man before. Except for my father, I'd never seen a man naked. Even on the television, they only showed the top half.

I found myself unbuttoning my sister's dress. I watched it fall to the floor. I climbed under the blankets, underwear intact, and felt the warmth of Paul's body, hot like a radiator, against my side. It was a tight single bed with a brown overlay in some rough fabric that was coarse to touch. Paul stripped it back along with the other blankets but I clung to the top sheet and pulled it up to my shoulders. Paul stroked my back, my arms and legs. I was relieved I hadn't plucked any pubes this week. With one hand he stroked the inside of my thighs, with the other he guided my hand to the knob of his penis, and slid it up and down.

I needed to wee. By now Paul had robbed me of my bra and underpants. I got up, pulled Juliana's dress around my shoulders and followed his directions to the toilet. It was at the end of a sunroom on the back veranda. Ferns hung down from wire baskets and stood in pots in every corner. There was a stained yellow couch pushed up against one wall and a pile of unsorted washing on a nearby chair. Someone had pinned a calendar advertising Nolan's Meats in Main Street Edithvale to the door. Someone had circled certain dates and scrawled names underneath. I looked for Paul's name and presumably his birthday date but the handwriting was indecipherable. The toilet flushed noisily and the water ran on even as I was getting back into bed with Paul. I could hear the sound of the running water blended with the murmur of the traffic on the highway and Paul's breathing. He was on top of me now and thrusting into me. A rip of pain. I held my breath. I clenched my muscles. I closed my eyes and it was over. There was a line of blood on the sheets and a trickle of liquid that ran down my legs when I stood to dress.

It was two o'clock, the fourth race at Sandown was about to begin and I needed to beat my sister home. I stood on the railway station at Edithvale and waited for the train that would take me back to Cheltenham and home. I looked across the station at the people standing there and wondered whether they might notice. I had a secret; I was a fallen woman.

If I had not gone to visit Paul that day, if I had not decided to hell with caution, to hell with my studies, to hell with propriety, I would not have lost my virginity. I would not have entered into the world of sexual experience that marked me, in my own mind at least, as an adult woman, no longer innocent.

The following Sunday, I went to Mass at St Patrick's Church in Mentone. I sat, stood or knelt in line with the priest's words, and chanted my responses to his droning. I listened to his sermon without taking in a single word and wondered why it was that cracks had not appeared in the brick walls of the church. Why a voice had not roared from on high to say that I had sinned so badly I deserved to be punished for evermore.

Even my mother who sat beside me on the hard pew did not seem to notice. She, whom I once thought could read my mind, did not detect any signs of my sinfulness. As the time for Communion drew near, I panicked. I could not take Holy Communion, given my sinful state but if I did not line up with everyone else come Communion time, my mortal sin would be obvious — the nature of it not, perhaps — but its severity, as plain as the Scarlet Letter around Hester Prynne's neck in Nathaniel Hawthorne's book.

On this day, I stopped believing in the power of the church to determine my status in the world as good or bad. St Patrick's Church on a Sunday morning in 1971 became a battlefield for me, caught between my desire to experience the love of a man and the rulings of the church: sex only after marriage.

Despite these rulings and my mother's misgivings, my relationship with this man continued to develop. After Christmas,

Paul moved out of his parent's home and he now lived in a brown-bricked one-bedroom apartment off the Nepean Highway. The walk from my parents' house in Warrigal Road to Paul's place took me a good forty minutes and by the time I got there I was exhausted. It had been scary walking through the streets alone at night, a young woman in the heat that lingered after a hot summer day but I stuck to the streets that were well lit.

Paul was not expecting me, which was risky, I knew. I could not be sure that he would welcome a visit from his would-be girlfriend. After all we had only known one another a few months then, but Paul had introduced me to the joys of sex just on my nineteenth birthday and I thought it only proper that he should have welcomed me into his life. Assuming he had not invited another woman into his life, I planned to spend the night with him in a bed that belonged to him and none other.

Paul was surprised to see me when I knocked on the door. But he ushered me in. I looked around his lounge room. The radio blared in the background, the end of the news, the sports events and given we were in the middle of the racing season, the voice of a race caller shouting out the results of the Caulfield Guineas. Paul had spread the sports page over his coffee table and had highlighted sections of the various races for the next day at the country meeting in Colac.

All this he told me as he ushered me into his bedroom and sat down on the edge of his bed. He was just finishing up for the night. He had an early morning ahead of a long drive for the race that began around eleven. But I was welcome to stay. He then took off for the bathroom.

I disliked Paul's bedroom in this new apartment. I disliked the way the floor to ceiling cupboards at one end of the room, the end opposite the bed, consisted entirely of mirrors. Mirrored doors that slid against one another to give access to the wardrobe. When the wardrobe was shut the doors became a single mirrored wall in which I could see myself from head to foot.

My body still bothered me, especially from behind. I raced through undressing and flung myself onto the bed and under the blankets undetected except by the mirrors while Paul made noises brushing his teeth, pissing and flushing the toilet.

By the time he turned off the light I was ready for him. No blood and plenty of desire for a night's passion, only we lasted long enough for several kisses before Paul rolled over into sleep and I soon followed. I had not thought to ask Paul to set his alarm but I didn't need one. I slept badly and woke often to dreams of being chased downstairs. To dreams of my mother's face red with rage at something I had done and after one such dream when I checked my watch and saw it was five o'clock in the morning and time for the birds to start their song, I leapt out of bed and dressed in a hurry, hidden from the mirrors in the almost dark.

I needed to get home before the rest of my family woke up. I had not told anyone where I was going. Juliana back home now from boarding school and with whom I now shared a room back in the house on Warrigal Road was asleep and I didn't want to wake her.

The sun was a blur of yellow on the horizon hugging the surface in a soft glow and the air was fresh but still warm enough for me not to need anything beyond my t-shirt. I walked briskly along the Nepean Highway and down through the back streets and factories in Chesterville Road. By the time I reached the old people's home a few blocks from my place on Warrigal Road, the traffic was beginning to hot up.

It was close to six am when I tried the front door handle. My mother got up at 6.15 on weekday mornings. I had only minutes to spare. For a moment I worried the door might be locked but it gave way without any resistance and I slipped through the hallway and into my bedroom undetected.

Juliana stirred after I closed the door behind me.

'Where've you been?' she asked.

'Can't you guess?'

She rolled back over to face the wall and grunted. Juliana didn't like this new man in my life. Since Paul had entered the scene, she complained I had no time for her anymore.

I dragged my nightie out from under my pillow and slipped it on as fast as I could then crawled into my bed. I left my clothes draped over a chair, something I worried about later. Worried it might have given my mother a clue as to my bad behaviour.

How could she not know? I wondered as the bedroom door handle turned and my mother stuck her head through.

'Time to get up', she said and looked directly at me as I opened my eyes and rubbed at them.

'I hope you slept well', she said, with special emphasis on the word 'well'. She could not have known that I had spent the night out. Could she?

Leaving home

I DID not say a word about my plans at breakfast. Instead I watched the others eat. Thick slices of white bread covered in butter or jam, the jam my father still brought home from the Monbulk factory. The business of jam did not trouble me much that day. I had bigger things to think about. Besides, I had decided to stop eating jam and bread and butter. From then on I would eat only fruit and seeing as the fruit bowl was empty of anything except a few dried out grapes, I would settle for a cup of tea sweetened with saccharin. I had taken to using sweetener in my tea in my last year of school.

My father had used saccharin in his tea ever since he developed diabetes when we lived in Healesville. It was all the stress that did it, my mother said. In those days my father drove every day into the city for over an hour from Healesville to get to his job as an accountant. I calculated on my fingers the number of times I had moved. I counted the places in my head under my breath so no one would notice me counting. First Greensborough, where I was born, then Healesville, Camberwell and Cheltenham, then back to Camberwell and the foster home on Pleasant Road with the Dijkstras who did not want Juliana and me anymore, and then back to Cheltenham again. From there I went to boarding school in Richmond then back to Cheltenham to Parkdale and back again to Cheltenham. I was about to embark on my tenth move, which seemed a lot to my mind, compared to the other girls from my school who lived in the same house all of their lives. Nineteen-years-old and ten different homes.

My mother was still in her dressing gown, pink quilted and raggedy from years of use. By now, all the buttons had fallen off. She was pouring tea when she heard the front door slam. My father had left for work without a word, as usual. My mother made sure that everyone was breakfasted and ready for school or work or wherever we were going before she dressed herself and got ready to go to work down the road at the old people's home.

One by one the others left, and I was home alone with my mother. I was still on holidays and in only a few days time my life at university would resume. My mother knew my plan but had agreed to keep it secret. She did not want to stir up trouble, any more than I did. She sipped her tea, read the newspaper and crunched on the scraps of her toast. I could hear the food swill around her mouth and tried hard not to think about food. I made a second cup of tea with two saccharin tablets and plenty of milk. That way I would fill up fast and have all the energy I needed for the day ahead.

'You can take your bed,' my mother said. 'And that small chest of drawers in your bedroom. The rest you'll need to get yourself.' My mother did not include my clothes and my books in the list of things I could take. These were a given. My bed included my mattress and three sheets, which I could rotate weekly as I had done all my life. Once a week the bottom sheet went to the wash and the top sheet went on the bottom.

My mother gave me the money to hire a van and a person to help me to move our belongings to Caulfield where I would move into a quarter of a house near the Institute of Technology and the railway station. There, I would have my own room shared with Juliana opposite the room of our friend, Helena, and together we would have the use of a tiny kitchen and lounge room. Helena and Juliana, who both finished school that year, had been offered studentships from the Education Department, so they planned to become secondary teachers, while I had been offered a cadetship with half the money a studentship allowed and a commitment to work for two years for the government in social work once I was qualified in three more years time.

Time stretched ahead like infinity when I thought it would take another three years before I could earn enough money to buy a fridge and a washing machine and all the things people had in their houses to make their lives comfortable. Helena, Juliana and I would use the Laundromat around the corner from the station and Helena's aunt had offered to lend us an old fridge that lived in her garage. She was happy to part with it even though she stored her lemonade and beer in there. So Helena, Juliana and I were set. We each had a bed and a chest of drawers, and Helena said we could share her wardrobe, which we would shove into the hallway of our new home.

A week later, after we had moved out, I rang my mother on the telephone.

'Your father is upset,' she said. 'You didn't say goodbye, but more than that, he thinks you shouldn't have taken your bed. You should have asked first.'

It took me several weeks more before I went back home one weekend during the day when my father was up and awake. He sat in his usual chair at his usual place by the fire, which was not burning that day because by then we were on the edge of summer's slide into autumn and it was not yet cold.

He looked up when I walked past the open doors that led into the lounge room. I looked in. I nodded but walked past the lounge room and into the kitchen. If my father wanted to talk to me, he would need to make the first move. But he said nothing.

'Go talk to your father,' my mother said as I sat down at the kitchen table with a cup of hot black coffee in my hands.

Why should I?' I said. 'I don't respect him any more.'

My mother looked sad. 'You're getting too thin,' she said. 'If you go on like this you'll look like someone from Biafra.' A new sensation crept through me then. A sense of triumph. At first I thought it had to do with the idea my mother had finally noticed me, that I was disappearing, but then it occurred to me that my mother and I were in some strange sort of competition, as to who was the most desirable, and now at last, with Paul in my life, I was winning.

BEFORE I started my second year at the university, I spent another eight weeks of the summer holidays working at Halls. They closed the book store early on Fridays before late night closing began, which was a good thing this night given Paul's train was due to leave Spencer Street at seven and I hoped to have time to say goodbye before the Southern Aurora took off for Sydney.

I had settled into a fast paced afternoon upstairs in the second hand books, filling out orders for secondary school kids about to go back to school when a heavy rain started. I could see it through the windows but I paid it no regard and imagined it would stop by the time of closing time; only it went on, in great grey swathes against the window glass. At times, I could hear it roar above the clatter of the cash registers and the babble of voices from the folks at the counter waiting to get their orders filled.

I fancied myself as a friendly shop girl, one given to do her best by all customers, only I had a secret system whereby I'd reward the pleasant shoppers with bargains and the demanding ones who were rude would suffer a limited discount. It gave me a secret power, one I'd not enjoyed before and one that soothed me given Paul's insistence on doing things that pleased him, going places that left me out and going off to places like Sydney, unannounced.

If anyone had told me then I was behaving like my mother, a slave to the whims of her husband, I would not have believed them. Paul may have been unpredictable. He may have gambled his money away on horse racing but to me he was mostly kind and that was all that mattered. Besides he was happy enough that I should meet him at the station after work. He liked the idea of a send-off, he said.

By the time I'd stored away my grey store apron in the back room locker and said goodbye to Mrs Doyle who ran our department, I was out on the street. The rain was still heavy and had transformed the dry city streets into what looked like a river. A few doors down on Elizabeth Street I could see cars, those able to move through the traffic lights that were flashing amber, up to their tyres under water. The policeman who directed traffic mid intersection looked like an upright seal under layers of black rubber, arms to left and right as he tried to stop commuters running onto the street, given the torrents they were trying to avoid.

If I had been traveling home as usual to the three rooms in the quarter student house that I shared with Juliana and Helena I'd have needed to join those people down there on the river that was Elizabeth Street. But this day I was lucky to be going up onto high ground to get to the other city station, Spencer Street, from where the country trains departed, on my rendezvous with the man I loved, the man from novels, the man with the moon face and straight toothed smile, the man who taught me about sex and bodies and the way these things worked.

That I might only spend thirty minutes with him did not register as much as it should. I thought only of the pleasure of seeing him again, nothing of the pain of our goodbye. By the time I caught sight of Paul under the boarding on the station, where all the times were displayed on clocks with moveable arms, which were controlled by invisible forces behind them in the upper offices, I was soaked through. No umbrella and no coat. I had not thought to bring them in January, when mostly I expected the days to be dry and hot. I lived from moment to moment in a welter of expectation and hoped only for the next good thing and here it was in the form of Paul who told me it was fine for me to come on board the train as his guest.

He ushered me into the dining car where we sat against a narrow window at a small round bar table and looked out onto the people scurrying like beetles across the platform. Paul ordered me a Pimms and lemonade while he drank his beer and the two of us sat and talked about his trip ahead to visit friends in Wollongong, his horse racing buddy, Mick Head, who lived there with his schoolteacher girlfriend.

I watched Paul's back as he walked towards the bar. I watched the rise and fall of his shoulders as he dug his hand into his back pocket to slide out his wallet. Paul had a strange relationship with money. He could give it away as though it was water and at other times he could be as tight as a screw. I'd have been happy to buy him gifts galore, anything he wanted if only it made him happy.

Paul beamed at me as he slid the two freshly filled glasses onto the table.

'I thought you might like to try something else,' he said. 'A Brandy Crusta.'

'What's in that?' I asked.

'Brandy, bitters, ginger beer and a dash of lemonade for sweetness.'

My insides heaved. Saliva filled my mouth. I couldn't tell him that there were only two foods I hated and one of them was ginger. Ginger beer was a close cousin with the same taste. I could see my mother in my mind's eye, dipping her fingers into the grey stone jar of ginger she had received as a gift at Christmas time.

'Thanks,' I said, and held my breath as I took up the glass between my fingers. I sipped through the thin crust of sugar that the bartender had coated around the edge. The sweetness took away the bitter taste but it was not enough for me to like the stuff.

Paul swallowed his beer fast and much as I'd have liked to keep up with him, I decided I'd have to slow down if I was going to get more of this stuff into me.

'I've never been out of Melbourne before,' I said.

Paul smiled. He liked introducing me to new things. He liked to have the authority of one who knew more, or so it seemed to me. I scraped at the sugar on the side of my glass.

'I won't be seeing much of Sydney,' Paul said. 'I won't get out of the station. 'And Wollongong's not much. Just another town, a bit like Geelong. But they have a pretty good racetrack.' He smiled at me. 'I plan to pick a winner this time.'

I took another sip of my drink and tried to hide my grimace as I swallowed.

'This is good,' I said. 'But next time, I'd prefer something with Coke, or straight lemonade.'

A voice called over the loudspeaker 'all visitors must depart the train,' and I stood to go, filled with regret.

'If only I could come with you,' I said and Paul's 'Why not come, too?' reversed every image I'd had in my head of traipsing back through the city and the rain to my room alone with my sister. We did not talk about the how of it, though Paul had a plan. I followed him to his compartment and we sat on the edge of his tiny bed, which fitted into the wall like a low lying bunk as the train pulled out of the station.

'When the ticket inspector comes around, you get inside the toilet.'

The toilet was the shape of those cubicles you find on aeroplanes, only narrower. Everything in this compartment was designed to minimal specifications. It was fun to squeeze up tight, curled on the lid of the toilet while the inspector knocked on the door and pushed his head through to examine Paul and his ticket.

Getting off was trickier when the train pulled into Sydney after a night lulled to sleep by the swish swash movement of the wheels on the tracks and squeezed against the wall in a bed that was already too small for one person only. I didn't mind. We breakfasted in the dining car with other commuters because as Paul reasoned there were too many people on the train for anyone to recognise a stray in broad daylight and the ticket inspector only looked at tickets on departure and arrival. As people left the train and the inspector wanted one last look at our tickets, Paul distracted him with a conversation about the train journey, while I slid in with a family group already leaving the train after their ticket inspection.

Paul and I met up moments later on the main platform at Central Station before a brisk walk across several platforms towards the country trains and Wollongong. The rain of Melbourne and those steel grey skies had turned to the bluest of blue in Sydney, made brighter by Paul's decision to buy me a ticket for the Wollongong train. He was happy to part with an extra ten dollars given I hadn't been paid yet that week and he was convinced he'd make it all back the following day at the race track.

I had never travelled this far before. Never travelled with a man before. Nineteen years old and my thoughts secretly tied to this one man, this man who brought sunshine into my otherwise drab world; this man whose voice alone evoked great swathes of joy that raced through my overloaded heart and left me breathless.

This must be love, I convinced myself, in line with the song, nothing more, nothing less and nothing else mattered. Not my sister at home who had no idea of my whereabouts and who must have been worried sick and might have called in the police by now. I did not give her much thought. She'd have had the sense to imagine the only place I could have been would be with the man of my desires and if not, no matter. On the train to Wollongong with Paul through the sunny countryside dotted first with houses and factories and then fields, my life was complete.

Mick Head and his teacher girlfriend, who went by the name of Jo, were not fussed when Paul arrived at the door with me in tow. I could share a bed with him in their spare room and for the rest I could muck in with them all. Between our trip to the races, where Paul and Mick both won modest amounts, and the Saturday night when they took us off to a friend's party, we played cards. Gin Rummy or poker for money, five cent pieces in piles. Paul and Mick could not manage many activities without a gamble attached. Don McLean was singing 'American Pie' on the radio again and again, till I knew the words by heart. 'Bye bye, Miss American Pie, drove my Chevy to the levee but the levee was dry.'

My levee was full up until that night at Mick's friend's party where something happened. Some strange mystery, whereby for the first time in my six months of really knowing Paul, he shifted from the kind though sometimes unavailable lover, to a man of steel and ice, a man in a rage with me for something I did not understand.

The party happened in someone's back yard near to where Mick and Jo lived. We drove there by car and mingled with people none of us knew, though Mick had met the person holding the party at a racetrack sometime before. The men outnumbered the women and while Paul stood near the browning sausages on the open flamed fire, I came to talk to a man who stood nearby, who seemed friendly enough and who leaned into me as if to hear me better. Nothing happened between us, but from the other side of the back yard I figured that Paul had seen us in silhouette and must have felt jealous.

What else could it have been that caused him not to speak to me all the way home and as we prepared for bed and all night long and all the next day at breakfast when we went out to buy more bread and all afternoon as Mick and Paul played more poker against Don McLean's plaintive voice and Jo and I sat in the background watching our boys?

Could I have done something wrong to cause Paul not to want to speak to me? Jo had no idea.

'Men are like that,' she said after two years of living with Mick. 'He'll get over it soon enough.'

I worried that Paul might not get over it. How could I get home again if he did not help me stow away on the Southern Aurora? I might be stuck in Sydney for good. I needed to go back to work on the Monday. I needed to let Juliana know I was safe. I needed to go back to my other life, dull as it was.

The several times I tried to engage Paul, to ask what had happened, why he was unhappy with me, he refused to answer and when he finally turned to speak to me around six o'clock that night when it was time to make our way to the station for our return trip, I had the sense not to ask again. When the Southern Aurora pulled in to Spencer Street Station early on Monday morning and I snuck off again, hidden within another group of people while Paul distracted the driver, the sun had come back to my hometown.

I rang Juliana from the station and she was only just getting out of bed.

'I was worried sick,' she said, 'but I figured you must be with Paul.' Her voice was scratchy across the phone line. 'You should have rung me, though. If you hadn't, I'd have called the police today.'

Paul took the train back to Edithvale and I dawdled back down Bourke Street to the bookstore early for work, and in the same clothes I had worn on the Friday. I hoped no one would notice.

Guilt is a terrible thing

QUEEN VICTORIA Hospital rose like a grey elephant along Lonsdale Street. I walked through its metal gates, up the entrance steps in blue stone, to the reception desk. My father was in the men's ward. Four North, the receptionist told me, and I followed the yellow painted line to the lift.

My father rested against a pile of pillows in a high cast iron bed with an empty chair on one side and a window on the other. He looked out over shop rooftops to tall city buildings that threw shadows against one another like a pile of children's building blocks. I did not know how to approach him. He was captive in bed. Now I had the power to turn around and walk away, but it was not so simple; I had decided I needed to visit him before he died.

Since the time I had left home, whenever I rang and my father answered, I hung up the phone and then felt furious with him for being there. I did not want to speak to my father. I imagined him looking into the silent earpiece wondering why someone should have hung up in his ear. Could he have known it was me? Known that I had left him with the dull burr of the cut off tone, the line dead and the discomfort of being shut out? But in the hospital then, I could not hang up; I could not run away. I was bound to stay for the duration.

My father smiled when he saw me, a wan smile but one that suggested he was pleased. I decided against leaning over to kiss him on the cheek. Even as I decided against it I imagined his rough beard against my lips and shuddered at the memory

So I resisted. He seemed happy enough with that, too. At least he did not reach out his arms, which were lying in prayer position in front of him on top of the clean white sheet that bordered the green hospital weave blanket.

'Have a chair', he said, and I pulled it closer towards the bedside as if I was attesting to my intention to confide. Even so I did not want to get too close, just close enough to take in the old man smell. His long grey hair, which he had grown out since retiring from his work as an accountant, looked less oily than usual. I imagined the nurses had washed it.

'How are you?' I asked. What to say to this man I had avoided since I left home three years ago? What to say now that I was a twenty-two-year-old and he was a shrivelled-up old man? A man who could no longer hurt me, a man who could no longer threaten me as he had when I was a child, when I had wanted him dead.

'I have pleurisy', my father said. 'Do you remember I had it once before?' He paused, then asked, 'What are you doing these days?'

After I left home, I was angry with my father for a long time. I now realise my father's rage at his idea we had stolen beds was a cover for his disappointment that we had left home at all. As each child left, one after the other, my father became more distressed and resentful. Worst of all was when my youngest brother left. My father wept.

We did not speak about beds in Queen Vic or of leaving home. I had been away too long and my father had given up drinking, 'For good', my mother said and I thought maybe this time she was right, but it was not a miracle as she would have once had us believe.

My father had stopped drinking alcohol because he could no longer bear the ravages of his mind and body. He had, as all the textbooks say, reached rock bottom. In his sixtieth year, he agreed to rehabilitation, weeks of drying out in Delmont Hospital. He came home and began building a doll's house for his granddaughters by way of reparation.

'I have done terrible things to you children,' my father said to me as I sat at his bedside and looked into liquid grey eyes that were red around the rims from too many years of drinking and cigarettes.

My father had taken up studying Hebrew. He had gone back to the church. He hobnobbed with the charismatics, not in the fanatical way they did, chanting and speaking in tongues, but from an intellectual position of curiosity.

When I was little I had worried that my father did not come to church with us, that he stayed away from Mass. I saw his rejection of our religion as a mark of his wickedness. If he had gone to church then I had reasoned he would not do the hurtful things he did. He would not get drunk. He would go to confession and would be able to examine his conscience. As long as he did not practise his Catholicism he was free to carry on regardless and there was no one who could stop him.

Now that I had given up the church myself I was disappointed in his turning back to God. Maybe my anger had shifted from my father onto this thing we call God. What sort of God? I did not know. God had become the brick wall of my mother's distance. I could not talk to her without God coming into the picture. Her God, her beliefs, and I could not connect.

Even here I see I have capitalised God when lower case would do. I capitalise out of my childhood respect for a God I no longer believe exists.

My father's skin was like parchment. He had grey bags under his eyes and his false teeth did not fit. They clicked when he talked. More so when he sipped on the cup of tea the assistant had just then wheeled in on a trolley. My father was in an eight-bed ward. I had tried to tune out the presence of the seven others, all old and wheezy men, sipping on their drinks in a strange cacophony. My father was silent and thoughtful for long moments.

'I'm sorry for what I've done to you children.'

I did not reassure my father that it was okay. It was not. The sixty-year-old man was coming to the end of his life—so he told me.

I did not bend to kiss him when I went to leave but offered the brush of my fingers against his hand.

'Guilt is a terrible thing,' my father called after me, as I walked the length of the ward to leave.

'I know,' I said. 'I know.'

Another home

BY NOW, Paul and I had become a couple, and my time spent with him was no longer a secret from my mother. Paul's flat mate was going overseas indefinitely and I could move in with him as soon as the last of Ivan's possessions were cleared and then we could be as husband and wife, although we didn't talk of marriage, but chose instead to 'live in sin'. To me living in sin was as good as being married, though my mother frowned upon the arrangement. My father had no say.

When his first lease expired Paul undertook to find us another place and unbeknown to me he chose a half house bang smack on Beach Road, a stone's throw from the sea, in Black Rock.

'You'll love it,' he said as we drove from his parents' place in Edithvale where we'd decamped those past few weeks until we could find another home. 'It's much bigger than our old place and much cheaper.'

I should have guessed then that Paul had chosen under the weight of that word 'cheap'. He had decided to live the life of a professional gambler and given I was still studying and not earning any money at all except during the Christmas holidays, we relied entirely on his peripatetic income of wins and losses. It was not good enough for a horse to lose by a half a whisker, Paul told me. The horse had to win, otherwise our electricity might get cut off or we'd have to live off yogurt and bread for a week.

The place looked better from the outside and that was saying something. It had the quality of one of those cracked paint weatherboards on the beach built fifty years ago, before Black Rock had become a genteel suburb for people who might have used it as a holiday shack or else for others who might have lived there long term because they could not afford accommodation closer to the city. In any case, its veranda sagged and the driveway that led to the back of the house where a second occupancy held sway, was crumbling at the edges, its gutter rusted through. Tufts of grass sprouted from the lip of the gutter to give it that unused look as if it had been uninhabited for decades. The front door opened onto a lounge dining area of dark unpolished boards with an open fireplace in the centre and to one side two small rooms, one you stepped into that formed the kitchen and the other, with a lockable door, the toilet-cum-bathroom. This place was so old they had not yet installed an ongoing supply of gas to heat the water. Instead there was a contraption above the shower into which you needed to feed twenty-cent pieces in quick succession for the length of your wash.

To one side of the living area a corridor led onto the two bedrooms, the first one for us, the second could be a study or a guest room as we fancied. It took to the end of summer and into autumn for me to realise that this place over the road from the sea, which could not be heated by anything other than electric heaters, which were too expensive to run, exuded cold air and damp in winter; warm air and damp in summer. With it came a mould so blue and filleted like lace, it covered all my shoes and handbags except for those I used regularly. All the books I made the mistake of leaving in the study turned green under the weight of this mould that settled on anything that rested there for long.

Ferdi gave us some unwanted off cuts of an orange shag pile that nobody in their right mind could have wanted even a decade before during the hippy sixties given its ghastly colour. But it was clean and thick and gave the illusion of warmth and comfort we'd otherwise not enjoy on those bare boards.

One day after I had taken my usual shower while Paul was away at the races, after I had spent the usual tense ten minutes panicking that I did not have enough coins to keep the flame alight over the escaping gas, I decided to explore the rest of the place, the place down the back out of view from the world. There was a sign above the hot water contraption onto which you fed your money that warned of an explosion in the event of letting the gas run without coins or flame. It was a tricky business and by the time I was showered and dressed I longed for something to take my mind off my studies in the back mould-filled room where I had set up my desk.

It was grey and overcast when I took off on my journey. I figured I was safe to go snooping as I'd heard the people who lived out back take off earlier. I figured they consisted of two men who rode motorbikes and entertained a good deal, other men mainly who also rode motorbikes and the occasional young woman in tight jeans who travelled pillion behind one of the men on bikes. They all travelled down the sideway of our house invisible to us, their faces hidden under heavy black helmets. The grass was damp underfoot. The landlord relied on his tenants to mow and given none of us had the wherewithal to buy a mower, nor the inclination to push one of those old fashioned non-motorised double blade contraptions, which we could have borrowed from Paul's folks, we let it grow high. It matched the decrepit look of the place and gave me heart that at least no one would bother to burgle us, not that we had much by way of valuables.

But out back they did, or so it seemed to me, as I turned the corner and saw there on the veranda a pile of boxes sealed off and from the labels on the outside, filled to the brim with cigarettes. These blokes must be in the tobacco trade, I reasoned, only it seemed a grungy place in which to store precious cargo like cigarettes. I peeked through the non-curtained windows into what must have been their kitchen, given its central table and sink to one side. A bong sat in the centre of the table and ash trays filled with dead butts alongside a filthy tea towel and a number of oddly assorted tea cups and glass jars and bottles empty or half filled with whiskey by the look of it.

Something about the place gave me the heebies and I began to worry that one of the men might soon come home and that I'd be in trouble or that he'd force me inside and tie me up and hide me in their spare room for fear I'd dob on them to the police for something I wasn't sure about. But the place oozed decadence and illicit activities and all things bad in contrast to me, a good student, working her way into a job with her also good, though careless at the races, boyfriend.

That night I told Paul we had to leave. We were not safe with just a thin wall between those reprobates and us. We could move, he promised me, as soon as this next lease expired around Christmas time.

For the last six months of the year, I lived in fear for my life. I could not abide the idea that these men lived so close and when Paul decided even before the lease had expired that he would take himself off to Sydney to complete a six week training course with the Commonwealth police I decided to move in with friends. I would not live on the Beach Road in that shack alone. Paul came back from his course and this time he included me in the negotiations on the next place where we might live, a brown-bricked second floor apartment on Westbury Street in St Kilda, again with two rooms but this time without mould.

Gamblers

WHEN I told the university counsellor, a tall thin man called Bryan Brown that because I was living with a gambler my life was uncertain and I was not sure I could finish my studies, he raised his eyebrows. We met in the Old Arts Building, in an office as small as a broom cupboard.

I went because Delys Sargeant who took us for Social Biology had rung the week before to tell me I had failed my Social Biology exam because I 'didn't answer the question.'

It came as a shock. It was one of those open book exams where you get the question a week before the exam with time enough to prepare and then on the day you go into the exam room and you have an hour in which to answer the question. The question was about pollution and its effect on a community's health. I had laid out my answer before the exam, then rote-learned it for the exam. I finished in half the time allowed but stayed till the end rereading and refining it into what I thought was a fine essay. But I had still failed.

'You'll be okay if you do well enough in your final exam,' Delys had said.

It freaked me out. It was cruel I thought to ring a student with such news in the middle of swot vac, with exams just around the corner. Besides, I was fearful I might be pregnant. I had not bothered with contraception while living with my gambler boyfriend, because not eating much had somehow stopped my periods. I told the counsellor I might be pregnant.

'You're not using any contraception?' he asked.

'No,' I said.

'Not even condoms?'

'No.' I did not tell him about my eating habits.

'You're the gambler,' he said, and then recommended I start in group therapy as soon as possible. 'I'll arrange an appointment for you with our group therapist, Dr Turkle.'

I went home to Paul. I decided against telling him I might be pregnant and that I'd failed my exam but in the back of my mind I decided all would be well. I'd sit the end of year exams but, if I failed, I'd be pregnant. I could have a baby and all would be well.

As part of my social work training that year I was put in the care of Isabelle Conradi who worked with the Catholic Family Welfare Bureau in charge of young women who became pregnant outside of marriage and needed to give up their babies for adoption.

The week after my exams, I went with her one day to visit a group of women who were spending their pregnancies in a house in Carlton, in a secret location. It was a double-storey terrace in Grattan Street not far from the university. The Sisters of St Joseph who looked after women in their "sinful" state ran it.

Isabelle knocked at the front door and a young woman answered. She had a sad face, and a big belly, though not as big as the other women who sat around in the living room where we met the head nun who supervised them.

It was Isabelle's job to interview these women close to the time when their babies would be born and offer advice on the pros and cons of adoption.

'We're a Catholic agency,' Isabelle had told me when I first began my placement, 'and so we only deal with women who go through to the end with their pregnancies. We can't advise abortion. It's against the church's rules and we find it best to encourage the girls to give up their babies for adoption. There are plenty of good Catholic married women who can't have babies of their own and would be far better placed to care for these unwanted ones.'

My mind flitted to my body wherein I imagined I carried a tiny baby of my own.

'Of course they're free to keep their babies, too,' Isabelle said and flicked back a wisp of her otherwise perfectly held blond hair. She was not much older than me or the other young women who filed through this house, but she seemed older by a decade as if her role as arbitrator on the fate of these unwanted babies and mothers gave her an authority that aged her overnight.

That evening at home with Paul, while I cooked him a plate of battered fish and kept my own grilled and batter-less, I was relieved to think I had a boyfriend who would care for my baby and me, even though unmarried, and our lives insecure. I would not need to go into such a home with all those women, full of babies that they would soon need to give up to someone else and then go back into the world and try to pick up the pieces of where they had left off and pretend that none of it had happened.

Over the next week I swatted over my books. I rote-learned the theories of operant conditioning, Skinner's theory of learning and Pavlov's dogs, the way they would do anything on cue when given the right reward; I learned the rituals of case work as decreed by Florence Hollis, a pioneer in the social work field, on how to greet people at the door, how to conduct open ended questions during interviews, how to be empathic, and what to say to a client who gets angry with you. I read up again and again on Durkheim's anomie and Max Weber's theories of *Gemeinschaft* and *Gesellschaft*, and tried to remember the translations of these foreign words. There was so much to learn and I was still so uncertain about my future but I hung on in.

After the exams were over, I went to meet Dr Turkle, the group therapy doctor. He sat behind his desk and wore a thick red moustache and beard that covered almost all of his face, except for his eyes, which were beady like a bird's, leaving me fearful.

'We'll put you into the mixed group that runs Wednesdays each week for two hours.'

'Can I think about it first?' I asked.

Dr Turkle's eyes widened. 'You want to think about it?' he said.

I burst into tears, uncertain what those tears were about. Something to do with the certainty of this man about what was good for me, and my own uncertainty about this crazy world in which I lived.

I hadn't had a period, but by then I feared I might not be pregnant. Nothing in my body felt any different and I had read that pregnant women around six weeks begin to feel nauseous and develop swollen breasts. I felt none of those things.

'Well,' Dr Turkle said, and stroked his beard. 'We'll be taking a month off over Christmas. You could start mid-January.'

I wiped my eyes, aware of how stupid I might have seemed to go into floods of tears without an explanation, but Dr Turkle probably wouldn't have cared.

'You can make another appointment with my secretary on your way out,' he said.

When the exam results were pinned onto the notice board before Christmas, I held my breath. I couldn't find my student number anywhere on the list. Finally, I went off home to tell Paul about our new future as parents.

Before Paul came home that night from another day at the races, the phone rang.

'Congratulations,' the voice said. 'You got a second class distinction with me.' It was Damian, the man I sat next to in psychology lectures. He knew my number because he'd asked me to tell him so he could know how we both went.

The next day, I took myself off to the local doctor who did a pregnancy test and gave me the news I'd failed.

'Now is your chance,' he said, 'to start afresh, and protect yourself from the worry of an unwanted pregnancy.'

BY THE end of the year I finished my degree and took up a job at Prince Henry's Hospital, a short tram ride away, I came to question my relationship with Paul. He had elected to go on a further training course with the police. To give him credit, it was not his fault. He needed to get a job, since there was no future in his gambling.

One day, on the fourth floor of Prince Henry's Hospital, a young resident, tall red-haired Dr Mark Robinson, in the softest of voices asked me out to dinner.

I told him I was in a relationship. But then, as I walked back down to my office in the basement, I reconsidered. Why not? I thought. Why not indeed?

Not long after, I found a list under a pile of magazines in which Paul had written about the pros and cons of our relationship. He'd concluded that I had stopped loving him.

Over the next few months we tried our best to go our separate ways amicably. But, one night, after we had moved into separate apartments in Caulfield, the telephone rang, interrupting my fitful sleep.

'You fucking bitch,' Paul said. 'You fucking bitch.' His voice trailed off. Time slowed down.

Is this a dream? I wondered.

'Everyone knows what you've been up to,' he went on. 'Everyone, but me. I was the last to know.'

My words were croaky. 'What are you talking about?' I wanted to deny that I had betrayed him. Even though I had slept with another man.

Slept with. A euphemism. Had sex with, fucked, shagged, you name it, in biblical terms, "known". Gone off with another man while he was away for weeks on end. Somehow Paul had expected I'd sit at home, the good and loving girlfriend and partner, always faithful.

'I'm coming over now,' he said. 'I've got your stuff. You can have it back. I never want to see you again.'

The dial tone buzzed in my ear. I held onto the phone. I could not believe he had rung off. I dragged on my dressing gown. He'd be here soon. Good. I'd settle him down. I'd soothe him. A few gentle words. I heard his car pull up in the carport below. I looked through the blinds. He opened the car door and flung the books and clothes that I had left behind as a mark of our friendship.

I pulled up the blinds and swung open the window. 'Come up,' I said. 'Don't just throw stuff there. Come up and talk.' He did not stop throwing books, then my old grey cardigan, my CD case and my sunglasses. I kept my voice low. I did not want to wake the neighbours.

'Please talk,' I called again to the silent man whose arm moved up and down like a piston as he threw the last of my shoes onto the pile. He slammed his car door shut. He had not even cut the engine and reversed without looking up to see me.

Endings

I NEVER saw Paul again. He disappeared from my life around the same time my father gave up alcohol. For the last five years of his life my father lived without it. He became a different man, a sad man, a broken man, whose emphysema grew worse to the point he could only walk short distances before needing a break. He had retired from his job at Cooper Brothers and could only potter around the house. He made dolls' houses for those of his children who had girl babies, including Hannah, who by then had married Jon, with whom she had five children.

My father shaved every day until he stopped drinking. He gave up his suit. He took to letting his beard grow long, grey and messy, a lookalike Eric Berne of *The Games People Play* fame, a man whose books on Transactional Analysis my father took to reading, as if he had finally found means to be free of the torment of his childhood, of his time during the war, of migration and of all those pressures that drove him to alcohol in the first place.

He also refused to wear the white shirts of his years of servitude as an accountant. Instead, he insisted on coloured shirts, the pale pastels of the mid seventies that became popular with other men who tried to brighten up their wardrobes. My father never wore a tie again, except to the weddings of his children.

He died when he was sixty-five after a series of heart attacks in Canberra on a visit to Dirk, who now lived there. We shipped his body back to Melbourne by plane, with Ferdi, who arranged the flight, paying for the extra seat. The box was long, given my father's height, and it seemed a lonely way to travel, like a dead soldier coming back from war.

THERE IS a story behind my father that I learned only after he died. The story goes that my paternal grandfather, chief archivist in Haarlem for Births Deaths and Marriages, and a man who switched religions often, wanted to follow in the footsteps of Joseph Smith, the founder of the Mormon religion and fancied being married to several wives. To this end, he treated his two daughters, Nell and Rie, as though they were married to him. But, during the war in 1942, when she turned nineteen, Nell, the younger of the two, reported her father's activities to the police, whose investigations eventually led to my grandfather's imprisonment. My grandmother was also imprisoned on separate charges.

I knew little of this as I was growing up, but sensed something was not right in the way my father denied the existence of his family of origin. For all his denial, he could not escape his own past.

In a yellow lunch box in which I collected the negatives my father left before he died, I came across a single shot cut loose from another longer line of negatives, which I later sent off to be developed.

I imagine my father took this photograph in the days after he had bought the device that enabled him to take the equivalent of today's selfies. In this photo, he sits side on, profiled against an otherwise blank wall. He is naked except for his glasses. It's a grainy shot and my father's pose is typical of olden day photos in that he faces away from the camera unsmiling. Most remarkable of all is his nakedness.

My eye is drawn to the thin line along his crossed leg, the way it travels across his body to emphasise the thinness of the man. And his glasses, the only other item in the photo beyond the edge of the chair, his body and the wall, are strangely heavy and grey. His shadow falls to the front. It highlights his profile and perhaps it's this shadow he was trying to recreate. I still shudder at the sight of his nakedness.

IN THE 1970s, when Alex Comfort published his *Joy of Sex* and consciousness-raising groups had swung into fashion, with bodies and gender inequalities at their centre, I began to explore the possibilities of a different kind of relationship to my own body and began to wonder whether my fears were exaggerated, linked as they were to my father.

They need not have applied to every man I met. I knew this to be true, but even then my body could not forget the fear and the impulse to hide, the sensation of walking into a room as if I was made of stuff lighter than air, as if I consisted of mind and brain matter only, as if my only protection was the smile I wore to keep others at bay.

I thought of myself as the Barbie doll I played with as a child, all angles and smoothness, but made of plastic. No matter how hard I tried I could not be rid of this need for protection in the presence of others.

LONG AFTER he died, I wrote my father a letter:

Dear Dad

I know it's against the rules to blame anyone, but I blame you. I'm all grown up now and should know better, even so, it's hard to get beyond the sense that I keep chasing you in all these men I've met over the years who turn out wrong, not because they themselves are wrong but because they're not you, the one I needed when I was little.

You even spelled my name wrong on my birth certificate,
not that it was you who spelled out the letters. You must
have gone to Births, Deaths and Marriages in Melbourne to
register my name and sat in a small office with a clerk whose
job it was to take down the details. And you got it all wrong,
my name spelled in the English way and not the European,
and even the births of my other siblings, the ones who came
before me, you listed in the wrong chronological order.

How could you do that? Were you addled, too overwhelmed by the birth of your seventh child, your sixth
child living, to notice that the clerk put down a 'z'
instead of an 's', to notice that the clerk listed your
first born daughter as older than her older brother?

These things matter, to me at least, even if they did not matter to you. It's the order of things. The way we're put onto this
earth to live out lives in a certain order in families from oldest
to youngest, but you paid it all little heed. We could all be just
one mess of children, each one indistinguishable from the other.

And then that decision to name me after my mother, your
wife. What about that decision? Did you have a say in it?
I found out later I should have been named Petronella after
your mother, but my mother told me you hated your mother
so much that you wanted none of your children to be saddled with her name. That was good of you. Bad enough to
be saddled with my mother's name but then to cop your
mother's name, the one you supposedly hated, far worse.

You were tall and intelligent enough to beat Barry Jones
on Pick a Box, not that you'd have tried. You'd have had
to front up on the television screen before all those view-
ers. Not for you the performance, at least not one held in

public. You preferred your own company but then, from time
to time when you grew lonely, you took off in search of one
of your daughters, one would do, preferably the oldest but
if she was not available and my mother was nowhere to
be seen you'd go after me or one of my younger sisters.

But I was smart, Dad. I knew how to avoid you. I knew
how to make myself invisible, as thin as a sheet of paper.
I knew how to slide from room to room on tiptoes, silent as
a beetle and just as small, and you did not see me as I slid
down the hallway past those double glass doors that led
into your chamber whenever you called out my name.

You called and called and the more you called the more
I plugged my ears and hid from view, from you, from everyone. Out back to the laundry toilet with the door closed
tight even without a lock where I read books. You refused
locks in our house. You wanted access at all times but you
could never access me, could you Dad? You could never get
to me, inside my body, under my skin or into my brain.

I held firm. I held you at arm's length and now
I have to suffer the consequences, the guilt that
slides like treacle down my back and sticks to every
pore of my skin, making it hard to breathe.

My younger sisters weren't as smart as me. They came
when you called. They went into your bedroom and closed
the door behind, and even though they were five and eight
and I do not know what happened behind that door, nor
am I ever likely to know because the older one of those
sisters has sealed her lips tight like a clam and she will
not speak to me nor to any of the others and the younger
one cannot remember other than to tell me how ten years

later when she was fifteen and we older ones had all left
home, she heard you at her doorway late one night.

She knew you were there. She knew you were naked.
She could see your silhouette against the hall way
light. She knew it had reached the stage it was her
turn, but our mother arrived in the nick of time.

'Leave her alone,' our mother said and you skulked away like
a rodent. Never to pester her again, except in her nightmares.

As for me, you still appear in my dreams, not as often as before.
I can still feel your presence at night in the dark when I tread
over cold tiles to the toilet and hold my breath fearful of your
touch. Always your touch, the touch I avoided throughout my
childhood, the touch I feared that has made me now into a
woman afraid of closeness, afraid of penetration, a woman who
has sealed herself off from too much bodily connection. And
I could not reclaim my body long after you had left. No body,
no chance of penetration, no chance of invasion, no chance
of the burning touch that drives even stronger people mad.

Your daughter

I WAS invisible to my father, even as he sought to objectify me,
along with my sisters and my mother, as I imagine he, too, was
turned into someone else by troubled parents, while still only
a child.

There are still times when I practise invisibility, when I try to
slip away like a wisp of smoke that curls under the door, slides
along the walls and out into the day light. I slither into this light,
where I can resume bodily shape, safe in the company of others

who do not wish me harm, and far from the ones, past and present, who might terrorise me in the empty night.

MY FATHER lies deep underground in the Cheltenham cemetery in a grave covered in white pebbles from Healesville. The graveyard slopes down into a valley and runs alongside a golf course. I imagine that by now the worms have eaten him away, even the coffin is rotten. Nothing is left but his bones, hair and teeth. My father's name is inscribed in gold letters on a shiny piece of granite, testimony to his life and death, but he lives on in my memory, hovering there in the dark.

The other night he came to me in a dream. Drunk and argumentative. He had that way of stepping forward to provoke and then retreat when we somehow managed to withstand his onslaughts. I was there with Juliana and Jacob.

'What's wrong with you, you stupid children,' he said. And without touching an inch of his being, I pushed him away with the glare of my eyes.

'Leave us alone,' I said in words my mother was never able to muster and my father skulked off to his bedroom only to return minutes later with more insults. He was unsteady on his feet and his words were slurred into nonsense.

'You think you're so smart. You think you're so good, but you're nothing.'

Jacob huddled in the corner in tears. He couldn't bear these insults, as if they were directed at him. My father lunged towards me and was about to swipe my face but I ducked and hid behind the kitchen table. He waved his fist at me, helpless to reach me, unless he began a chase around the table, one only I could win. Juliana took off to the other end of the room and put her arms around our little brother to protect him.

My father skulked off and Jacob began to shake in great sobs. He was eight years, old but not too heavy for me, seven years older, though in my dream I was an adult, and I carried him into his bed and pulled the blankets around his shoulders and stroked his body, still quaking under the bedclothes.

'It'll be okay, I said. 'We won't let him hurt you.'

And so my dream came to an end.

I believed those words: 'It'll be okay', even as I knew my father would once again reappear in my dream, staggering on his drunken legs, ready to provoke and insult and hurt once more, but I could withstand him now. He had lost his power.

Now, in the daylight, I no longer need to disappear. I have come out of hiding.

The people in this book are real and the stories true, in so far as I can remember or others have remembered and reported them to me. From time to time I have added descriptive detail for literary purposes, to help bridge gaps, and I have also changed names for privacy wherever necessary.

CPSIA information can be obtained
at www.ICGtesting.com
Printed in the USA
LVHW04s1608070618
579959LV00002B/447/P